*Y*ou are entering a world as exciting as a vampire's kiss and as wild as a witches' sabbath. It is a world where fairy tales of flesh and fantasy are for adults only. And with this intimate and knowledgeable guide you will be able to explore the outer limits of this world—its intriguing depths, its hidden meanings, and its special thrills. . . .

THE ROQUELAURE READER
A Companion to Anne Rice's Erotica

KATHERINE RAMSLAND, Ph.D. teaches philosophy at Rutgers University. A close friend of Anne Rice, she wrote the biography of the bestselling author, *Prism of the Night,* available in a Plume edition, as well as two other guides to Rice's work, *The Vampire Companion* and *The Witches' Companion.* She has also been widely published in journals such as *Psychology Today.* Ms. Ramsland currently lives in Princeton, New Jersey.

ALSO BY KATHERINE RAMSLAND

Engaging the Immediate

Prism of the Night: A Biography of Anne Rice

The Art of Learning

*The Vampire Companion: The Official Guide
to Anne Rice's "The Vampire Chronicles"*

*The Witches' Companion: The Official Guide
to Anne Rice's "Lives of the Mayfair Witches"*

The Anne Rice Trivia Book

THE
ROQUELAURE READER

A COMPANION TO ANNE RICE'S EROTICA

Katherine Ramsland, Ph.D.

Written in cooperation with Anne Rice

A PLUME BOOK

PLUME

Published by the Penguin Group
Penguin Books USA Inc., 375 Hudson Street, New York, New York 10014, U.S.A.
Penguin Books Ltd, 27 Wrights Lane, London W8 5TZ, England
Penguin Books Australia Ltd, Ringwood, Victoria, Australia
Penguin Books Canada Ltd, 10 Alcorn Avenue, Toronto, Ontario, Canada M4V 3B2
Penguin Books (N.Z.) Ltd, 182-190 Wairau Road, Auckland 10, New Zealand

Penguin Books Ltd, Registered Offices:
Harmondsworth, Middlesex, England

First published by Plume, an imprint of Dutton Signet,
a division of Penguin Books USA Inc.

First Printing, February, 1996
1 3 5 7 9 10 8 6 4 2

 REGISTERED TRADEMARK—MARCA REGISTRADA

Library of Congress Cataloging-in-Publication Data
Ramsland, Katherine M.
The Roquelaure Reader : a companion to Anne Rice's erotica / Katherine Ramsland.
p.   cm.
Includes bibliographical references (p.).
ISBN 0-452-27510-5
1. Rice, Anne—Criticism and interpretation.   2. Women and literature—
United States—History—20th century.   3. Erotic stories, American—
History and criticism.   I. Title.
PS3568.I265Z82   1996
813'.54—dc20   95-34847
CIP

Printed in the United States of America
Set in New Baskerville

Designed by Jesse Cohen

For Michelle, Corey, and Lori,
who helped me have fun with this book

And for Steve,
for his sense of humor

CONTENTS

INTRODUCTION

Erotic appeal is different for everyone. It is stronger for some than others, and what arouses one person may alarm someone else. There is no doubt, however, that eroticism is part of the human imagination. We crave stimulation and often use our fantasies as sources of arousal. Even negative emotions like fear and anxiety can offer a potent edge. Fictional frameworks allow us to get closer to "dangerous" feelings without the risk of real harm so that we can experience the excitement such emotions provide.

For Anne Rice, who writes as sensually about vampires as she does about naked pleasure slaves, the experience involves heightened awareness as a quality of erotic connection. She views much of life as erotic, feeling a spiritual rush in the presence of such diverse things as a work of art or the pattern of fine china. "Everything is eroticized for me," she insists. "I fall in love with men and women. I fall in love with cities. That's the way I see life." As she traverses new literary territory, she gets as close as possible to the electric moment of spontaneous authenticity. Erotic excitement for her involves much more than just sexual heat: It is an encompassing fusion of mind and body yielding increased energy, self-knowledge, inner power, and possibility.

All of Rice's novels contain erotic elements. Beginning with *Interview with the Vampire*, she brings to the vampire image an engulfing sensory experience of immortality. In her other supernatural series, *Lives of the Mayfair Witches*, Rice develops the powerful sexuality of generations of women associated with an incubus-like spirit. This hovering sexual entity belongs to a species of highly erotic creatures called Taltos. Rice also wrote two historical novels that follow the developing sexualities of various characters, and

The Mummy, which features an immortal man with insatiable appetites. However, none of these novels match the explicit sexuality of the five that Rice wrote under two pseudonyms.

As Anne Rampling, she developed a relationship of heterosexual dominance and submission in *Exit to Eden,* and in *Belinda,* she described an older man's love for a sexually mature teenager. A. N. Roquelaure penned the three "Beauty" books, *The Claiming of Sleeping Beauty, Beauty's Punishment,* and *Beauty's Release.* Rice described this trio as "elegant sadomasochism," viewing them as wholesome and playful fantasies.

The Roquelaure Reader focuses on the Beauty trilogy. It is intended as a guide for readers who wish to know more about Anne Rice's "gender politics," who would like a resource guide, or who just want to refresh their acquaintance with Rice's characters. In the first part, the novels are placed in the context of Rice's erotic imagination, which has roots in her childhood experiences. While writing them, she was aware of the political climate surrounding pornography, so her own reaction is included. Her other novels are acknowledged only for the parts that relate to themes in the Beauty books; there is no attempt to present them in full. *Exit to Eden* gets detailed treatment because Rice wrote it while finishing the Roquelaure series and because she had originally intended that it be like that series. This essay is more overview than biography, noting the various personal and social influences on the way Rice developed her fantasies. It is more thematic than sequential, with attention to the issues that most influenced Rice's work.

The second part is an A-to-Z concordance that lists and describes characters, places, implements, and themes in the world of the pleasure slaves. Some background information is provided, but by and large, the material derives from the novels.

Last is a trivia game comprised of queries for those who want to test their "mastery" of Beauty's world.

The appendix offers readers a look at the two "missing" chapters from *Exit to Eden,* cut from the original draft because they were too similar in tone to the Roquelaure novels. Thus, they deserve a place in this companion.

ACKNOWLEDGMENTS

For their comments, support, and assistance, I wish to thank the following people: Frank Corey, Daphne Hobson, Donna Johnston, Jim Kerr, Kathleen Mackay, the late John Preston, Sue Quiroz, Steven Ramsland, Stan Rice, Michael Riley, Ben Spedding, Michelle Spedding (especially about the h. c.), Susan Strassberg, and Gail Zimmerman.

My agent, Lori Perkins, was especially delighted about this book, and assisted me in the bookstores.

Also thanks to Peter Borland and Elaine Koster for seeing the potential and eagerly embracing it.

And most of all, my gratitude to Anne Rice, for writing the novels, and for supporting me with her enthusiasm and rich responses.

PART I

THE EROTIC IMAGINATION OF ANNE RICE

Pornography stands outside accepted cultural values; it thrives on excess, spurns convention, and strives for intensely provocative descriptions. As a person long acquainted with the strength of her own sensuality and affinity for extremes, Anne Rice was a natural for this medium. Her first adult writings were about relationships with a highly charged sexual component, and although these early expressions were lost, Rice went on to incorporate her erotic perspective in novels that did get published. Contemporary social currents merged with personal events in Rice's life to influence her artistic directions. Beginning in childhood, Rice's erotic imagination gathered force from many diverse contexts.

EARLY INFLUENCES

"I loved the saints for their excessiveness."

As a child, Rice was highly attuned to the sensory aspects of her environment. Growing up in the sultry climate of New Orleans, she felt the moist air press against her, smelled the fragrant flowers, played in the cloying cemeteries, and learned in church the power of imagining intense experiences.

"I grew up in the only Catholic city in the country," says Rice, "and I was taught by nuns whose orders came from Catholic countries, and by an order of priests that originated in Italy. You sit there and you imagine what Christ felt as he walked down the street carrying the cross. I went through a lot of that in my childhood; there were many such spiritual exercises. It's very common to sit in church and visualize what the thorns felt like going into Christ's forehead and what the nails felt like going into his hands. All of this involved using your imagination, trying to make the leap into something else.

"My religious education was filled with sensuality and with preoccupations over good and evil. It was natural to come out of that environment writing the kind of fiction I do. That's why it feels authentic to me."

Rice was particularly enthralled with the lives of the saints because of their courage, dedication, and intensity. "I loved the saints for their excessiveness, their going out on a limb, their willingness to fight everybody, and the misjudgment they endured." She learned about the punishing exercises of the medieval flagellants, how they stretched the resources of their bodies to increase their pleasure in God by increasing the degree of pain they could bear. She listened avidly to stories about the asceticism of St. Francis, the extreme devotion to holiness of St. Teresa of Avila, and the self-inflicted brutality of St. Thérèse (the "Little Flower"). Such saints were known for their avowals of self-negation in the face of God's presence and power. They believed that only true humility could bridge the abyss that separates mortals from God, and sometimes their own bodies manifested their spiritual intensity with the startling blood of the stigmata.

"The lives of the saints were very sadomasochistic," Rice points out. "They drove themselves into a state of ecstasy that was erotic. They went to extremes."

Contact with God, according to one of Rice's heroines, Teresa of Avila, became a "delectable pain," or "the wound of love" that "leaves the soul yearning once again to suffer that loving pain." Enamored of martyrdom, Teresa had a vision of an angel piercing her heart with a fiery tip. She preached that only total surrender of the will and continual supplication to God for mercy reaped the fullness of heaven. The end result was a rapturous transport into the arms of God.

"I loved St. Teresa and read lives of her constantly," Rice admits. "I have a statue of her in my house. It seems natural and inevitable that Catholic mysticism and eroticism have much in common. The mystics would surrender in ecstasy to Christ, be pierced by his arrow, and feel a sublime trance state akin to sexual fulfillment. It's all dominance and submission, and it's quite beautiful. I read a lot about mysticism when I was a Catholic girl, about meditation, about visions, about surrendering the mind to Christ, about meditation on Christ's passion, his wounds, the Stations of the Cross, all of it. It never seemed erotic to me, but obviously it had a profound influence, and I'm eroticizing these things now in my writing."

Rice was so transfixed by the lives of the saints that she begged her father to design an oratory for prayer and meditation. He converted an unused bathroom at the back of the house. Inside, she spent many hours imagining the suffering of the martyrs and hoping to experience the stigmata. "I believed I was going to be a Carmelite and a saint," she says.

"Anne's temperament was such," her father later recalled, "that when she embraced something, she had to exercise real restraint not to become a zealot or a fanatic."

Perhaps the central image of her daily religious education was the ceremony of Transubstantiation—the transformation and spiritualization of physical substance. The mystery and magic of the Holy Communion, wherein bread and wine become Christ's body and blood, was conveyed in secretive Latin by priests in colorful robes. Rice observed all with the impressionable, wondering eyes of a child. Adding to this experience was the injunction from her mother, Katherine O'Brien, to honor Christ's sacrifice with daily devotion. Katherine had saintly aspirations for herself and her four daughters, and she urged them to be good Catholics.

Rice often lost herself in the desire to be a holy instrument of God. As she walked down the aisle at church, she imagined Christ inside her and took pains to live up to the church's ideas. "I was pretty repressed," she admits. "If they said it was a sin to have dirty thoughts, I'd agree with them. If they said it was a sin to touch yourself, I'd agree with them." Yet she also "had a great feeling of sexually and sensually responding to things." These opposing emotions confused her: "My mother always said such feelings were normal but sinful." In autobiographical terms she describes the conflicted childhood of her character Lisa, in *Exit to Eden*—someone who was raised in a similar environment. Lisa has "dark, strange" sexual feelings and wants to be touched, although she feels ashamed of such desires. She thinks they set her apart from other children. "That was sort of based on me," Rice admits.

The contradiction between holiness and sin proved to be stimulating, and Rice began having masochistic fantasies. "I've had those fantasies since I was very little. I think lots of children do. Some children find that stuff sexy right off."

As she developed, Rice's fantasies became more complex, evolving into several imaginary worlds. "I've had these dream worlds since I was a kid, and they're very active," she affirms. Each "world" was peopled with numerous characters of all ages. One fantasy was a contemporary drama about people who shared many of Rice's own aspirations, while another—destined to become highly sexual—was set in ancient Roman times. "It might be," Rice admits, "that if I wrote down everything that was going on in that imaginary world, it would be very psychologically revealing. But if I wrote down my personal fantasies, they'd just be fragments."

Rice provided details of how this Roman scenario developed for her when she described Elliott Slater's sexual fantasy in *Exit to Eden*: Elliott imagines himself as a young boy in Greece. Every few years, seven boys are sent to another city to serve as sexual slaves. The priests tell them to submit to everything asked or demanded of them, then consecrate their genitals to the gods. Naked and forbidden ever to speak, the boys are auctioned off to the highest bidders. As symbols of masculine power and fertility, they become mysterious objects of both scorn and veneration. Although their masters cherish them, they are not considered fully human. "We were utterly subservient," says Elliott, "meant to be played with . . . meant to be beaten . . . and sexually tormented and starved—driven through the city for the amusement of the master. . . . It was a religious thing to torment us, while we kept our fear and humiliation inside."[1] For this fantasy to be powerful to Elliott (and Rice), there had to be coer-

[1] *Exit to Eden* (New York: Arbor House, 1985), p. 24.

cion without force; only with consent did it become a good fantasy. It had to be humiliation "with a struggle inside between the part of you that wants it and the part of you that doesn't; and the ultimate degradation is that you consent and grow to like it."[2] Ultimately the master who buys Elliott falls in love with him, even as he continues to abuse him.

Elliott confesses that his mind is a three-ring circus, echoing how Rice felt about her own, and his sexual mentor tells him such is the case with all sadomasochists. Excessive, complex fantasies are part of their nature.

"I wanted to be like everyone else."

Rice's mother encouraged and supported her with affirmations of her own power to be whatever she wanted. It did not matter that she was a girl; she could still strive for greatness. With no real emphasis on living according to role expectations, and having a firm belief in her own special worth, she came up hard against the gender biases of the Catholic church. As an adolescent, she soon realized that girls were socially ostracized for exhibiting sexual feelings and behaving in any manner other than what was prescribed as demurely feminine. Rice was later to write an article for *Vogue* magazine in which she yearns for the androgynous endowment of her youth, "a wise innocence that embraces the power of both sexes and uses it effortlessly before adult gender distinctions clamp down."[3]

"In early childhood," says Rice, "when you're sexually undifferentiated, before all this crap descends on you, that's when you're a pure character and heading toward strengths that will manifest themselves as an adult. Adolescence is a treacherous period where all of that can fail. Up to that point in my life, I had been a free spirit and could do anything I wanted."

Just as frustrating were the inequities between the genders. The boys were more privileged, and it soon became obvious that having a relationship entailed giving over power to them. Fe-

[2]Ibid., p. 24.
[3]"Playing with Gender," *Vogue*, April 1983.

males obviously risked more. Rice longed for love with an equal, but her perspective seemed contrary to the experiences of the girls around her. She felt she might never be part of "normal" society.

Nevertheless, she developed an attraction to boys, and her attention to their physical beauty was just one more thing that made her feel painfully unique. She later wrote about her secret enticement in her master's thesis, "Katherine and Jean." Katherine, an adolescent in boarding school, experiences curiosity about sex and men's bodies. She wonders why the other girls fail to share her desires. "The girls at school felt that you loved a man first, and then tolerated his body. You fell in love with him because he was 'cute' or 'wonderful' and then you giggled and turned red talking about the size of the bulge in his trousers."[4] As with Lisa Kelly in *Exit to Eden*, Rice felt about herself that "some vital imprinting had never taken place, some message about sex being bad had failed over and over to reach its destination in my head."[5]

Rice sensed she was unable to express, without censure, who she truly was. This feeling of being unlike others—"more physically there"—gave her a sense of being different, an outsider. She wanted to be one of the crowd but felt she was out of step with the way the other girls talked and viewed themselves. "I wanted desperately to fit in," she recalls. "My individuality was almost irrepressible, but I wanted to fit in." Intimidated by seeing the girls around her developing into women, she was envious of their knowledge about makeup, high-heeled shoes, and fashion. Yet she was horrified by the rigid expectations of female roles. "It was like a storm descending," she remembers. These painful adolescent experiences gave added impetus years later to her sympathetic portrayals of sexual rebels.

"You loved all the sexual adventurers."[6]

When she was nearly fifteen, Rice lost her mother to alcoholism and had to learn to take charge of her own life. Her father

[4]"Katherine and Jean," unpublished master's thesis, 1972, p. 92.
[5]*Exit to Eden*, p. 280.
[6]Ibid, p. 179.

moved the family to Texas, where she went to public schools for the first time. As she began to write in an atmosphere of greater freedom, a new element crept into her stories, about which she became aware only in retrospect: She was becoming fascinated with same-sex attraction between males. "If I go back to stories I wrote in high school," she recalls "it was there. I just didn't know what it was. Anyone reading the stories would have seen how the males talked to each other, and the emphasis on their appearance, and the slight idealization of them. It was latent."

Around this time, Rice had the experience of seeing a flasher and feeling a strong sense of kinship with him. She spotted him in a park, across the lagoon, and realized he was holding his penis in plain view. The sight of it upset the girl who was with her, but Rice felt that as long as the man was hurting no one, he was harmless. This encounter would eventually become part of the character development of Lisa in *Exit to Eden,* a young woman who loves sexual outsiders for their boldness in seeking their own form of pleasure. Lisa views the flasher as a mirror of herself. Rice, too, identified with such nonviolent sexual outlaws. Between her feelings of ostracism, her erotic fantasies, and her appreciation for people who reached for the most heightened forms of experience, she was well on her way to becoming a writer with a flair for unique sexual themes.

RICE'S INTRODUCTION TO PORNOGRAPHY

"I just didn't click."

In the early sixties, Rice moved to San Francisco. Once again, she was in the uncomfortable position of feeling removed from people around her. "I got flack for looking and sounding like a square," she remembered, "and for saying things that were unfashionable. I just didn't click." Against an anti-intellectual trend, she wanted to study and learn. Among funky artists, she dressed like a Catholic schoolgirl, yet she was also aware of the cultural changes. She got caught up with both the emergence of gay culture and the new directions of erotic expression. Each had its distinct influence on her writing.

Behind the Puritanical facade of an American middle-class, family-dominated culture, a recognition of primal sexuality was developing. In the late 1940s Kinsey had provided startling evidence of sexual practices among Americans that belied what they wanted to believe: Homosexuality was more widespread, masturbation had no negative mental effects, and premarital sex could produce better marriages. While Rice had been a teenager during the fifties, personalities like Tennessee Williams, Marlon Brando, Hugh Hefner, Marilyn Monroe, and Elvis Presley had drawn attention to a restless undercurrent of dissatisfaction with "proper" sex. The 1953 advent of *Playboy* had associated sex-for-fun with the good life. In 1956, *Peyton Place*, Grace Metalious' notorious novel about lust and intrigue in a small New England town, became one of the top best-sellers of the year. Three years later, the U.S. publication of Nabokov's *Lolita* opened doors for other erotic novels.

There were voices of resistance, particularly against challenging the feminine role of the happy, monogamous homemaker, but the tide was turning in favor of sexual expression and freedom. Birth control gained appeal as Margaret Sanger continued to promote the rights of women to take control of their own bodies. The youth followed the lead of rebels like Jack Kerouac and James Dean, losing confidence in moral codes blandly prescribed by an out-of-touch older generation. Within a few years, erotic works by the likes of Henry Miller, the Marquis de Sade, and Jean Genet would be available.

Rice moved into Haight Ashbury with Ginny Mathis, a friend from college. She developed a crush on a young Catholic student named Ed, who resisted her advances. It was her first experience with a man who would later realize he was gay. However, it was not long before Rice had reunited with a boy from high school with whom she had fallen in love. His name was Stan Rice. He came to San Francisco to see her, she seduced him, they carried on a steamy correspondence, and he soon proposed. They got married and made their home in San Francisco.

Although they worked and went to school at night, they found time to mingle with artists. Stan developed his flair for poetry while Rice dabbled with writing. She contemplated turning out steamy romances for money but could not sustain her interest. When her cousin, Allen Daviau, suggested she read Vladimir Nabokov for his "cinematic" writing style, she responded enthusiastically. Her choice was the controversial novel *Lolita*.

"*Lolita* has had a huge influence on everything I've written," Rice admits. "I fell in love with Nabokov's language when I read *Lolita* and his memoir, *Speak, Memory*. His way of writing erotic scenes, so eloquently and elegantly, had a huge influence. I wanted the elegance of his books. I wanted the mood. I wanted his skill. I have reread *Lolita* several times in the past few years. I reread it before writing *Belinda*. I turn to it often, just to dip into the language. I also loved Nabokov's wit, and his compassion for most of his characters."

Like Nabokov, Rice wanted to write about the intensity of a devotion that transcends physical desire, and to explore emotional realms fraught with psychological risk. "The mixture of love and erotic attraction is frightening and overwhelming," she explains, "and that mixture interests me." Such relationships, she thought, provided opportunities to build up heat with language, and she wanted to write stories that would deeply affect people.

Stan also broadened her appreciation for the richness and pliability of language by exposing her to contemporary poetry. "I've been influenced a great deal by Stan," Rice admits. "I think a lot of his rhythms, phraseology, and music are deeply ingrained in my own writings." Stan believed that poetry was sensual and physical, "the most physically immediate form of literature." As a poet and later a teacher, he viewed his work as having a "raw-meat, spontaneous" style. "If you trust the words, they'll do the work," he explains. "If you trust the rhythm, the sense will follow."

In school, Anne Rice studied the styles of such diverse writers as Shakespeare, Woolf, and Hemingway. From them, she grasped the importance of linking the emotional and physical in the most intense moments, and of expressing that connection with subtle and poetic nuánce. However, few of the Rices' friends took her efforts seriously. Her desire to write linear narrative seemed unadventurous to them, and obviously Stan was the one who had the important career. They thought Anne should concentrate on taking care of him.

For her part, Rice found the repressive role of the good wife to be stifling and the role of women in general to carry many liabilities. She resisted the pressures to act a certain way simply because she was female. "I think it's oppressive being a woman," she responded. "It's a terrible thing to be from every standpoint. I've never been comfortable as a woman. I thought I was an imposter. I was told I didn't talk like a girl or walk like a girl, and I was very upset."

In her fifth vampire novel, *Memnoch the Devil*, she gives the same opinion to the devil. When he first acquires physical form, he chooses the guise of a male. He quickly dismisses the other option as unthinkable. Lestat agrees that Memnoch made the best choice. He mentions several times in this novel how vulnerable women are in a man's world.

"The feminist movement has done wonders to alleviate the situation," Rice admits, "I was glad to see it happening. But there's so much more to be done that it's appalling. I think the position of being a woman is still one of daily outrage. I didn't realize it until I was fourteen and I started learning all these dreary Catholic rules, that you weren't supposed to let boys do things or they'd think you were cheap. There was not a thing in all of that about what women were feeling; it was all about how to play your cards right so they didn't think you were a whore. No one ever said anything about whether you were entitled to any kind of pleasure or whether your desires represented anything other than something not to give in to. I remember being horrified by the whole thing. I realized that women weren't really like men and were not entitled to do what men were entitled to do.

"I went through those phases that people went through in the sixties where it was a common thing for women to say they didn't like other women. It was a natural step to take to think that women were second-rate people and to think you only liked men. It was only with the beginning of feminism that we were able to say perfectly well that we liked women. I've always had women friends, but they were always the strong ones who felt that they didn't like women, either."

Rice believed in equality and liberal ideals, but to her chagrin, some of her friends who identified with the feminist movement began to dictate her behavior. They reminded her of the strict nuns from her childhood, who laid down all the rules.

"The radical feminists I knew were strident and aggressive. They believed I should be writing about women's experiences. I believed a woman should read and write what she wanted to read and write." Even with the new freedoms for women, Rice realized she still did not identify with her gender, particularly with those women who tried to dictate her thoughts and behavior. "I feel like my intellect is masculine or androgynous."

In years to come, she was to claim that she would happily be a six-foot, blond, blue-eyed man. However she did not identify fully with men, either, because she was appalled by the aggression and violence of heterosexual males. In interviews and in her novels she alludes to the dangers of testosterone and the way lust seemed to control men: In *The Mummy*, she hinted that men need to hurt; her character Khayman in *The Queen of the Damned* can commit a rape he despises; Lestat has no awareness of a woman's distress as he rapes her; and *Belinda*'s sexually aroused Jeremy Walker senses a wild animal inside him. Rice allows only one female character to react aggressively: To finally terminate patriarchal dominance and cruelty, the vampire Akasha in *The Queen of the Damned* decides to annihilate most of the men on the planet. Although Rice did not agree with such a hideous strategy, she did believe it would work. Despite her attraction to heroic and symbolic violence in fiction, she viewed male criminal behavior as evil.

It seemed to her that due to innate differences and the inferior status of women in the culture, heterosexual men and women could not achieve equality in a relationship. So she idealized gay relationships. Although she wondered briefly what it would be like to be sexually involved with a woman, she pursued it only in fantasy. Her real fascination was with two men loving one another, equal in their strengths and weaknesses.

"I enjoy scenes between equals more than any others," she says. "You learn the most from equals. That's why it's fine to make love to someone of the same sex."

Gay men, to her, were like angels or saints because of their courage and ability to transcend the negative aspects of gender boundaries. It gave them more options for pleasure and self-exploration. Gay men seemed to develop spiritual resources for overcoming powerlessness and adversity, and they thought sex was good—that was another plus. "The gays care about the sexual revolution," Rice insists, "about free speech and sexual aggression. They remain curious about what we really feel." Such relationships came more vividly into her imaginary worlds and later into her writing: "To write about male–male sex feels normal; it feels free. I can get to deep nongender things like affection and commitment."

"I felt like a gay man in a woman's body."

Some of Rice's early attempts at writing short stories in college involved themes of complicated romantic and sexual feelings between males, particularly between older men and young boys. This type of erotic bond offered an opportunity to explore the sacred aspects of mentoring and initiation. For example, one story from the sixties, called "Absolution," was about a man living in a sexual relationship with a young boy. The man teaches the boy about sexual experience. "When the boy turned nineteen," Rice explains, "he ran away. He returned after many years and wanted absolution for running away, but the man was very cold to him." She also wrote repeatedly about a beautiful boy named Jean who had emerged from her adolescent fantasy world. Jean is constantly involved with older, more experienced men.

A gay friend of hers, Michael Riley, noted the repeated image of sexual mentoring whenever he read her work. As an English professor, his own interests centered on the creation of self in art, and he saw a consistent theme: "This combination of man and boy, older and younger, innocence and experience, has, in my opinion, always compelled her," he says about Rice. "Interestingly, the innocent is usually not an innocent at all so far as sexual experience is concerned—just the opposite—but the innocence survives and even seems to define the youth."

As early as high school, such relationships had fascinated Rice, and while she lived in San Francisco and observed the gay men around her, her imagination took a more personal twist. "I knew when I was young, about twenty-four, that I wished I was a gay man," Rice admits. "That was a common fantasy of mine. I felt that the physical response I had to men must mean I'm like a gay man. I identified with the way gay men talked about other men. I felt like an imposter as a woman. I read that story by Gorky called 'The Nose,' where one man steals another man's nose, and I wrote a humorous version of it. I see a beautiful gay man in the park and I say, 'That man has my body.' "

Rice was able to accurately intuit the male point of view, although she did ask Michael Riley about his experiences.

Having come into the gay culture as an older man with a reserved, intellectual bent, he felt that he was a bit atypical. "In a gay bar, I might as well have been a creature from the moon. I felt like an outsider who could understand the language when he heard it spoken but who could not speak it himself." However, he was eager to discuss his feelings and ideas with someone as responsive and sympathetic as Rice.

"She showed an absolute fascination with everything that had to do with being gay," he remembers. "She seemed to have an intuitive understanding of what my experience was like. I felt a great empathy from her, and a kind of passionate conviction on her part that embraced not only the fact of my sexuality, but also the personal pressures and displacement that inevitably went with it. I think Anne actually identified with it, that in some way she felt her own passionate (even erotic) nature put her on the outside. It was a bit as if I was a surrogate for her. She asked many questions about what I felt like, and she often interpreted my experience, as if she were trying to put it into her own words. There was one occasion when she asked me if I would write an account of what I considered to be my most perfect sexual experience, but I found myself completely unable to write it."

They talked about men that they both found beautiful, such as the French actor Alain Delon. Rice cherished beauty that was androgynous rather than effeminate and that seemed infused with both bisexuality and some inward spirituality. "It always has an immediate, intense emotional impact on me to see androgynous figures," says Rice. They also discussed Mary Renault, whom Rice considered a wonderful novelist on the topic of same-sex relationships. She loved Renault's descriptions of affection and erotic desire between men.

"We talked at length about *The Charioteer*," Riley recalls. It was a book about an emotional relationship that developed in a

British military hospital between a young soldier and a conscientious objector.

"This is not to suggest that Anne had homosexual desires of her own," he points out. "There was nothing in the least like that. But in some fashion it was as if my sexual nature and the way I had to live it out in the world spoke to something in her own sense of herself. Stan was such a charismatic figure, and the center of so much attention, that Anne felt herself something of an outsider. In a sense, sexual attractiveness was a kind of power that Stan had, and certainly Anne saw him in those terms. With that power also comes a kind of freedom. Male physical beauty was like an inspiration to Anne. It stirred her in ways that must have been erotic but also went beyond that."

Rice herself explains her identification with gay men as being multifaceted:

"I feel like a gay man in a woman's body because I'm attracted to men. I identify with gay men in their taste. I like much of what is called 'the gay aesthetic.' But I really must say, out of respect for gay men, that I really don't know what they truly feel. I am not visually aroused, as a man is; I am not a Y-chromosome person. But I often see men in the bluntly sexual way that gay men do. I find in conversations with gay men my visceral attraction to Tom Berenger or Arnold Schwarzenegger, or other hunks, is understood—really deeply understood—by the gay men. In my youth, I frightened other women when I spoke bluntly about men's bodies and how I liked them. I was told repeatedly that 'women don't feel like that.' I was given the impression by other women that I was abnormal. I wanted to see naked men. I wanted to feel their muscles and hammer on their chests, and feel their penises. I wanted to be a gay man. I want to run with gay men. Be one of them.

"I have come to the conclusion that the gay aesthetic is only part of our overall aesthetic, that it is not separate at all—that the entire culture now responds openly to the things which only gay men once cherished. I speak of flamboyant dress, violent colors, cross-dressing, S&M imagery, the blatant androgyny of figures like Prince, Michael Jackson, the boldness of Madonna. Madonna's porno book resembled gay men's magazines in its motifs, its use of leather, its love affair with grunge, et cetera.

Much of what we see in rock music was once the private fantasies of gay men. These are all mainstream now, when once, they would have been confined to gay fantasies, they would have been more esoteric. Now the world loves kink, and kink speaks to the world about free will and self-expression. That wasn't always so. During more conservative times, the gays were the ones who experimented with style and entertained visions of the androgynous. It's all open now. We know that the gay aesthetic is our aesthetic. The gays are us.

"Gender influences everything but determines nothing. What we share is more important than what sets us apart from one another. The possibilities are endless."

Eventually Rice and her husband bought a Victorian house in the Castro District, San Francisco's predominantly gay neighborhood. She appreciated what the gays had done to restore the old Victorian houses, and she was attracted to the vital, yet mellow quality of life there. She also loved watching the beautiful people walking around. Kathleen Mackay, a friend and writer, visited her there and recalls being with her during a Gay Rights Parade. "Anne and Stan watched it with great relish," she says. As a published writer, Rice made herself fully accessible to gay bookstores, supported gay rights, and was happy to have a large gay readership.

> *"We want our madmen and our*
> *madwomen to be offensive."*

Rice's exploration of gay experience and her own sexuality paralleled the increased sexual freedom in society at large. In the 1960s and '70s, more explicit sexual depictions in novels and films brought the pornography debate into new perspective. Decisions by the Supreme Court that allowed publication and distribution of sexually explicit material made it increasingly available, generating concern among conservatives about deviant behavior. Novels like *The Story of O* and *Candy* were widely read. Anne Rice and her friends were aware of the controversy over censorship laws in the recent past, and they fully supported freedom of speech and greater access to sex education.

"Many of us who considered ourselves liberal, intellectual,

and literary types," says Kathleen Mackay, "had read stuff like *The Story of O* and the Marquis de Sade's work. People in Berkeley had *The Joy of Sex* on their coffee tables. We had been pioneers in the sexual revolution. Women were proud that they could openly enjoy sex and rather casual encounters with the same gusto and aplomb that men did. The sexual revolution in San Francisco was a natural outgrowth of the hippie movement and part of the counterculture of the late sixties. Rock was a vibrant force in San Francisco and it was very, very sexual. The time was one of experimentation, of progressive ideas."

Originally, pornography had been written about and by whores to arouse lust in men and get more business. It represented erotic acts with no moral or aesthetic justification, and such was the state of much of the hard-core commercial porn in this century in America. One of the questions raised in the sixties concerned its increased prevalence as a sign of cultural decline: Was it merely evidence of the need for stimulation or did it show a new vitality and a more daring exploration of the forbidden? The artistic community examined the status of pornography as literature, and some claimed that pornography debased language and had no function as art.

In reaction, there were people who believed that social conflict was the soul of art; the role of the artist was to contact the forbidden and open up new awareness on behalf of society. Pornography did just that. Anne and Stan Rice aligned themselves in support of keeping the artist's options open.

"In my opinion," says Stan, "there is a ladder of literature. On the highest rung is the poem or novel which uses images to increase the ambiguity of truth. As we go down the ladder, the images start to limit the truth. On the bottom rung, we are still in the realm of art because we're still working entirely with images, but the images have a single function rather than a richly multidimensional one. On this last rung, we have advertising, propaganda, and pornography. Each of these images has a single intent: advertising's single intent, to persuade to sell a product; propaganda's single intent, to persuade to a particular political view; and pornography's single intent, to sexually arouse. Pornography does not debase language. It simply limits and reduces the images out of which it is made to a single function."

Feminist writer Susan Sontag stated that most of the arguments against pornography as literature could be used against other literary works as well. No aesthetic principle exists that would exclude pornography. Since artists are explorers of spiritual dangers, they inevitably advance into transgressive places. Art is about authenticity even if it is deviant, and sexual arousal in literature should not be considered a defect.

Rice agreed with this point of view: "Our artists and writers on all levels should be able to be madmen and madwomen. That's the function of art. We want our madmen and our madwomen to be offensive; we need them to be obscene. That's the way culture works. It's only when you have a free artistic marketplace that people have freedom to create the classics of tomorrow."[7]

She did not see how pornography could debase language. It was her opinion that repressing sexual expression kept people ignorant of the spiritual benefits of fully surrendering to that part of human experience. Rice was uninterested in sleaze written by hacks, but she felt there was value in having competent writers like Henry Miller and Vladimir Nabokov explore the deep realms of erotic desire.

Having already read *Lolita*, she next encountered a very different type of pornographic material in a Sausalito bookstore. A friend had handed her a copy of the *Evergreen* review, an avantgarde journal. "She said to me, 'Take it over in a corner and read it where no one can see your face,' " Rice recalls. "And I just thought, 'Wow, terrific, fabulous!' " It was the first chapter of Pauline Réage's *The Story of O*, and it had a significant effect on Rice's direction.

The story involves a young fashion photographer, O, who becomes sexually subservient to her lover, René, and his friends at Roissy, a château outside Paris. O is humiliated, whipped, and sexually assaulted. She willingly submits to everything, although it often frightens her. At times, she feels as if she is an object rather than a human being. The brutality increases with the entrance of Sir Stephen, but O endures his demands and even grows to need him so much that she prefers death over parting from him. In one of several endings, O is nothing, and her very

[7]John Preston (ed.), *Flesh and the Word 2* (New York: Plume, 1993), p. viii.

emptiness has been interpreted as her means of achieving transcendence over human limitations.

Rice eventually read the whole book and thought that the story was simply too sinister. Sexual freedom, she felt, should not have to be punished with death. "There was something frightening about the way the book took itself seriously," she said. In reaction, she wrote an erotic story for entertaining her closest friends, called "The Sufferings of Charlotte."

Set in the nineteenth century, this masochistic fantasy featured a heroine saved from being prosecuted for murder by reluctantly consenting to join a sexual cult. Although she desired the captivity and all that it entailed, she had to be forced to consent to it. Rice liked writing from the submissive victim's perspective, and she was proud to produce something so transgressive. She thought, "This from a square!" She loaned her only copy to friends, who lost it. Attempts to rewrite it failed when she lost interest. However, she later took up similar themes in her Roquelaure series.

During the same period, Rice fulfilled one of her earlier ambitions by writing a romantic novella in response to Vladimir Nabokov's *Lolita*. Set in a castle on an island, "Nicholas and Jean" involved a man who fell in love with a boy with violet eyes—a real-life image that a friend had described to Rice. "I created this boy with violet eyes," she said, "and imagined a man in love with him, and then the story came out of the subconscious."

The first chapter of this novel was published in the college literary journal, *Transfer*, but the rest eventually disintegrated with the newsprint on which Rice typed it. In this novella, Rice brings together her dual interests in pornography and in relationships between men. Told from the perspective of the older man, the story begins with Nicholas, a photographer in his twenties, arriving at an isolated castle owned by a friend. He discovers the boy, Jean, already there. Jean lives on champagne and has a passion for velvet. Because of his delicate beauty, youth, and vulnerability, he has been since the age of ten the sex toy of wealthy eccentrics, but has run away from each of them.

Nicholas is aroused by the boy. He decides to take care of him, although Jean runs from him as well. Nicholas then finds him in a bizarre sex club, drugged and sexually abused. He rescues him and takes him back to the castle, torn between finding Jean's parents and keeping the boy for himself. He finally decides on the latter and asks Jean for a commitment. Jean kisses him in affirmation.

However, secrecy and deceit eventually destroy the relationship. "Nicholas made the mistake," Rice explains, "of telling Jean he'd been married. So Jean went off and got garbed in female clothing and came to seduce Nicholas. Jean then revealed who he was and their affair was destroyed." Nicholas sends Jean away to boarding school, but Jean gives him an ultimatum: "Come to your senses or I'll leave."

As she wrote this story, Rice experienced a terrific sense of momentum; exploring her obsession once again with an older sexual mentor and a sensual, androgynous boy, she felt real freedom in expressing herself fully and lyrically. When she finished, she showed the manuscript to her husband and a few close friends.

"It met the test of something sincere, articulate, and deep," Stan Rice recalls. "We all have an interior of sexual fantasies, which we normally forbid showing one another, but when we see it, I think we have to acknowledge it as being one of the wellsprings of mental activity that never gets outside our heads."

"People were tremendously encouraging," Rice remembers. "They were responsive to the excessive language, and rhythms, and the obsession of it. I was really letting my language go, and I wanted to achieve something with Jean, this little boy figure, like Nabokov had achieved with Lolita, and I was madly pursuing my obsession."

Michael Riley read it and was sincerely impressed. "I've never read anything that shocked me so much. It was dazzling and utterly different. I felt a shiver as I turned the pages that night, in the midst of a room filled with other people talking about other things. It was like suddenly seeing an astonishing secret laid bare and knowing that it was both terrifying and true. And that you would somehow never be the same for knowing it.

"The story seemed archetypal in the fullest Jungian sense. You couldn't read it without being pushed to the wall. There is something so startlingly sensual about her world, about the physical world itself and the feelings of the characters, and Anne is completely unafraid of it.

"There was a tension between a profligate innocence joined to a very knowing sexuality in the young person, on the one hand, and a contained dignity joined to a powerfully sexual nature that needs both that innocence *and* knowledge to awaken him, on the other. There was illusion and performance (but neither is unreal), and the highest emotional stakes; there was fear and fearful longing, and facing the terrible uncertainty of choosing between them. Which way lies the greater danger? There were mysteries and often betrayals that seemed not so much calculated as inevitable. And the characters were master and apprentice both.

"I truly believe Anne has touched and explored something like a universal truth about human nature in this aspect of her work. It has little to do with sex as it is rendered in most books and films, but it has everything to do with its actual place in who we most deeply are."

Rice showed the novella to her creative writing professor. He appreciated its originality but suggested revision. Rice never rewrote it. However, many of the themes and images found their way into later works, especially Rice's master's thesis, "Katherine and Jean," and her novels *Cry to Heaven* and *Belinda*.

Another piece that Rice attempted with pornographic images and themes was "The Tales of Rhoda." A contemporary story, it involved another young woman voluntarily brought into captivity. Rice was exploring masochism and how a woman's desire to be dominated could arouse her. Although such a theme was becoming politically incorrect in some feminist circles, Rice was not going to allow anyone to tell her what should or should not excite her: "I believe in fantasy and in the right of women to express themselves in erotic fiction. Let women talk. Let them tell what they really want. For the first time in history, women can express themselves as men have always done. For centuries the world has not trusted women or women's sexuality. It's taken the position that women must be properly indoctrinated and controlled."

Rice was attracted to masochistic images and wanted to write something that expressed them as hotly as she felt them. "The delicate balance between force and consent is hard to find for masochists," she explains. "I wanted to maintain that balance."

However, "The Tales of Rhoda," too, lost steam after only a few chapters.

Rice wrote several versions of some of the sections of "Rhoda," but essentially the story was similar to *The Story of O*, and many of its themes foreshadow the Roquelaure treatment of dominance and submission.

Rhoda is a bored, twenty-five-year-old student at the University of California at Berkeley. She reads erotic novels like *The Story of O*, but dislikes the way female sensuality seems always to be punished. She does not believe that death must be the ultimate goal of true masochism. She views suffering as a means to make some larger experience possible.

One day, a strange man who knows her name slips a nude photo of her underneath her door. She is stunned but excited by this novel event. Then he engages her in conversation about the nature of masochism, and when he invites her for coffee, she agrees to meet him at a restaurant. The man claims to represent an organization that provides female slaves to masters for a period of one year. He sees Rhoda as an excellent candidate for training, but it has to be by her consent. Should she freely choose it, she would surrender to captivity with no way out. This is a choice, he tells Rhoda, that will separate her from most other people. She will be able to live out her fantasies of surrender.

Rhoda decides to do it, and she is taken to a place where she finds herself examined and prepared with other beautiful girls. She begins to have second thoughts and to fear what may lie ahead. Her nakedness shames her, although her passion increases with the feeling of humiliation. In one room, Rhoda meets Richard, a handsome, blue-eyed man who assures her that she cannot escape and must relax in her captivity so that she can fully please her master. "You only protest because you feel you should," Richard tells her. In fact, he points out that Rhoda was born to be a flagellant.

Richard's own trainer, Patterson, joins him as he begins Rhoda's training and insists that Richard be more strict and harsh, but Richard wants to go easy on Rhoda at first. From both men she learns that her master is her sole source of pleasure and satisfaction. Richard sends her to another room, where she becomes a plaything for the attendants.

During her introductory sessions, Rhoda is jabbed with needles, paddled, probed, displayed, corseted, humiliated, and inspected, all actions calculated to make her ever more aware of her nakedness and helplessness. One of the attendants makes her play a mindless game of fetching flowers in her teeth and bringing them to him as he places each stem into her anus. Then he brings in two other women to pluck the flowers out while Rhoda attempts to escape them. Rhoda fails to elude her pursuers, so she is delivered over to them for the night. These slaves are then transformed into masters. They stuff chestnuts into Rhoda's anus and vagina, and she hates them even more than her original masters for their knowing cruelty. They make her remove the chestnuts from her own body with her teeth. "Rhoda cried because she was sure it was impossible. . . . She could barely grasp one of the chestnuts and with tears in her eyes, she removed it."

Rice's writing ended at this point with a gentle voice telling Rhoda he is her confidant and will tell her whatever she wants to know. Like Alexi with Beauty in *The Claiming of Sleeping Beauty*, there seems to be a secret person in Rhoda's world who understands her misery and who might become a source of solace and education. However, no more of "Rhoda" was written.

Along the same lines, but using only men, Rice wrote a story that seemed meant to be the start of a novel, called "The House." As in *Exit to Eden*, "The House" is a charming old Victorian wherein sexual fantasies are cherished and acted out. A thirty-two-year-old bisexual man named Alex has confessed his fantasies of wanting to be dominated to his friend Tony, who urges him to visit The House. Alex is frightened but determined to see for himself what this place is all about. Although the master of The House advises him to sign up for only one night for his first experience, he insists on the entire weekend. Like Elliott Slater in *Eden*, who signs up for a two-year stint at The Club, Alex wants to be immersed. He understands that once he makes this choice, he is at their mercy. There is no escape. "Once you enter The House," Tony has warned him, "you're in their hands."

Alex has placed himself in a situation of consensual captivity. He agrees, within limits of health and safety, to allow the masters to decide what he needs done to him, and then to do it.

He will have no further say in the matter. He trusts that they know best what to do. If you can't stop it, he is told, eventually you surrender. "Fear is what we feel when we are trying to control what will happen to us," Alex hears—a wisdom that is often repeated in the Roquelaure novels.

His master is a genteel dark-haired man wearing a smoking jacket (a sexy image of power for Rice). He interviews Alex, then announces that he himself will be Alex's master. Through alternating rounds of discipline and affection, the master ensures that Alex's dignity is peeled away layer by layer, as humiliation is fused with sexual pleasure. The master uses a paddle because it both hurts and humiliates, but the cane is reserved for real disobedience. He instructs Alex to take no initiative, save for kissing his boots should they be near at hand. Alex forgets this and gets punished several times.

Eventually, the master takes Alex to a room where he sees a boy bound to a stool. The master instructs him to wash the boy and prepare him for sex. Alex is appalled but must do as he is told. The novel fragment ends here, obviously intended for continuation.

The stories that Rice wrote during this period were explorations of various characters who were parts of herself. The narratives all shared a "weird quality" that felt normal to her because she felt off kilter herself and because she wanted to use her scenarios to explore things below the surface. "I enjoy literary pornography," she says. "I see nothing wrong with writing sexually titillating scenes that have no redeeming social value."

"Katherine and Jean"

For her master's thesis at San Francisco State University in the early seventies, Rice developed a story around the character of Jean, from "Nicholas and Jean." She made him more clearly bisexual by involving him with a young woman named Katherine, a naive Catholic schoolgirl from New Orleans. The novella was not pornographic but made many allusions to erotic subjects and involved a seedy underground world of sexual hustling. Rice did not know the details of such a world, so the story was difficult for her to write. "It was a novel about me yearning to know all kinds of secrets about life."

Katherine's character involved Rice's exploration of making the transition from passivity to action: Katherine has long had decisions made for her, but as the novella opens, she finally takes charge of her life. Upon her mother's death, she leaves her family and runs off with Jean, an androgynous, violet-eyed stranger. Jean has a secret life that he hints about from time to time. He often disappears and returns without apology or explanation, so Katherine decides to spy on him. She encounters male nudity for the first time when she catches Jean dancing naked for an older man. Again, he does not explain himself.

Because he is street-wise and obviously experienced, Jean becomes a sort of tutor for Katherine, despite his youth. Eventually his past relationships with dangerous men involve him and Katherine in an adventure: They must don disguises to enter a kinky S&M club in San Francisco. Jean dresses as a woman, giving Rice the opportunity to explore the transgender imagery that so strongly fascinated her. She goes into detail, developed entirely from her own imagination, about this young man's experience of transforming himself into a woman. In the end, it is his beauty that saves him from the violence of his former masters. The story ends with Jean and Katherine returning to New Orleans, their relationship strained and unresolved, echoing Rice's own feelings about her story.

"I think two forces have warred in me for many years," Rice explains. "As a young writer, I tried to force myself into a mold. I would start off with a novel like 'Katherine and Jean,' set in the boarding school where I went, but in would come this fabulous imaginative character, and he would take over. The elements of my real life would pass away because I couldn't work with it."

Katherine's life failed to inspire her, but Jean was a different matter. As a character, he held a certain archetypal fascination, because what intrigued Rice most in her writing was attending to a mixture of opposites that transcended both poles. "I can't get interested in dramatic extremes if they don't embody that mixture. The reason I like to write about people who are bisexual is that I see them as transcending gender. I don't see my characters as homosexual; I never have. They are people who have homosexual relationships, and they are written about without the kind of sinister guilt overlay that people generally put on homosexual characters. I see opposites coming together in the person: male and female, good and evil. I like going into the complexity."

Rice began to describe the human mind in general, not just her own, as bisexual. Once people grasped that truth, she believed, they could more easily bond with members of either gender. The immense popularity of the novels soon to come might be convincing arguments for this point of view.

THE EARLY NOVELS

"I saw as a vampire"[8]

While Rice was writing her master's thesis, she was also caring for her young daughter, Michelle, who suffered from leukemia. The child died just before her sixth birthday. This tragedy precipitated Rice's first published novel. Called *Interview with the Vampire*, it was an erotic depiction of a supernatural creature's experience of immortality.

During the mid seventies, when Rice was writing about vampires, people all around her were seeking alternative ways of viewing the world. They explored new paths to enlightenment, spiritual peace, and transcendence.

"I was in what was called a hot center—the Bay area and Berkeley," she says, "so I was in the thick of whatever was happening in terms of trends and attitudes, but the emphasis for me was very personal. I was out of step with everyone because I wasn't writing a novel about hitchhiking to Big Sur or dropping acid in the Redwoods." Nevertheless, Rice's first novel uniquely expressed in metaphorical terms the restless longing of that decade. She sensed a primal undercurrent, which emerged in her work.

While the story became a cathartic vehicle for dealing with grief over her daughter, it also provided an arena for Rice's obsession with eroticized relationships. Her vampires experienced

[8]*Interview with the Vampire* (New York: Alfred A. Knopf, 1976), p. 20.

a heightened degree of sensory stimulation and were able to love one another regardless of sex. Rice saw a natural link between horror images and erotic experience. "I think the connection is profound," she acknowledges. "I am writing about the same themes, dominance and submission, and there's an erotic tone to everything. The vampire story echoes the sex act, with the seduction of the victim."

She believed that as outsiders, vampires were free of role restrictions of any kind. Their nongenital eroticism, rampant lust, bisexuality, and tendency toward incest made them sexually transgressive. They easily crossed hypothetical gender boundaries, allowing multifaceted identifications for readers. Using voluptuous and imagistic language, Rice created an aura of charged sensuality and subliminal tension that could find no ultimate release. She brought to this supernatural genre a deeper sense of the vampire's complex point of view, particularly with regard to the extreme degree to which these creatures could feel pleasure and pain.

"I think the vampire is an erotic image," she says. "It echoes the old lusty vegetation gods. Religions used to have sensuous gods and goddesses, but they're gone now and what lingers in our imagination is the vampire. He demands from us a sacrifice—but there's also great rapture—and we respond subconsciously."

Rice admitted that the female experience of orgasm influenced her description of the ecstasy that accompanies the vampire transformation: "I think I swapped the male orgasm for the female. The pleasure [Louis] gets in killing is an overall swoon like women feel, a surrender." She was also influenced by the erotic tones of the relationship between mentor and novice that Carlos Castaneda portrayed.

"The one contemporary book I read at the time that had a profound influence on me was Castaneda's book *The Teachings of Don Juan*. I really fell into that book. I was enthralled with the writing and the simplicity of Castaneda's descriptions."

The vampire telling his story in *Interview* describes how another vampire, Lestat, initiated him into a secret world of death, darkness, and addictive compulsion. Although Louis appreciates the richness of his new experience, he mourns his lost mortality. When he and Lestat eventually create a five-year-old vampire child, Claudia, they become a family bonded by love and hate. Louis and Claudia try to destroy Lestat, then search for other vampires. They find Armand, who falls in love with Louis. Together, Louis and Armand explore what it means for the damned to love the damned, but Louis eventually ends up alone. The novel is a chronicle of unrelieved suffering and the desperate search for love and identity.

"The vampires are us," Rice insists. "They are us in our loneliness, in our fear, in our spiritual and moral isolation. They are us in our ruthlessness, and in our desperate quest for companionship, warmth, love, and reassurance in a world full of gorgeous temptations and very real horrors. They are fallible beings with the power of gods, and that is exactly what we are, all of us."

Over the next twenty years, four other vampire novels became part of this series, beginning with *The Vampire Lestat*. Each made even more daring use of Rice's political agenda of freeing the vampires from gender baggage. Lestat, becoming her new hero, is clearly bisexual and eager for erotically charged relationships. On his various adventures, he makes his mother a vampire, is attracted to males, and has sex with a waitress and a nun. He also finds the devil rather appealing.

In addition, in 1979, Rice wrote a sensual vampire story for *Playboy* magazine. The editors had sent her several photographs of a romantically garbed male vampire in various poses with two nude women. She used the vampire Armand to tell the tale of a vampire's loneliness and search for love. Armand is a gentle seducer, bonded to his victims through their dreams but ever aware of the violence of eroticism: "All embraces, no matter how tender, are surfeited with violence. Violence is the throbbing of the unsatisfied heart."[9]

As a result of Rice's unique portrayals of vampire sexuality, her novels have been the focus of critical controversy. Some reviewers claimed that the first novel was a contrived and obvious metaphor of gay life: Louis's descriptions of alienation from his own nature, his guilty awakening to what he is, and his initiation into a secret subculture paralleled the experience of the gay man in America.

[9]Anne Rice, "The Art of the Vampire at its Peak in the Year 1876," *Playboy*, January 1979, p. 388.

Indeed, this novel found a huge gay audience. A few critics were offended by the erotic license implied in the vampire's existence. Even years later, when the 1994 movie *Interview with the Vampire* visually explored the sensual relationships between the vampires, issues were still raised about Tom Cruise's depiction of a "homosexual vampire." The critics seemed to miss the point of the vampire's transcendent freedom. However, Rice was undaunted.

"Fiction has to be vital," she claims. "Vampires enable me to talk about something larger than themselves. Fantasy and horror can embody and reflect the most dreaded pain that we all share. The ambition and potential of these genres is limitless."

For Rice, the vampire mythos offered metaphors of the complex power relationship between seduction and surrender in the context of the titillating images of dangerous sex. Rice spiritualized the vampires' transformation, linking it to the imagery of the Transubstantiation. Blood was as central to the vampires' essence as it was for Christ's sacrifice and for the believer's redemption and union with God.

"I remain impressed with how rituals work in life," she explains. "Many things are ritualized, and I retain, in retrospect, an appreciation for the power of the rituals of the Catholic church. Those images run all through literature."

More politically, Rice also viewed the child vampire, Claudia, as a statement about the plight of women. "I saw Claudia as a woman in a child's body. There are women who are eternally called girls, when in fact they have a ragingly strong mind that's very threatening. She's the person robbed of power."

From the first book on, Rice emphasized the idea that all wisdom lies in the flesh; substance is its own teacher, and it teaches that pleasure is life's prize. The experiences of the body, along with its appetites, reveal truth about human existence. This idea, combined with the imagery of forced consent inherent in the vampire story, helped her to sharpen her own sense of the erotic.

"Outsiders give us a different perspective on life."

After Rice's first novel, she wrote two works of historical fiction, *The Feast of All Saints* and *Cry to Heaven*. The first was about the free people of color in antebellum New Orleans, focusing on the stories of a gay writer and of several adolescents dealing with the upheavals of their personal maturation.

Christophe, the writer, faces prejudices in New Orleans over his sexual orientation, although he does not press it on the fourteen-year-old quadroon boy, Marcel, whom he grows to love. Eventually Marcel offers himself, but Christophe refuses him.

"Christophe and Marcel made love in the original *Feast of All Saints*," says Rice, "but it was 'off camera.' I didn't follow them into the bedroom, and I thought it really was out of character for Marcel, so I didn't include it later. I thought it was far too romantic, the idea that a straight boy like Marcel would seduce Christophe out of romantic love for him. They were supposed to go to bed and consummate their relationship, but the editors talked me out of it. I wrote the scene, only they don't go to bed. I repressed a lot of those elements."

Marcel's younger sister, Marie, must also face the demands of her own hungry body. Like Rice at her age, Marie feels religious shame over her orgasmic capacity. However, after being gang-raped and flinging herself into a house of prostitution, she learns from an older woman the nature of love and sexuality: Having broken out of social roles, they are truly free to be who they are. Rice absolves Marie of her religious guilt.

Rice thought about writing a sequel in which she married Christophe to one of the female characters, and she asked Michael Riley what he thought of the idea. "I told her," he recalls, "that I hoped she wouldn't use that. I had so seldom read a novel of any merit in which the gay character was 'permitted' to find happiness or fulfillment. I remember thinking that she had 'heard' what I said." There was no such sequel.

The next novel, *Cry to Heaven*, was much more explicit, joining issues of sexual freedom to the world of art. Having done thorough research to support her ideas, Rice described the libidinous affairs of castrated opera singers in eighteenth-century Italy. One young castrato, Tonio, who was mutilated against his will, allows intimate advances from other boys training with him but resists the feeling that he is no longer fully a man. He moves through numerous sexual scenarios, including one with a cardinal, variously playing male and female roles. However, for a long time he denies his unique ability to defy gender for gaining self-empowerment. For Tonio, sexual freedom borders on chaos and loss of control. He needs to have a number of diverse liaisons and meet an exciting woman who easily switches roles before he appreciates the possibility inherent in gender ambiguity. Eventually, Tonio grasps his advantages and discovers the wealth of potential in the abnormal life of the castrato. As another type of outsider, he illustrates a concept dear to Rice, that such people may have lives as full as those who play out socially approved roles.

In this novel, rather than berate religion for its role in repressing sexuality, Rice made the bold move of subsuming the symbols of the church into Tonio's erotic experience. The cardinal makes surreptitious, guilty love to him, but Tonio views their coupling as a holy encounter. The relationship reveals Rice's feelings about the spirituality of sex when Tonio approaches the act of oral sex as a sacrament. "You're taking the power of the male into your mouth," Rice claimed, "and that's what you're supposed to be doing in Holy Communion—getting the male into your mouth and getting that power."

When Rice gave the novel to Michael Riley, he told her it was audacious. "She found her way to a profound statement of her conviction," he says, "that in art and sexuality we have the most at stake and can find absolute and liberating fulfillment of the self. She had in a sense taken a staple of historical novels—sexual 'license' in an earlier age—and made of it something not only different but profound. In her characters the search for the self was intricately bound up with their sexuality—not merely their having sex, but their sexuality as a mainspring of their identity no less than their creativity. There was always a sense that the characters' very self was on the line, whether they necessarily knew it or not. For Anne, sexuality and creativity (even in a spiritual sense) are indivisible. One of the strongest traits of Anne's erotic imagination is that she truly joins the flesh and the spirit."

These three early novels were joined by a common thread. All of them were about outsiders who developed profound inner resources. Rice showed that their lives were potentially as rich as so-called normal life, and in some ways better. Nevertheless, as outsiders, they felt cheated of some of their options, and their desire for community or family drove them to seek others like them.

Rice wanted to continue to explore this theme, but she felt oppressed by the darkness of the characters she had used thus far. In addition, writing historical novels required so much background material that it interfered with getting to the "heated realities" of the relationships. Rice also wanted to recapture the fun she had experienced writing pornography back in the sixties, so she pondered making a major change in her creative directions.

THE PSEUDONYMOUS BOOKS

"I had three voices"

In the 1980s, the previous decade's pursuit of pleasure clashed with a counterrevolution fed by fear. Ronald Reagan's eight-year reign in the White House brought with it a strong conservative tide. More sobering was the discovery of AIDS, which closed many sex clubs and shrank the "swinger" subculture. Rock music was subjected to ratings, sexual expression became suspect, and some safe-sex campaigns promoted chastity. There were even recovery groups for sexaholics.

Nevertheless, more women were writing erotic material than ever before. Sexual fantasies of all types were becoming acceptable. Nancy Friday's *My Secret Garden*, Lilli Pond's erotic journal *Yellow Silk*, and the best-selling *Ladies' Home Erotica* were readily available; clearly, women were getting more adventurous and aggressive. The idea that "girls just want to have fun" gave momentum to liberal feminism, but spurred a backlash from within its own ranks.

From the feminist Right, Andrea Dworkin and Catharine MacKinnon spoke out against the way pornography sexually demeaned and abused women. Dworkin argued that pornography was brutal, ill-conceived, and simple-minded, defining women as being reducible to what was between their legs. She and her cohorts urged women, for their own self-respect, to resist the trend to make pornography acceptable and available. Otherwise they were buying into the violence. The organization Women Against Pornography demanded that the Meese Commission, formed to study the relationship between sex crimes and smut, acknowl-

edge that the pornography industry depended on the sexual ex-
ploitation of women.

Critics of the feminist Right's position claimed that it actually insulted women; it failed to credit women with the strength
or intelligence to make up their own minds about pornography.
Women as a group had diverse tastes, and no single group
should legislate this for all others.

For political purposes, a fine distinction was drawn between
pornography—predominantly associated with male fantasies—
and *erotica*, the softer, more romantic, and more acceptable variety of sexually stimulating media. Gloria Steinem pointed out
that pornography was like rape, whereas erotica involved a genuine sexual relationship.

Feminism continued to be divided on the issue, as many
women pushed the envelope of female sexuality. Anne Rice was
among them. Antipornography crusaders, she felt, were fools in
their misunderstanding of sexual desire and tyrants in their attempts to dictate behavior. "You can't change the mentality reflected in pornography by censoring it," she insists. These
women had no respect for free speech or free will and were no
better than the men who, for the past two thousand years, had
been telling women what to think and feel. "These feminists
have the same old contempt for women's feelings," she said,
"the same horror that women might really enjoy sex." It was
time to allow women to express themselves, to read and write
whatever they wanted, and to discover what they really do feel.
She told an interviewer for *The Advocate* that sex was the most
important subject to write about.

"I regard my writing of pornography to be a real moral
cause," she says. "And I don't want a bunch of fascist reactionary
feminists kicking in the door of my consciousness with their
jackboots and telling me that sadomasochism isn't politically
correct." To her, the sexual revolution of the 1960s and '70s was
"the most important revolution of our time."

"Anne felt quite passionately about the feminists who were
antipornography," her friend Kathleen Mackay recalls. "She felt
they were violating the First Amendment. I think some of that
passion helped fuel the Beauty books, because Anne felt, in her
own way she was defending our rights to these precious free-

doms, which others wanted to deny us. I felt she didn't want these antipornography crusaders to speak for all women. She wanted other voices to be heard."

In *Exit to Eden*, Rice addressed these political issues when she discussed how human history is replete with violence. As a survival mechanism, the subconscious has transformed these racial memories into sexual fantasies for people to act out harmlessly. "They can't sanitize or legislate our sexuality out of us," Elliott says in the novel. "It's got to be understood and contained."[10]

"The best of our art contains violence," Rice points out. "The violence I enjoy is pretty much wrapped up in the idea of heroism. I enjoy seeing people in complicated conflict. I love to see one person against the odds."

Since the sixties, Rice had been searching for satisfying pornography. "I was always enchanted with the transgressive. It always seemed to raise my temperature a bit mentally when I glimpsed something others called perverse, especially if I saw deep feeling involved. I always felt that a door was ajar on a world that was more vital than our own, that in perversity lies a great secret: true love."

She had read histories of sexual customs and looked over much of the explicit material that was available. "I read one Henry Miller book, and it went right through me," she says. "I can't remember a thing in it. I've read de Sade and Anaïs Nin, and also *Candy*. I've read lots of Grove Press reprints of anonymous pornography from the Victorian era. I read *My Secret Life*, by Walter X, a famous Victorian masterpiece about erotic life, and I've read plenty of cheap pornography over the years. I read *Delta of Venus*, but I hardly considered it porn. I thought Nin's words and images were pretty, but I wanted to do something stronger and to my taste. I've read some pure pulp trash involving lesbians and spankings and such, but I was always looking for good porn and could never find just the right thing."

Candy, published in America in 1964, was a satire on pornography and contemporary fads. The innocent and sexually generous Candy Christian has her first encounter with her college ethics teacher, and her erotic adventures go from there. The

[10]*Exit to Eden*, p. 224.

work of the Marquis de Sade is more hard-core. He believed that human nature was both forceful and vulnerable, innocent and cruel, and he depicted the extremes of sadomasochism in violent relationships that often made sexual arousal contingent on mutilation or death. Victorian pornography was also sometimes sadomasochistic and no less urgent, but less violent, and books like *My Secret Life* concerned primarily the male point of view. None of these books adequately described the scenarios that Rice envisioned as being hot.

"I am turned on by elegance," she says. "I adore the promise of a unique personality, unique demands, and subtlety."

She wanted to read about people who cold do 'bad' things but still be good, who could submit to degradation and even desire it without losing their integrity, beauty, or dignity. "What interests me," she says, "is creating exceptional, heroic people who are larger than life and who triumph." She wanted imaginative pornography wherein body and mind were focused together, totally possessed, and lost into something larger and more glorious than the individual ego. And most definitely, she did not wish to read about getting punished for going to sexual extremes to achieve spiritual ecstasy.

"I believe pornography can be literature," she says. "I believe the Beauty books have as much or more significance than anything I've ever done. No subject matter can debase language. Language can elevate any subject matter. The power lies in the language and the perspective, not in the subject matter.

"Pornography is an escape, a chance to live in an imaginary realm that we might not want to visit. I have no interest in acting it out. Good porn teaches you something. It takes you someplace in the imagination, and when you return, you know something more.

"I believe we must free sex from superstition. People have a right to enjoy sex. The closer we move toward that, the better off we are."

Since she could not find what she wanted, she decided to return to the themes that had always intrigued her by writing her own pornography: "I was frustrated and burning with ambition to do a number of things." She put aside all constraint and plunged in. Some fast, spontaneous writing, she thought, might get her closer to her emotions and help her attain the intimacy she felt she had lost in her recent writing.

One of the novels that emerged during this time, *Exit to Eden*, reveals her full motivation. The character Elliott Slater signs up for an extreme sexual experience for the same reasons Rice wrote her pornography: "I'm doing it for pleasure, the word made flesh. And it is something else too . . . some harrowing of the soul, some exploration, some refusal to live on the outside of a dark and heated inner world that exists beyond the civilized face I see in the mirror."[11]

"She was at a kind of crossroads in her career and in her art," Michael Riley explains. "Something in her knew that she had to breach that barrier. And when she began, she discovered zest and exhilaration and a kind of extremity that was genuinely liberating. Somehow, [the pornographic novels] made everything that came afterwards possible."

The Claiming of Sleeping Beauty

Rice sat down to write a sexual fantasy set in a fairy-tale castle with fairy-tale characters. "I have no idea why the Sleeping Beauty myth inspired me," she says. "I just wanted to take those fantasies and put them into some form, being true to what they were and making the least possible concession to literary form or the market." Her own fantasies led in that direction. "When I wrote the first part, I had no idea it was going to be a whole book or a series."

She wanted Beauty, her heroine, to have fun with "forbidden sex," and to allow herself to be dominated by others without being harmed. The idea throughout the novels was for the characters to learn to surrender to their desires, to achieve a brief mindless state that could result in a stronger sense of self. They are granted license under "force" to experience a sexuality that is otherwise secret and taboo: they must please their masters, who want to see them explode from the build-up of powerful feelings.

"In the midst of the worst humiliations," Rice explains, "they

[11]Ibid., p. 32.

can attain the feeling of freedom and power because they went through with it. It's similar to the saints and the mystics. Their bodies were no longer important. They transcended the physical to become one with Christ."

Rice strove to create a "one-handed read" that would be hot on every page and would appeal to both male and female masochists. Wanting the novel to be elegant but so eccentric as to defy editorial intervention, she set up a duality of dominance and submission within the master-slave hierarchy of the medieval world. "It was an experiment," Rice explains, "a way of dealing with a range of things I wanted to do." Breaking down walls of inner resistance created by family, society, and religion was her goal.

In an aroused state herself, she wrote quickly, finishing the first book in three weeks. "I paced the scenes with my natural feelings," she admits. She believed that for pornography to have integrity, the writer ought to share the fantasy and be turned on by it.

"The idea was to create a book where one didn't have to mark the hot pages," says Rice, "where every page would be hot. It was an attempt to get to the very heart of that fantasy, to really reach the moment of pounding intensity and to take away everything extraneous, as much as could be done in a narrative. The concept really involves intensity—a sense of being absolutely alive to what you're writing at that moment being very crucial. I think it's hard to achieve a consistent contact with that in fiction. You get swept up with building a scene and you have to continuously try to get through that to make the book more totally 'it.'

"It's a feeling that what's happening on the page really, really matters, is almost climactically important, and yet it can go on for pages. 'It' is the moment of really important truth that you would want to utter on your deathbed. It's the most important thing you can say about our struggle in the world. Since I do write in an instinctive way and I do access the subconscious, for me to discover a truth that makes your hair stand on end can be a very surprising, spontaneous development.

"There wasn't anything I didn't include in the erotica that didn't produce that feeling in me. I was batting a real good score on that. Almost any orgiastic scene involved it. When someone writes an authentic erotic book, when elements of the fantasy cohere with real feeling on the part of the writer, you have a window into the psyche. If you look up S&M literature in the library and read the case histories where psychiatrists have studied patients' fantasies, the Roquelaure books have the same value. There's almost no literary dilution or distortion. The Roquelaure books are really close to the true fantasy of S&M freaks. I believe someone could pick up those books two hundred years from now, and they could learn what one kind of S&M mind is about.

"There are moments in my books when the most powerful feelings about exposure and sexual revelation are being examined. Some of that stuff parallels mystical writing. You get out of yourself, you become the thing that is happening to you. Part and parcel of the sexual revolution was the knowledge that it was spiritual."

Rice talked over her new direction with her husband, and he was a bit apprehensive. "At first," he admits, "I had trepidations that it might be dangerous for her reputation. Those were little fears having more to do with family than anything else." In the end, however, he fully supported her artistic freedom. "I thought it was powerful stuff: honest, unique, and sexy. It met all my expectations for something that was successful in its mode."

Sending the novel off to her agent, Lynn Nesbit, Rice woke one night with the nervous awareness that some people just did not get the idea of the masochistic fantasy. Editors who looked at it might not realize it was a mental game of temporarily giving up power to experience freedom: "If you think S&M is sexy, it needs no explanation. And if you don't, you won't have the faintest idea why anyone else does." She felt exposed, but the tension made her realize how alive she was to her work. It would not matter how anyone else responded. She trusted her instinct.

Vicky Wilson, Rice's editor at Knopf, read the manuscript and thought that the "love slaves" that Rice described should want to try to escape such a place. She could not get behind such a novel. It just did not appeal to her. Rice realized that her editor simply did not understand the appeal of masochism. However, although Wilson felt the fantasy was claustrophobic, she made a referral, and Rice soon met Bill Whitehead, editor-in-chief at Dutton.

Originally from New Orleans, Whitehead was known as a witty, sexy man with a sense of style. He was a pioneer in trade paperbacks for literary works. Whitehead liked what he read of Rice's manuscript, felt it worked for him as pornography, and agreed to publish a series of three with elegant covers.

Lynn Nesbit strongly recommended that Rice publish under a pseudonym, and Rice agreed to for several reasons: She wanted to keep these books secret from her father, prevent fans of her other books from buying something that might shock them, and gain the freedom a pseudonym offered to write anything she wanted. So she chose the name A. N. Roquelaure. She had seen the word *roquelaure* in Sheridan le Fanu's ghost story "Mr. Justice Harbottle" and had learned that it was a French word for cloak. Thinking it sexy, she became "Anne under the cloak."

The book was dedicated to S. T. Roquelaure. S. T. was Stanley Travis, Rice's husband. "It was a family joke," she explains. After writing the novel, she mentioned the dedication to him and they laughed about it.

The Claiming of Sleeping Beauty was published in 1983.

It opens with a handsome Prince taking Beauty's virginity while she sleeps, awakening her physically and sexually, and commanding that she accompany him to his mother's castle to become his love slave. He wants to possess her, to make her submit her will completely to his. He observes at once that Beauty has the capacity to be a fine slave: Punishment "softens" her and inspires her to yield more fully.

This was the first of Rice's published novels to describe a predominantly female experience, although it was not told from a first-person perspective. "For years," she explains, "I felt so enraged about repressive forces that it was easier to write from the viewpoint of a male." Now she was exploring a new type of character and would continue to recognize the need to describe her version of female sexuality.

The fifteen-year-old Beauty has no idea what to expect. At first she is frightened, but the humiliations she suffers as the Prince parades her naked through the streets also excite her. She surrenders to him in stages. Beauty experiences some degree of power over the Prince's desire for her but feels entirely vulnerable to the unknown that lies ahead.

"In erotic experience, anticipation and expectation are everything," Rice explains. "We draw out our erotic lives with foreplay and fantasy. It is our great gift as humans that we can do this, that we can dream erotic dreams, lead up to sex slowly, and do it the way we want. Our intense and prolonged elaboration on sexual desire may underlie all our social actions and institutions more than we could ever know or would ever want to know."

Beauty sees other naked Princes and Princesses in the Queen's castle, all of whom are pleasure slaves like her. To her mind, the Princes are more vulnerable because their erect penises are exposed for anyone to touch or slap. Unlike some of the Princesses, Beauty is quite passionate and ready for pleasure. She soon learns what it means to be disciplined by the Lords and Ladies, even as they lovingly care for her. The Queen takes an interest in her, as does Lady Juliana, and Beauty is forced into silly erotic exercises that test the limits of her tolerance. Although people repeatedly tell her that surrender is best for her own enhancement, she is inclined to rebel. Nevertheless, she finds herself strangely stimulated by the tasks demanded of her.

She meets another slave, Alexi, who tells her how his own rebellious spirit was tamed and what it means to be possessed, mind and body, by the Queen. He has become an object, with no control over his own desires; he has transferred his power to his Masters. Through a series of degrading experiences, he grew to crave the discipline they dealt him and to learn serenity in the face of his helplessness. He has been examined in every crevice, probed, whipped, slapped, raped, exposed, left in the garbage, and treated like a circus animal. Yielding to the worst humiliations he could ever imagine, he claims, proved to be a source of great strength for him. For example, when all of his private parts were exposed to a group of villagers, he endured the shame and eventually tolerated the debasing postures. He realized then that he could endure anything.

Alexi was the epitome, for Rice, of the male masochist. To defy the stereotype of female passivity and illustrate how strongly masochistic desires can affect men, Rice went into lengthy detail about his experiences. Throughout his ordeal, Alexi exhibits the anxiety, weakness, fear, and subjugation normally associated with women. He cries over things done to him but also finds them arousing and craves more.

Alexi also portrays the power of attitude over the quality and intensity of experience. Pain does not in fact correlate with the degree of injury done to the body, and Alexi's story illustrates how pleasure and pain are influenced by the meaning bestowed on them. In the end, he accepts his lot as a pleasure slave by finding a way to make peace with it. As a result, he becomes a model of serenity.

"Alexi was my favorite character in *The Claiming of Sleeping Beauty*," says Rice. "In his story I got the most erotic detail. I just loved it. The shift to first person with him worked very well. I was going by temperature gauge. It seemed very hot to have him telling all these stories to Beauty. . . . I just followed the red brick road."

One of the central themes in the Roquelaure trilogy, which plays out in the vampire novels to a lesser degree, is the idea of being intimately examined. It is the essence of being under someone else's power, made an object for possession and scrutiny. The slaves are constantly put on display, probed, touched, and evaluated—in part for pleasure and in part to determine their capacity to be slaves. They are to keep their legs apart at all times and their private areas exposed for handling. Often they must confess their deepest feelings as well. Being the focus of such concentrated attention excites them. The experience is that of a child under the loving but firm and constant discipline of totally devoted parents.

"I was going by instinct, as always," says Rice. "The master forcing the slave to examine his own feelings, discuss them, and confess them is very sexy to me. I suppose it's just another form of submission for the slave to have to do that, for the passive one to have to deliver his soul over to the master. It was simply another variation on the same thing. It intensifies the relationship between the master and slave because the master is so interested in the slave; from the slave's point of view, it's pretty narcissistic having this person want to know what you're feeling every minute.

"Masochists occupy center stage always in my pornography. All eyes are on them. They run the show, really. I'm almost never writing from the point of view of the dominant one. I have no interest in it. I think those who love porn generally love writing that is from the masochist's point of view. The masochist is king or queen—the object of desire, the one worth tormenting, studying, loving. Masochism is very self-centered and openly childish.

"I do think being treated as a specimen, being spoken of as if you were 'for sale,' or there for pleasure, is very sexy. We see it a lot in films about ancient Rome—handsome masters talking about the demure slave girl as if she were an object. Obviously, it's a common idea."

Cultures that emphasize sin and repress sexuality, Rice believed, inevitably generate people who equate punishment with pleasure. "Many people have fantasies about dominance and submission, but they can't bring themselves to tell anyone." She believed that S&M fantasies were more closely associated with trends in human consciousness than with any particular incident in childhood. Rice wanted people to have permission to enjoy their pleasure as a natural extension of who they were, so she continued to write. It was not long before she thought she might like to become one of the most famous female pornographers in the country.

Beauty's Punishment

In the second Roquelaure novel, published in 1984, Beauty rebels against the Prince and the castle nobility, and gets sent away from the castle to the Queen's village. It is a place that the castle slaves all dread because they hear stories about its harsh discipline and extreme humiliations. However, the routines of the castle have become dull to Beauty. She seeks increased excitement and danger. On the way to the village, Beauty meets Tristan, another disenchanted slave, and together they face their new fate.

Beauty winds up with Mistress Jennifer Lockley, an innkeeper with a reputation for breaking rebellious slaves. Beauty decides to test this woman's limits, with harsh results that surprise her. She realizes that she now has a Mistress who will spare nothing to keep her slaves in line, but who also knows how to show moments of affection. Mistress Lockley clearly comprehends the masochist's need and knows how to meet it. At the same inn Beauty also acquires another Master, the Captain of the Guard. He wants her for himself but willingly passes her around to his men from time to time. Yet even as Beauty's sensual adventures continue, Rice was clearly more interested in her new character, Tristan.

Rice suddenly breaks the frame of the third-person narrative style to present Tristan's experience firsthand, not in dialogue form as she had done with Alexi, but as its own narrative. She had first learned this kind of stylistic freedom by reading Jack Kerouac. "He would say anything he wanted to at any particular time," Rice recalls. "He would just break the frame of the book to put in his own conjectures."

More comfortable in the male perspective, and more excited by it, Rice reached for greater intimacy by telling Tristan's story as if it were hers. However, she felt a little more reserved than she had creating Alexi's story. "I got more inhibited in the second book when people found out I had written the first, and even more inhibited in the third. Nothing in them touches Alexi's story for sheer sexual madness."

Nevertheless, Tristan talks freely about the importance of loving his Master, Nicolas. He discovers from Nicolas that it is easier to surrender to a Master he can trust to know what he needs even if that Master seems brutal. Nicolas understands that a true Master realizes how a slave needs love and suffering interspersed. The slave's captivity allows him to feel everything fully—to push against his bonds, as it were—and the Master must find ways to take him to the edge without pushing him over. Each slave's tolerance level is unique, but some, like Tristan, need excessive punishment.

Nicolas puts him through a series of debasing punishments that test his physical and psychological tolerance. Tristan fears what may happen, but loves Nicolas all the more for it. He hallows the pain and uses his powerlessness to increase his inner resources. Tristan's worst trial occurs when Nicolas asks the Public Whipping Master to whip him unfettered. That means that Tristan must exercise supreme self-control to mimic the leather restraints and prevent himself from trying to escape. To admit he cannot endure it would be the worst shame of all. To endure it will be to become enhanced.

"Putting people under the jeopardy of constraint," Rice explains, "sets up conditions for them to feel incredibly alive under limitations. It has to do with being constricted and bound. Knowing your limitations allows you to be totally free."

Tristan feels secure in this newfound love, as if its very existence drives back chaos. That is the experience he seeks. "I've found my Master," he tells Beauty, "the one who brings me into harmony with all punishments."[12] Beauty fails to comprehend this concept, but sensing that her own experience lacks something, she believes it might be the love that Tristan describes.

"Love between dominants and submissives is just about the only thing that interests me in my porn," says Rice. "I've written scenes in which the love complicates and heightens the experience for both people. I think that's all through the Roquelaure books. Only occasionally did Beauty deal with some dominant person she didn't like, but then she would grow to love that person. *Thrall* is the key word. The dominant and the submissive hold each other in thrall.

"Love between the dominant and submissive totally shapes the experience. I can't analyze it too deeply. I have no interest in strangers getting together in my books. Emotional content amid sadomasochistic motifs is what interests me. Like many women, I find all kinds of scenes erotic that don't even involve genital sex . . . they just involve two people becoming intensely involved."

Tristan's deeper experience of that love involves the feeling that he is part of a greater scheme. It diminishes his ego to the point that he experiences himself as nothing. All he possesses is his capacity to feel. He finds inward peace because he envisions a purpose for himself and a reason for his suffering conveyed by some larger power. He can transfer meaning and responsibility to the whole. This perspective is similar to Rice's notion of the "continual awareness" that the vampire Marius describes in *The Vampire Lestat.* He wants such an entity to exist so that nothing will be forgotten and even the smallest details will be embued with some degree of significance. Rice herself found the concept seductive: "There's a great promise of order, and of all suffering and pain being redeemed in a moment of great illumination and understanding."

Tristan and Beauty both experience more exacting punishments in the village than they had in the castle, yet the extreme discipline only attracts them to remaining with their new mas-

---

[12]*Beauty's Punishment* (New York: Dutton, 1984), p. 206.

ters. However, Rice decided to take them to yet another level of humiliation, so she has them kidnapped by raiders from a foreign land, the Sultanate.

Just before this happens, Rice introduces a new character, Laurent, who livened things up for her. "He saved the book for me." She had grown tired of Beauty, and Tristan's story had reached a sense of closure, so she needed a new perspective on the masochistic experience. Laurent is kidnapped along with Beauty and Tristan, and he looks forward to the adventure.

Beauty's Release

In the third Roquelaure novel, Rice concentrated on Laurent's story, telling it, as she had done with Tristan, from Laurent's point of view. More than any other character, he is the image of the man Rice wanted to be. Laurent is more adventurous than Tristan, possessing Beauty's rebellious spirit, albeit more aggressively, as a man. He also embodies the complexity of being both dominant and submissive in equal doses and is clearly bisexual. Laurent does what he can to get the Masters' attention. To be noticed is delirious for him and he loves the intensity of being punished, so he continues to provoke the masters in whatever way he can. In the midst of his pain, he feels transient moments of utter tranquillity.

The captured slaves find themselves prisoners of the Sultan, a foreign sovereign who, in this version of the story, had originated the Queen's practice of using love slaves. He steals six prize slaves to keep for two years. Beauty, Tristan, Laurent, and three others must get used to being treated as even less human than they had at the hands of the villagers. They are not allowed to speak at all or to show any evidence of the power of reason, and they are mostly used for decoration.

"Slaves as decoration is an old motif in my imagination," Rice explains. "Also I remember slaves as decoration in de Sade. I read that years before I wrote my own pornography."

Each of the grooms want the slaves in his care to stand out because only thus will he himself gain the Sultan's attention. Beauty is placed with the women and finds a lover in Inanna, the

Sultana, while Tristan and Laurent come into the hands of Lexius, the Sultan's Chief Steward.

Beauty discovers that the Sultan's women have been genitally mutilated. In the Sultanate, the clitoris is routinely removed, preventing the women from experiencing their own pleasure. Beauty offers Inanna a way to achieve orgasm, and thus becomes a symbol for Rice herself, who offers her fantasies in the Beauty books to free other women from social restrictions so they can enjoy themselves.

In this novel, there is more emphasis on switching dominant and submissive roles. For example, when Laurent perceives that Lexius, his Master, wants to be a slave, he makes the switch and dominates him. With Laurent's encouragement, Tristan also masters Lexius, and they both get a taste of another part of themselves. And even though Lexius deeply desires to be subjugated, he still holds his power as Master when his public persona demands it.

All three of these characters express Rice's ability to take both perspectives. Although she preferred the point of view of the masochistic slaves, she had to think up the various torments as the author of the novel: It is in effect *she* who impales Tristan on a horsetail dildo, makes Alexi dance naked for the Queen, whips Beauty down the Bridle Path, and hangs Laurent on the brutal Punishment Cross. In each scenario Rice indicates how the masochist's fantasies control it. As Laurent points out, going back and forth between being dominant and submissive sharpens both sides of the experience, and Rice fully appreciates the interlacing motivations.

The Queen's men eventually rescue these slaves, albeit against their wills. At Laurent's command, Lexius accompanies them. He soon becomes one of the castle's prize slaves, while Beauty returns home at the request of her parents, and Laurent and Tristan are sentenced to the supreme humiliation of being rented out as village ponies. Laurent thoroughly enjoys this demeaning role, but when his father dies, he must return to his Kingdom as sovereign. He learns that Beauty has remained unmarried, so he claims her, taking her to his Kingdom to be his secret slave.

With this third book, Rice was now finished with Beauty's

world. She had grown tired of the repetition. Nonetheless, she was pleased: "I'm convinced that the work has a wholesome overview and a gentle approach. The Roquelaure books are fun. They're tame. I was trying to create a safe fantasy of fully realized locales and characters in which readers could move without fear of something ugly happening.

"The most interesting of those books is the second one, because the village is the most interesting place. I kind of got locked in with the Sultan's palace. I didn't really care about it, so I had to get them out of there fairly fast. I think it had really run its course. I like the third book because I like the character of Laurent. That was my hero. But by that third book I had done what I wanted. I was sick of trysting. I was almost sick of Beauty, but I liked Laurent. To me those books were a wonderful experience to write. It was just going into that stuff and forgetting any question of what anyone would think."

The Roquelaure books created quite a stir among readers of pornography. Reviewers speculated about the identity of the writer behind the pseudonym, and in the *Village Voice* one journalist suggested it was Joyce Carol Oates (who quickly denied it). Reviewer Dorothy Allison thought the novels were the "best one-handed reading" she had found in years, although she thought the lesbian scenes were weak, while Gayle Rubin stated in *The Advocate* that the Beauty books were the S&M of the eighties. Rubin especially appreciated the bisexual elements and the fact that women were portrayed as dominant as well as submissive. *Dungeon Master* called the Beauty books "elegantly written," and *Playboy* acknowledged their articulate, "baroque" quality. There were some critics who suggested that A. N. Roquelaure was a literary writer, but others thought such praise an exaggeration. The series was not widely reviewed in the mainstream press.

When Rice eventually did own up to her authorship, she received a variety of responses from fans. She was gratified to see women with baby strollers bringing these novels to book signings and confessing that Rice had accurately expressed their own fantasies, but there were also fans who were angered by them or who claimed they simply did not work as erotica. Rice felt that such diversity of opinion merely reinforced what she already believed, that sexuality was complex and not easily categorized. What worked for her was not going to work for everyone, but she was happy that both men and women claimed that the fantasies had been hot. Whether readers and critics loved these books or hated them, there was no doubt that they stirred up controversy at a time when pornography was under the gun and brought attention to one's right to read or write whatever form of sexual expression one found appealing.

"Arguing as I have for the right of people to read and write pornography, I've never talked much about the deeper meaning of the books," says Rice. "But I know that the deeper levels of meaning are there. I saw my task as the opposite of analyzing them—to go like a warrior into the land of S&M and to fight for the truth. I never sat back and thought about the whole thing. I went into it.

"I trust that if I create with a feeling of authenticity, the things my characters say about their sexual lives will have some element of universal truth.

"The erotica is saying that all these random experiences of the flesh are not evil, they're wonderful. If you can act out your fantasies safely with a consenting adult, or you can fantasize them, they're fine. Whatever your flesh is wanting is not necessarily bad. It's time to explore it, to listen to it.

"Women who come to my signings tell me they're very happy with those books. They're happy someone put down those fantasies.

"I believe sex and sexual fantasy is good. I believe the sexual side of our nature is powerfully mysterious and not to be despised, and I wish more people would write true sex scenes rather than writing according to convention. There are moments in the Roquelaure books where the most profound feelings about exposure and sexual revelation are being examined. I experience them as a gradual transcendence and opening up. You get out of yourself, you're turned into something else, you become the thing that is happening to you. Only after I wrote those books did I come to see the connection between the erotic and the supernatural. Then it all fell into place for me. I think this nation had a sense of that in the sixties. It was part and parcel of the sexual revolution, the knowledge that sex was spiritual. We've lost the intellectual edge of that in the dreary era of censorship and repression. Unfortunately feminism has played a very large role in that because of the inability of some women to understand that there are all kinds of feminine experiences."

Although the Roquelaure books were finished, Rice was not finished writing about sexual relationships. She had other ideas that developed away from the mode of the Roquelaure series, but which were also unlike what she called the "European" mind-set in which she had written her first three novels. She discovered a new voice, a new persona. The new characters were as present to her as any others, and she felt fully involved in the writing, but clearly this novel was different.

Exit to Eden

After writing the first two Roquelaure novels and while working on the third, Rice created *Exit to Eden*. It was another S&M fantasy, but less sexually explicit, and it was set on a remote island in a contemporary context. Since this novel was written in a new voice, Rice used another pseudonym. She adopted the name Anne Rampling after the stylish actress Charlotte Rampling.

Initially, *Exit to Eden* had been closer in tone and imagery to the Roquelaure series, but Rice had found herself falling in love with the characters. To her they were more like people. She wanted to tell a story that precluded constant attention to sexual games and S&M experiences and gave attention to romance. "I started *Exit to Eden* and it was wonderful because the novel was totally unplanned," she explains. "It began as a planned pornographic novel, but the characters of Elliott and Lisa came alive for me. I fell in love with them right away. It ceased to be just pornography, or it became a heightened form of pornography because it involved not just the same kind of infantile sex scenes that are in the Roquelaure books, but it involved real people doing them. I just got sexier and sexier, and when I was finished, I felt terrific.

"Everything in *Exit to Eden* was derived from my own fantasy world. I didn't write anything in that book that I didn't think was a pure turn on."

The main character, Lisa Kelly (the "Perfectionist"), is the sensual mastermind of an exclusive luxury resort known as The

Club, where members can safely act out their wildest sexual fantasies with the "slaves" who serve them. The slaves sign on for a specified period of time up to two years, and each is a "thoroughly sexualized being, ready to serve your every whim in bed."[13] This is the first of Rice's novels in which a female character tells her story in first person.

Having experienced the roles of both slave and dominatrix, Lisa becomes the ultimate masochist: She sacrifices her desire to be dominated and serves others instead by playing the Mistress role. Using rituals to maintain control and prevent herself from being vulnerable, Lisa eventually grows restless. Even in this ultimate zone of arousal, she wants something more. Enter Elliott Slater.

Elliott is an adventurous bisexual man, twenty-eight years old, who has learned that exploring his fears through symbolic violence is preferable to placing himself in real danger: he was nearly killed on an assignment as a photojournalist in El Salvador. He signs up to participate at The Club as a slave. Elliott seeks an experience in which he can be totally engulfed, knowing that to be possessed by another yields an intense orgasmic feeling. Giving his mind and body over to someone else relieves him of the responsibility to try to save himself. However, his greatest fear is to be dominated by someone weaker than himself, particularly a woman. As luck would have it, Lisa selects him for her personal attention.

Lisa seeks what Elliott seeks: a person who can thoroughly understand her secrets, accept them, and even love her for them. "Each of us has within him a dark chamber where the real desires flower; and the horror is that they never see the light of another's understanding."[14] If they can accept each other's masochistic needs, they can form a truly loving S&M relationship, because, Rice believes, the best slaves make the best masters. They know what the slave feels and needs—when to exert pressure and when to offer tenderness and affection.

In a bold move that breaks her own rules, Lisa decides to kidnap Elliott. She takes him from The Club and asks him to accompany her to New Orleans. For Rice, this destination meant

[13]*Exit to Eden*, p. 11.
[14]Ibid., p. 105.

encountering her own secret places, where past memories of pleasure and pain mingled together. To explore New Orleans was to move closer to "it," that mysterious feeling of the erotic unknown which she strove to contact in her writings.

"In my Rampling novels, I was able to bring my characters to walk through areas of New Orleans from my childhood," she says. "They really covered the turf. It was like going deeper into my roots. It means something very deep. It means a lot about battering down doors and drawing closer to something you really want to explore."

Lisa and Elliott have intense, complicated feelings for each other. In their lovemaking they constantly change roles and Elliott grows disoriented. He cannot tell for a moment whether Lisa is a man or a woman. "That's a powerful moment to me," says Rice. "His reaction to Lisa was so strong that her gender didn't matter." He is able to experience a broader range of feelings because he is not playing out a gender-specified role, and the sense of balance for both means equal potential for accelerating and fulfilling their desires.

They have a discussion about the psychology of S&M, in which Elliott describes symbolic violence as a cathartic way to work out the dangerous urges inherent in human sexuality. Lisa agrees, feeling affirmed in the fantasy that made The Club a reality. Both parts of this conversation echo Rice's reaction to much of what has been misunderstood about S&M fantasies. Sexuality is not going to be erased from men or women, and it needs to be recognized for what it is so that it can be channeled into safe scenarios.

"I think a lot of what we respond to sexually is in our genes," Rice explains. "What I'm trying to say is that sadomasochism has almost nothing to do with the way one is brought up, or one's religious background, or any particular incident in one's childhood. People from all different walks of life and all different kinds of backgrounds enjoy masochistic fantasies. If we look for a cause, we would have to look into something like racial memory, something encoded in the genes, some way in which, after thousands of years we've turned experiences of violence and violation into something erotic, as we've tamed it. We have a vast history of war and pillage and rape, and obviously the fantasies of sadomasochism play with all those images. Rape is an arche-typal fantasy. It's part of our racial memory. To fantasize about it doesn't mean we literally want to be raped by some stranger, or that we will act it out. It seems to me far more likely that the ex-planation is in some sort of racial memory or genetic response. No environmental approach to it makes much sense."

Elliott learns that Lisa has taken him from The Club without telling anyone and that, essentially, she has run away. She soon realizes that she must face her conflicts so she tries to convince him that he should go back. This turnaround stuns him. He has told Lisa he loves her and had expected a similar commitment from her, but she cannot face what such feelings mean. She is not even aware that she is in love. Elliott reluctantly leaves and Lisa sits in a transsexual bar to ruminate about her pain. In this place, her thoughts echo Rice's own feelings: Rice loved the fe-male impersonators for the way they put their sexual feelings on the line. She herself has often felt like a female impersonator, and she views them as angels: "You have transcended everything into the pure theater of yourselves."[15] Watching them, Lisa un-derstands that she has not been true to her own needs and must do something to change her life.

She confesses her conflicts to her former sexual mentor, Martin Halifax. He tells her that she is in love and should yield to the feeling. Frightened but determined to surrender to this overpowering emotion, she flies back to The Club only to dis-cover that Elliott has left. Locating him, she confesses her feel-ings. He asks her to marry him, which he insists carries as much risk as anything they've ever done. She agrees and both of them realize they have found a lover who accepts their secrets: Elliott needs a woman who understands his deepest masochistic desires before he can surrender to a deep love, and Lisa needs someone to penetrate her dominant stance to lay out the truth of her masochism. Genuine exposure and vulnerability, Rice felt, meant "to really know the one who shares your most savage desires."

Elliott and Lisa both represent to Rice the most interesting type of character. "The bisexual being is my ideal," she says, "be-cause he or she can care about the person who is being loved, in

[15]Ibid., p. 268.

an overwhelming way. My mind and heart are bisexual. I fall in love with all kinds of people. I'm captivated by their energy. The exploration of sensuality is my personal obsession as a writer. Complexity feels natural.

"In a lot of my books now the woman's point of view is in there. I think the breakthrough was in the Rampling books, in Lisa. In a way, she was a stereotypical woman because she was a terrible masochist—she allowed herself to be a dominatrix to serve other people. The masochists really could take over. They don't have to do this for other people. The S&M world is filled with masochists begging people to be dominant. The dominatrix is the creation of a male masochist. That's the way masochists run the show. So many misunderstandings surround that world. S&M to me means games between consenting adults. It doesn't have a thing to do with literal sadism. I don't think most people understand that.

"I believe most people who like S&M have some masochism in them. I think very few are sadists. A genuine dominatrix is hard to find. It's usually someone doing it for a living to cater to someone else's fantasies, like Lisa. The ultimate form of masochism is to service someone else. People want to be passive, they want to be ordered about, controlled, worked on, dominated, insulted, made love to, ravaged, and they want to be in the focus of that intense devotion and attention. Masochistic fantasies transcend gender, but men are more aggressive about getting it."

Rice knew she was taking a risk with *Exit to Eden* being misunderstood: "S&M in this novel is a type of exotic love, as sex play, not as something sick. But if people have no acquaintance with sadomasochistic fantasy, they're not going to understand it. One of the great mysteries of sexuality is that not all people want the same thing."

She asked a few people to read the novel and her husband responded affirmatively. "I thought *Exit to Eden* was a fine book about a person who has lost his will to live," he comments, "whose strength has failed him, and who regains his soul by 'submission' to a force stronger than his own isolated and self-disciplined will. We have to 'submit' to love. I think this is probably more true of men than women."

Her friend Michael Riley noted the romantic qualities in

Rice's novel: "Anne's way of dealing with homoerotic relation-ships is fully romantic, in the nineteenth-century sense of the word. She remarked that Lisa said something to the effect that sadomasochistic pleasure at its greatest should be like one was actually touching the beating heart of another human being. That's what eroticism is to her, an intimacy that exceeds any other realm between two people."

When an anthropologist who was into S&M invited Rice to ex-amine her collection of whips and handcuffs, she decided to inves-tigate. This woman also wanted to point out what Rice was getting wrong, such as whipping slaves in the back of the knees. However, this realistic approach to her fantasy dampened Rice's interest.

"She invited me to a group," Rice remembers. "They had a meeting where they were going to go see each others dungeons, and I just couldn't do it. I didn't want to know them that well. And then the Janus society invited me to their meetings, but I never went. I didn't want to be connected to them. I'm a writer and that's it. I think that meeting those people resulted in the closing down of the Beauty series with three books. It was very interesting to hear what they thought, but I had no interest in getting involved. I wanted to meet the dominatrix and just pay the hourly rate, but they said I'd probably have to take her hy-giene course, and I thought, 'Bullshit.' " That was the extent of her personal exploration of the actual S&M world.

When Rice submitted *Exit to Eden* to Bill Whitehead at Dutton, he was unimpressed. "Bill Whitehead didn't care for it," she says, "and he didn't want to publish it. As I recall, it was conveyed to me that Bill didn't care for the way Lisa switched from dominant to passive. He wasn't interested in the story of Lisa and Elliott."

Shocked but undeterred, Rice took the book to John Dodds at Arbor House. She had worked with him previously on *The Feast of All Saints* and thought he might appreciate this new novel. Dodds liked it and wanted to publish it in hardcover, but since the focus was on the developing love between Elliott and Lisa, he requested some changes to make it closer to a softcore erotic novel. Explicit sexual scenes between Elliott and other men were cut. (See the Appendix for the full version of these two chapters.)

There was immediate critical reaction. *Publishers Weekly* found *Exit to Eden* "pornography pure and simple," and not of the quality of Rice's other novels. Dorothy Allison, who had called the Beauty books exquisite, thought the story of Lisa and Elliott was flawed. The disciplinary practices seemed unrealistic to her, and she found some of the sexual descriptions impossible. "The masochistic indulgences . . . read very much as the extended fantasies of a woman who has never tried anything of the kind herself." She was also dismayed by the lack of lesbian passion between Lisa and one of her personal slaves. However, part of Allison's negative reaction was based on her misunderstanding that Elliott was gay when Rice clearly described him as bisexual. Nevertheless, she did appreciate Rice's attempt to show how people might find pleasure in the wake of a successful sexual revolution, even if she viewed *Exit to Eden* as only a partial success in that regard.

Penthouse called the novel "a really good read," and other critics noted the skillful writing that could bring respectability to the genre, as Henry Miller and D.H. Lawrence had done. Not as hard-core as the Beauty books in its explicit sexual content, *Exit to Eden* was interpreted as erotica with a message—that symbolic S&M was part of the human psyche and ought to be accepted and explored. Many of Rice's male readers told her it was their favorite novel and wanted to know when it would be made into a movie. Rice hoped that if such a thing ever happened, it would be lush and rich and true to the fantasy.

THE VOICES UNITE

"Everything is passionate with her."

While *Exit to Eden* was still in manuscript form, Rice met another writer who would have a significant impact on the way she viewed the S&M scene. In September 1984, Bill Whitehead gave Rice's phone number to John Preston, told him that Anne Rice was the author of the Roquelaure series, and urged him to meet with her on his trip to San Francisco.

A former editor of the gay newspaper *The Advocate* and a prominent writer of gay pornography, Preston had his first break in fiction with *Mr. Benson*. He also wrote adventure novels under the name Alex Kane. With the progressive court decisions of the

1970s, Preston had eagerly witnessed the increased availability of pornography, particularly for gay men. Since publications about homosexuality had once been few, with miserable endings, Preston had joined those writers who wanted to explore happy and satisfying gay experiences. He hoped to be taken seriously but soon learned what a struggle it was to get respect as a writer of pornography.

One of the exciting aspects of being gay, he believed, was the emotional and sexual stimulation that comes from being able to perform as either the active or passive partner—to desire as well as identify with the sexual object. Preston founded the first gay community center in the country, in Minnesota, and openly became a gay activist. With the advent of AIDS, he lectured widely and wrote about safe sex practices. It was during this period that he met Rice.

Preston first encountered Rice at the Café San Marco near her home in the Castro District. He was ready to have lunch, but Rice had other plans. "It was really weird," Preston later recalled. "She evidently didn't expect to stay. She'd already eaten, so we sat down and started to talk. She had read some of my books and we just clicked."

"I'd read his pornography, *I Once Had a Master*," says Rice, "some of *Mr. Benson*, and sampled his Alex Kane novels."

They soon found themselves talking easily together. Rice had the galleys of *Exit to Eden* with her so she offered the manuscript to Preston. As he read it, he was impressed with the way she worked at blurring the lines between types of sexuality and with the way she developed extravagant secret worlds.

"One of the reasons we're best friends," said Preston, "is that I also write pornography, so it just isn't a big deal to me that she does. Everything is passionate with her. I think that's one of the reasons she has so few friends, because to be involved with her is to be *involved*.

"I think it was painful for her to establish a relationship with another writer; there were lots of trust issues, and she's very concerned about reading other people's work for fear it might influence her. One of the experiences we have in common is to have written porn and to have owned up to it, then gone through the experience of having people assume it's autobiographical. That's true for me, but not for her. Lots of people want to believe that we have done these incredible things in dungeons together, but she doesn't do them.

"We're most likely to talk about where ideas come from. For example, there's a great scene in one of the Beauty books where a prince slave is kept in a garbage pile by the servants of the castle. Anne has childhood memories of nuns in her grade school punishing a young boy by making him stand in a wastebasket. She'd always thought that was just a horrible thing, and it was a very powerful image of humiliation in her mind. It came up for her in the pornographic imagination."

As their relationship progressed, Rice sent Preston the finished manuscripts of her novels, with the understanding that she was not asking for criticism or advice. He understood how anxious she was about being blocked, so his critiques were careful and sparing.

"I do remember him telling me a few things he liked and didn't like," Rice recalls, "but he was very tactful."

Preston gently pointed out that some of Rice's descriptions would fail in the real world: "He said that if you tied a person's arms up, hands over his head for hours, then the person would lose the use of his arms. In other words, the scene with Elliott on the ship where they tie up his arms for the night is fantasy. In practicality, no one could survive that. Their arms wouldn't work for hours afterward. I think I do a lot of things like that in the porno and in *Eden*. It sounds like fun but physically it would be far too strenuous to be fun."

Preston had many political connections and was well aware of how popular Rice's work was in the gay community, particularly her vampire books. "Many gay men see the vampire books as metaphors of being gay," he explained. "The passages about initiation and the concept of being separate from society— perhaps even above it, but always estranged by it—fit most gay men's self-images. Many gay men find the descriptions about becoming a vampire to be parallel to coming out, especially involving the welcome seduction by a being who holds the secret to the future. Her take on how it feels to be in a gay relationship is very strong and accurate. It reads *right* to a gay man.

"Gay men also relate to the voluptuousness of the descriptions and the heavy sensuality. Gay men, in general, pre-AIDS, have desensitized S&M, so it's not as alien to our experience as it might be to the rest of society's.

"Also, Anne's never turned away from gay society—something *very* important to a group which perceives itself as stigmatized. She lived in the Castro area in San Francisco, which many gay men knew, gave interviews to the gay press long before it was stylish, signed books at a gay bookstore when others—even gay writers—would have been skittish about the identification. And, quietly, she immediately saw AIDS as something terrible.

"She thought that gay men were vanguards of a sexual revolution that she thought very important. She saw AIDS as something that threatened the revolution. Her take on it was adamant, supportive, and angry. She was horrified for a while about her public making a connection between AIDS and the vampire books. I told her about friends who were dying who were reading them, and she wondered, 'How *can* they?' One man said he loved the books because they helped him to 'go over' and to do so with dignity. I think that made a huge difference to Anne. She loved the men of the Castro, and she loved stories people like myself could tell her about parties and back-room bars and so on."

To Rice, Preston represented a window into the S&M scene. "After we first met," he recalled, "when she became comfortable with me, she shyly asked me for one favor: Would I take her to a leather bar? We never did it, alas, but it was a chance to enter into a fabled world that she very much desired."

As a pornographic writer himself, he was able to place Rice's Roquelaure novels in a cultural context: "I think Anne's Beauty books are utterly and historically unique. There are elements of the sexual which she's written about which simply were never seen before, or at least hadn't been seen or written about out-side of gay male culture—the vulnerability of a man with an erect cock, for example. She turned the feminist perception of what a cock was upside down, from the symbol of power to a deep, deep vulnerability. No one in the mainstream culture had reenvisioned that before her. Not even the most marginal porn writers who would address male submission in low-grade fan-tasies did as much [as she did] with her perception of the penis;

occasionally they would write about it as a symbol of shame but not of defenselessness, as she did. Those are brilliant moves. And Anne's biggest thing is never to equate violence with sex. That's her own definition of pornography."

This relationship with Preston became an important part of Rice's life. They carried on an extended correspondence about their careers and concerns and she grew to view him as her best friend.

"The fantasies are all in the books."

Although Rice had written her pornographic novels under a pseudonym, it was not long before her actual identity was revealed. She had told some friends, so John Preston urged her to go all the way. She allowed Arbor House to reveal her as Anne Rampling, and in a speech at the Clift Hotel in San Francisco, she publicly owned up to the pornography. When people asked her how much of her description was from her own experience, she was dismayed. She had no intention of revealing her private life with her husband, but she wanted people to realize that she had created these S&M worlds out of her own imagination.

"I don't see any reason why I should have a room with whips and handcuffs," Rice says. "Agatha Christie didn't try to solve real murders and Raymond Chandler wasn't Philip Marlowe. Writing isn't the real world reflected in a mirror. My books are my fantasies.

"I never wanted to try out anything I wrote about. I love plain 'truck-driver bang' when it comes to sex. I can't get enough of it. I'm not much of an experimenter at all and certainly can't even imagine acting out the fantasies. I just like to think about them a lot. I like to imagine. I have no weird sexual practices. The fantasies are all in the books. I suspect being paddled hurts too much to be fun. But there are all kinds of people who do S&M, and they seem to know how to have fun with it."

Such questions were put to her husband as well. "Anne is no more sadomasochistic than she is a vampire," he responds, "but she has the capacity to empathize with and imagine a whole range of things that are so intense in her mind they don't require experience. No one could have that many experiences. She has to be making it up, and she is. It's all an act of imagination drawn from her unconscious, her thoughts and fears and imaginings about sex all the way back to when she was a little girl. Every aspect of her life is just fomenting mentally all the time."

"I was totally there in every voice," Rice agrees. "I felt a terrific rush of energy with the Rampling books. It was an outpouring of something that was subconsciously profound enough to be tremendously exciting to me."

Now that her identity was known and much of her freedom curtailed, Rice decided to move on. "I'm proud of the Beauty books and happy with them," she says, "but they're over. I did what I wanted to do. Those books could have gone on, but it would have simply been different costumes, different colors of satin and velvet, different faces. There was plenty enough to have accomplished what I wanted to accomplish—the silky, soft, delicious fantasy I couldn't find in any published pornography. I'm very happy that I went all the way with them, making them fairy tales of erotic detail, which are outrageous, really. I wanted to go deep into the fantasy, no matter how childish or embarrassing it might seem to someone else. I just loved it. But I couldn't write them now. I have nothing to add now to the genre. Whatever I write now must transcend the genre and is not porn. I'm not really interested in that world anymore. I completed those books, and it was powerfully cathartic to me, and I just don't think about it anymore."

It might be as Martin Halifax told Elliott in *Exit to Eden*, that sadomasochism is merely a phase for some people, a means of searching for something else. For Elliott, it was the search for love. For Rice, it may have been a search for sexual expression and perhaps a more authentic form of spirituality than what she had found in religion.

"It was what I really wanted to do," she says. "I felt that no one else had ever examined those fantasies in that way, and I wanted to create the books I couldn't find. I wasn't at all surprised when people from all over the country came to me and said, 'Those are my fantasies,' and they were glad that someone had written them down. I was surprised they ever got published. And sometimes when I see *Exit to Eden* on a shelf I'll open it up

and read some of the scenes and think, 'We published that between hardcover in America! What an accomplishment!' And it
was even more outrageous when I first wrote it. We had scenes
in there that were just unbelievable, like stuff that Elliott was put
through at The Club. It was really awful what happened to him,
the poor guy, but he loved every minute of it."

Despite revealing the secret of her authorship, Rice retained
the Rampling pseudonym for one more novel, but *Belinda* would
acknowledge Anne Rice as the author as well.

Exit to Eden: *The Movie*

Eventually, Rice was approached by a film company that wanted
to put *Exit to Eden* on screen, so she talked to Preston about writing the screenplay. "Anne was high on my doing it," he said,
"but the company that was involved was a real low-life outfit, and
she had no illusions about how well it would be done, other
than that it would provide us both with income. The deal never
came through, and there was never an offer."

Several years later, Hollywood director Garry Marshall made
a film of this book, the first one produced of any of Rice's novels. Released in October 1994, it starred Dana Delaney as Lisa,
Paul Mercurio as Elliott, and included Rosie O'Donnell and Dan
Akroyd as undercover detectives on the trail of a jewel thief.

Rice was appalled when she read the script. Her novel was being made into a comedy with an extraneous plot about an interna-
tional crime to make it move faster. Although she had initially
been supportive, she soon distanced herself from the project.

The parts of Lisa and Elliott remained intact, but the toned-
down fantasy clearly exhibited a male heterosexual bias and attempted to do the very opposite of what Rice had intended: the
film explained that Elliott had developed a spanking fetish from
his childhood experience with a voluptuous maid. In the novel,
Elliott quite clearly dismisses such pointless attempts to analyze
sadomasochistic desires. For Elliott (and Rice) sadomasochism
was infinitely more mysterious and profound than the film portrayed. Rice also believed that the film was too flip about S&M,
and that some practitioners would be offended. She did not want

them to think that what happened in the film was what she had written. Marshall's version of *Exit to Eden* was a disappointment to Rice and her readers alike, and was generally panned by critics.

> *"Abnormal life can be as rich and wonderful*
> *as seemingly normal life."*

Although Rice had only published four sexually explicit novels, she had many other ideas on erotic subjects. She envisioned most of them while writing as Roquelaure or Rampling but preserved them only in her memory.

Before she decided to stop writing pornography, Rice had planned a Victorian Roquelaure novel. It was not the first time she had tried using Victorian themes, and as before, she quickly discovered that she "had an easier and more productive time in the fairy-tale medieval setting. So nothing ever came of my use of the Victorian settings."

Yet another Roquelaure novel had taken form for her, a turnaround of *The Story of O:* "I had planned a fourth Roquelaure book, but it began to darken in my mind; it became more philosophical and less purely pleasurable. I still think about it. I realized I wanted to transcend the genre and get into something very serious about the way masochists control their sadists, and make them play the sadistic role. I wanted to write a novel in which the masochist simply murdered the sadist when she was finished with him, and when he'd fallen in love with her and couldn't be sadistic anymore, but I abandoned the book."

Rice had described the book to Bill Whitehead, but he had been uninterested. However, he was intrigued with another idea she had proposed about a novel involving Catholic schoolgirls and a naive priest. Rice wanted to explore a sophisticated religious mind confronted by blatant, animal sensuality, tracing his evolution from spiritual mentor to sexual slave. The book was her answer to *Candy*.

"The Catholic girls inducted a handsome Italian priest named Santino into sexuality," Rice explains. "They were savvy but gentle with young Santino's innocence. They had orgies in the sacristy, seducing him until his faith was utterly confounded.

It was to be purely erotic, like the Roquelaure books. I was going to tell it from Santino's view, as a heterosexual romp. I just never got to it."

She had also thought about writing some S&M set in ancient Rome. She envisioned a young slave girl and boy who were paired together because they resembled each other. She wanted to follow them through the brothel world, while avoiding the brutal realities of Roman life. However, this novel, too, remained in her fantasy world.

Although Rice was hesitant about doing another historical novel after *Cry to Heaven*—partly because she thought her own had not fully succeeded and partly because she herself did not read such novels—she became caught up with an idea related to Oscar Wilde.

This late-nineteenth-century British writer was one of the most scandalous personalities of his time. Known best for his novel, *The Picture of Dorian Gray*, and the stage play *The Importance of Being Earnest*, he became one of London's most prominent literary figures, but his flamboyant aestheticism provoked hostility and ridicule. At the height of his career, Wilde had an affair with the son of the Marquis of Queensberry, and the Marquis accused him of being a sodomite. Wilde sued him for libel but lost, and the British government then prosecuted Wilde for indecent acts. He served two years at hard labor for his "criminal" offense.

Rice read about the impact his trial had had on London's gay community, and she became interested in the artists who had lived in that society. She was appalled at how the homosexual rights movement had been driven underground and how people who had thoughtfully examined the subject were silenced. "I adore Oscar Wilde," she effuses. "In the late eighties, I read everything on him that I could find. I wanted to write a novel set during the time of his life. I was totally in love with the whole idea of Wilde, his world, his neighborhood, and I was much wounded and dismayed by the horrible tragedy of what happened to him."

This novel, called "The Education of Richard Lockhardt," was set in Victorian times, and it was to be about a man who kidnaps a fourteen-year-old boy, Richard, and takes him to Egypt.

The man molests Richard until he grows up. Richard then returns to London and falls in love with another boy. They go together to a cathedral where people drop off babies for the church, because Richard wants to take one to raise himself. However, his young lover persuades him not to, showing him that his act would merely be a repetition of what had happened to Richard himself. He advises Richard instead to develop a relationship with an equal.

"I never wrote the novel I had in mind," Rice admits. "But I have pretty much used all those emotions, ideas, and sources of energy in other ways."

An idea for a novel with similar themes but a heterosexual orientation was "Triana Walker." Rice wanted to try out new textures, with a lighter mood and a contemporary setting.

She tried out several versions of this story, including one with a narrator named Nicolas, but wanted to keep one thing in focus: This novel would involve "sensual drench." She wanted to explore the sexuality of women even more than she had already, to get out from behind the mask of a gay man. She thought of herself as coming out of the closet as a woman, ready to confront forces, both traditional and feminist, that were repressing female sexuality.

Having always been strongly attracted to erotic relationships between adults and young people, she plotted this novel around a Berkeley artist named Jeremy. He tells the story himself in order to "rejoin the human race."

Jeremy paints a series of nude females which he titles "My Life as a Woman." While working out his own issues, he encounters a six-year-old girl, Triana, who has been abused by her hippie parents. To save the child, Jeremy kidnaps her, but then falls in love with her. Giving her a bath one day, he succumbs to her playful charms. She is too young to realize erotic attraction is not a game, so she seduces him. He indulges in a guilt-ridden affair until she is seventeen and eventually wants to die because of it, but Triana insists that he accept what they have done. She grows up to be bisexual and becomes highly educated, aware that, had it not been for Jeremy's intervention, her parents might have killed her. She insists that her relationship with Jeremy was not one for regret or shame.

In this novel Rice experienced difficulty with the scenes of child molestation. She wanted to make them sympathetic, but she was aware of the moral problems of having adults take advantage of children. Triana was mature for a child, but she was also very young. The idea of this relationship was shocking, Rice realized, and she felt certain that she would never be able to publish the book.

"I wanted to write that novel but never did," Rice admits. "I felt it very strongly and I understood what it was about—the idea that abnormal life can be as rich and wonderful as seemingly normal life." However, some of the themes, images, and characters ended up in *Belinda*.

Another idea that remained unexpressed involved Rice's fascination with male ballet dancers. They suffered from the same social prejudices that always had drawn her attention and shared many of the artistic concerns of the castrati, but she could utilize a contemporary setting. She attended the ballet frequently and read books on the subject, noting with pleasure the intense dedication required of the dancers. Yet their lives seemed full and satisfying. Rice immersed herself, searching for a way in, but found no real inspiration. "It just didn't take root in my imagination."

A second Elliott Slater novel was also planned, involving him in a scam with a minister, but that, too, did not get written. What began to take up Rice's time was the sequel to her vampire novel.

"You are the man in me."[16]

While Rice was working on *Exit to Eden* and *Beauty's Release*, she also had *The Vampire Lestat* on the back burner. She had already signed a contract for it before she took up the pen as A. N. Roquelaure, but she had experienced trouble getting Lestat's character right. Through writing the erotic books, she found the voice of her future vampire hero. Both Elliott Slater and Laurent had exhibited spirited and rebellious qualities while able to play out the dual roles of dominant and submissive. Lestat shares these features, and his growth as a character eventually

[16]*The Vampire Lestat* (New York: Alfred A. Knopf, 1985), p. 62.

took Rice away from the erotica. The vampire novels featuring this character were also partly instrumental in bringing her diverse erotic voices back into her writing as Anne Rice.

Elliott and Laurent had represented Rice's ideal of a man—the man she wanted to be. Lestat took over and became Rice's dominant male persona. As a vampire, he had more possibilities for leading a rich, adventurous life and for doing anything he wanted. Rice was excited by this aspect of his character. Just as Lestat's mother, Gabrielle, told him that he was her missing male organ, so it was for his relationship to his creator. Lestat provided Rice with an aggressive, heroic perspective, and she began to dream up adventures for him.

Unlike Louis, whom Rice had grown to dislike, Lestat accepts his fate as a vampire and finds a way to make it a powerful experience. He seeks out older vampires, learns what he can, then goes to New Orleans. There he makes Louis and Claudia, pays a heavy price for it, and eventually becomes a rock star. He awakens the queen vampire, Akasha, who uses him as a symbol of destructive male energy in her campaign to reduce the male mortal population. He resists her and assists in her destruction. Lestat always lands on his feet, despite adversity.

As a vampire, Lestat dominates many of his relationships, but he, too, desires to be dominated. He falls in love with various people, looking for one to whom he can yield his soul. Although he succeeds in this most strongly with David Talbot, David has his own interests and eventually wanders off. Like Laurent and Elliott, Lestat continues to find ways to put himself at risk, such as tempting the devil in *Memnoch the Devil*, so as to experience the most extreme emotions life offers. He even trades bodies briefly with a mortal in *The Tale of the Body Thief* and has several sexual encounters, but finds he prefers being a vampire.

"Lestat is my hero," says Rice. "He's determined to be good at being bad. I see everything through his eyes. If I were going to be a vampire, I would be Lestat."

As an extension of Elliott and Laurent, but with a broader canvas than S&M material, Lestat became for Rice a way of creating erotic fantasies that could take many forms. Lestat's bisexuality was clearly developed both before and after his transformation to vampirism. As a mortal boy, he was a "billygoat" with the village girls and developed an intellectual passion (possibly more) for Nicolas, another boy his age. They ran off together to Paris, sharing a room and a great deal of intimacy. Lestat then became a vampire in a highly sensual and spiritual embrace with Magnus. It was not long before he brought his mother over into immortality, calling her both mother and lover. Then he made Nicolas a vampire, felt an erotic charge for a rival vampire Armand, and went on a passionate search for the vampire Marius, whose compassion and wisdom excited in him intense desire. Eventually Lestat fell in love again, this time with Louis, then Claudia, then Akasha, then Gretchen the nun, and finally the mortal scholar David Talbot. His ability to cross gender boundaries so fluidly was due partly to his nature and partly to his heightened supernatural sensibilities. As a character, he provided Rice with a way to express a range of artistic, personal, and political agendas.

The Vampire Lestat was published in 1985, the same year as *Exit to Eden* and *Beauty's Release*. Rice's three personas—what she called "the divided self"—were represented side-by-side. They were poised to merge, but there was one more Rampling book to write. With it, Rice took on a more volatile political issue than the rights of women to write what they wanted. She supported the independence of sexually mature young girls.

Belinda

For this novel, Rice used ideas from the unwritten "Triana Walker." "I proposed to Knopf the idea of this painter falling in love with this girl and being destroyed by her," Rice explains. "Years later he met her in the lobby of a theater, and she asked why he had never shown the paintings he had done of her. He explained that he never showed them for her sake, and she says he should have shown them, and that was the end of the book. When I got to writing it, it had all changed. As soon as they get into their sexuality, they get released instead of going downhill. That always happens to my work. I have almost a political refusal to show sex leading to death. That book was really the first one that I felt was about art and life even more immediately than *Cry to Heaven*—that through art and sex, one is liberated."

Belinda, an older version of Triana, is a precocious sixteen-year-old girl, bright, articulate and accomplished. She feels mature enough for a sexual relationship with forty-four-year-old artist and children's author, Jeremy Walker. He is looking for a dramatic life change while Belinda is escaping a dysfunctional family situation. She wants to be loved, to feel like she's a person—yet another character who thinks love staves off chaos.

Belinda and Jeremy find what they need in each other, so they carry on a torrid affair. Rice describes their lovemaking in terms of the Holy Communion, linking sex and spirituality as she had done in earlier novels. To show his devotion, Jeremy paints twenty full-size canvases of Belinda in various stages of nudity. However, deceptions and betrayals eventually drive them apart. In an attempt to salvage their love, Jeremy displays his paintings to the public. When Belinda fails to respond, her family accuses Jeremy of murder. Just before his arrest, Belinda shows up, and they head to Las Vegas to get married.

Rice was disturbed by how American culture seemed to want to punish "abnormal" sexual desire. She used the novel to address and defy this position. At one point, Jeremy meets with a friend, Alex Clementine (based partly on *Belinda*'s editor, John Dodds), and they discuss the American attitude about sex. Jeremy believes the public wants the truth and that sexual scandal cannot hurt a career, but Alex, echoing Rice, insists that it has to be the right dirt in the right measure. "Sex, yes," he says, "as long as death and suffering comes with it, gives them the moral overtone they've still got to have."[17] Jeremy comes close to being arrested but finds happiness instead.

For Rice, *Belinda* was about freedom of expression and the need to view alternative sexual choices in a more positive way. Belinda describes her confusion and anger over being denied the validity of her true desires: She is fully developed and could have a baby, but it is illegal for a man to touch her. In defiance, Belinda takes her life into her own hands. She pursues the relationship with Jeremy, despite the outcry against them both, until she gets what she wants. Rice insisted that Jeremy and Belinda could have a legitimate sexual relationship, and that they could

[17] *Belinda* (New York: Arbor House, 1986), p. 48.

achieve love and success, as Jeremy did with his erotic paintings of Belinda.

"Belinda was prophetic," Rice indicates, "because it represented what was happening to me with the porn. People said, 'It's going to ruin your reputation. It's going to be terrible.' But it wasn't terrible. It kept opening doors. It didn't ruin my life at all. *Belinda* is a symbol of that porn and the way it meant breaking down barriers."

Some critics dismissed *Belinda* because they felt that the female character was unrealistic. She was not a typical American teenager. Rice was angry at this cavalier invalidation of female sexuality. Through Belinda, she had expressed her strong reaction to the American practice of criminalizing sexually mature girls who reach out for older men. "I believe in the rights of young women," she claims. "I believe young people are capable of loving older people. Our attitude toward adolescents in this country is fantasy. Young people have strong desires and feel shut out of the adult world."

In the earliest version of the novel, Belinda was even younger, and her character foreshadowed the sexual proclivities of the thirteen-year-old character, Mona, in Rice's next series of novels, *Lives of the Mayfair Witches*.

Entertaining a Master

At the 1986 American Booksellers Association convention in San Francisco, John Dodds threw a publication party for *Belinda*, and Rice invited her friend John Preston to attend.

"I had the idea of arriving with a group of utterly handsome men I knew in San Francisco," he said, "all of them stripped to the waist and dressed in leather slacks and boots, arriving by motorcycle. I didn't follow through, but I told Anne about it at the party, and she howled with delight at the image. She told me she'd have loved me forever if I'd done it."

They discussed ideas for books and wondered together whether the market could bear more pornography from Rice. She described a novel to John that she had in mind. It went back to a story she had written in high school about invaders from

Mars coming to Earth, but she had added a new twist: "Slowly the invaded town changes. First, there is no more violent crime. Then the men start softly asking the women if they can help with the housework. The men lose interest in sports, and gradually the heroine of the novel realizes that the men's bodies have been taken over by aliens who are feminine, and that if she doesn't stop them the whole world will be filled with gentle people who are really women regardless of what their bodies look like." This story was never written.

Rice and Preston also toyed with the idea of writing a pornographic novel together.

"As I recall," says Rice, "it was John's idea. It was to be a correspondence between a man and a woman. The woman was supposed to be what John called a sexual athlete, the man just emerging from the seminary where he had given up on the idea of becoming an Episcopalian priest."

"The idea was to get Anne out of a writing slump," said Preston, "and me to move into a larger arena. We were going to goad each other on with more and more writing. She would have written one character's letters and I would have written the other's. If we did it in letters, she could maintain the integrity of her writing. We were to be a brother and sister. The brother had just come out of a monastery and was going to explore the sexual world. Unbeknown to him, his sister was a very high-class madam. She was to instruct him on sexual adventure, and he was to report back about his experiences. It would have been on the level of the eroticism of *Exit to Eden*."

When Preston went back to the convention floor and mentioned this project, several editors made offers. "They *flocked* to me," he said. "People were talking hard/soft deals and the whole bonanza."

Aware of Rice's reticence over collaboration, Preston decided to go ahead and start his part. "I did a couple of the first letters about wanting to buy a sexual identity the way that one bought a suite of furniture for an apartment." He sent these to Rice. "There was immediately a great deal of tension about the project and Anne withdrew in a matter of days."

"I realized early on," Rice explains, "due to my extreme resistance to any sort of collaboration or editorial supervision, that I simply could not embark on the project. I could not work with someone else. I could not go into a project not knowing what the editorial approach would be. I just backed out."

"I understood," Preston emphasized. "What Anne can't stand is anyone messing with her words or her vision. She believes firmly that she, as a writer, must keep her words and vision intact. That there would be any back and forth about what we were writing appalled her. She was quite gracious about it and very upset for upsetting me—which she didn't really do. I wasn't surprised. She needs control over her work. It's that simple. She's also very cautious that another writer might influence her work."

He thought about going ahead and writing a book that still involved her but would not be a collaboration. He called it *Entertainment for a Master*. He would include it in his pornographic *Master* series and make Rice one of the characters. He asked her to pick her own name and design the appearance she desired. She named the character Adrienne and chose to be a tall, blond woman who dressed well and smoked unfiltered cigarettes.

"If Anne were to be any character in an erotic novel," Preston said, "she would be like Charlotte Rampling in 'Night Porter,' five foot seven with long, blond hair and gray eyes, deeply tanned, and smoking a cigarette and drinking only coffee. She would wear spike heels and a black dress with a Victorian collar and ruffles on the sleeves."

In the novel, Preston presented the narrator as a leather master organizing a memorable S&M party during the San Francisco ABA. His guests are Madame and Phil, two sophisticated friends from the sexual scene, and Adrienne, a distinguished novelist who cares about her literary reputation but who also writes pornography.

He describes Adrienne as confident and energetic. She is a married woman and mother who lives in a Victorian mansion in San Francisco and who carries on marathon conversations over endless cups of coffee. Her naiveté about the S&M world is obvious but nevertheless charming: "If her descriptions are less realistic, they are all the more precious for their eloquence."[18] Adrienne looks to her friends who actually participate in the S&M scene for details for her novels. "You know how bitterly

[18]John Preston, *Entertainment for a Master* (Boston: Alyson, 1986), p. 10.

anxious she is that we discovered things in her books that weren't possible."[19] She refrains from actual involvement in S&M herself, but her intense interest drives her to ask questions about how certain movements are made, what implements are used, and how certain things feel. For example, she asks about the use of nipple clamps, and her friends graciously explain the dynamics of cutting off circulation to sensitive areas, then letting the blood flow back quickly to make the area more sensitive and create greater pleasure.

Like Rice, Adrienne's fantasy life is rich but her experience is limited because she prefers to remain an observer via literary expression. She re-creates her fantasies well enough that she does not need to act them out. She agrees to attend the party because she would like to see her words put into action, translated by a trusted friend, without having to compromise herself. It is a laboratory wherein she can see and feel and smell everything to record later. The party is a gift to her. "Just the sight, just the experience of the naked men serving," says the narrator, "was something that I knew she would admire for many years, forever."[20]

The novel records the erotic buildup to the party, as the organizer examines potential slaves for their beauty and worthiness. At the same time, he makes other elaborate preparations for the right room in which to present his "banquet." According to his ad, the male participants must be "well built and attractive, willing and able to perform servile tasks and endure moderate to heavy pain."[21] The party itself takes place in an old hotel near Nob Hill. The essence of the experience is the anticipation and preparation for it.

The men who have been chosen and prepared with such extreme attention to detail are used merely as decoration for the party. One of them becomes a food table, while the others are provocatively posed. The four "masters" converse, glancing occasionally at the prize male flesh working to remain sexually stimulated and aesthetically presentable to their demanding tastes. Adrienne flushes with excitement.

---

[19]Ibid., p. 109.
[20]Ibid., p. 151.
[21]Ibid.

Madame and Phil eventually leave, each with a slave in tow, while Adrienne departs with only an appreciation for what she has witnessed. Uninterested in crossing the line between fantasy and reality, she merely observes with an author's detachment. "Not that she wouldn't like to do it, but it's not her life."[22]

Rice did not read Preston's tribute to her. She was reticent about some of his early notes for this book, so she declined to take the risk of disliking it. "I told him to proceed, and I just wouldn't read it," she says. He published it to honor their friendship—the nature of which was about to change dramatically.

In 1987, Preston went for blood tests and discovered that he was HIV positive. The diagnosis was a terrible blow, and Rice commiserated. She wrote about it in her diary that day, August 20. They both knew that his condition had to remain a secret from the publishing world. Rice called him to say she loved him and wanted to help him get insurance coverage. The progress of his health became a central part of their conversations.

"Anne has been the main person to go through that experience with me," said Preston. "For a long time she was my sole confidante. I needed to talk, and she was remarkably good about it."

"We corresponded all the time about it," says Rice. "He kept me posted on everything. I suggested things like antidepressants, but he had good doctors, and he really took charge of what happened with his body."

Preston continued to write, dedicating several of his books to Rice, as she did to him. He produced more adventure novels, a comprehensive resource guide for gay men in America, called *The Big Gay Book*, and a series of anthologies of gay erotic writings, *Flesh and the Word 1, 2, and 3*. He included excerpts from Rice's work in all three. Eventually, he went public with his health problems so that he could bring more attention to the AIDS issue and promote safe-sex practices. Rice read the essays he wrote on these issues and strongly encouraged him: "I pushed him hard to write a serious autobiography. I always wanted him to tell the whole story of his amazing life."

They continued to monitor the progress of his health together.

[22]Ibid., p. 108.

"I sympathize with people loving each other."

After writing the third vampire novel, *The Queen of the Damned*, which followed *Belinda*, Rice focused on a novel she had started in San Francisco. It was about a family of witches, and she called it *The Witching Hour*. Its sequels, *Lasher* and *Taltos* would reinforce Rice's stand on the issues raised in *Belinda*.

Since much of the action in this novel takes place in New Orleans, Rice decided to return for a trial period to her native city. She wanted to recapture sights and sounds that would make the story authentic. The move became permanent, offering her a chance to face down childhood demons of old griefs and explore previously inaccessible areas of her imagination. As she had done in the Rampling novels, Rice took her characters all over the city. Moving to New Orleans, she felt, had put her in touch with an emotional intimacy in her characters that she had always wished to convey. Her three distinct voices finally came together.

The Witching Hour focused on a purely heterosexual romance between forty-eight-year-old Michael Curry—who was Rice's age and shared much of her background—and Rowan Mayfair, a powerful witch. Michael represented a new trend in Rice's writing toward masculine types and away from the earlier androgyny.

"When I'm writing about Michael," Rice says, "I'm having a wonderful sexual time describing a hunk of a man, his physical beauty and his boyish-gorilla appeal. It's a sex trip for me to talk about Michael. I always picture the actor Tom Berenger. I don't think I become Michael the way I become Elliott or Lestat. I just make love to him and hug him. I see him more from the woman's point of view. Maybe Michael is my sex object."

Rowan is a member of a family of female witches shaped by their strong sexuality. For thirteen generations, they have built their power with the assistance of Lasher, an incubus who has frequent sexual contact with them. Some of them are enslaved to him, while the stronger ones control him for their own use. Lasher is battling to acquire a body and become flesh—reversing the Catholic injunction to shun the flesh. Some family members view the liaisons between Lasher and his chosen witches as perverse, particularly when they are young girls, and for Rice this suspicion represented the traditional social fear of female sexuality. One of the witches, Deirdre, is even forced into extensive electroshock therapy to eradicate her "oversexed" obsessions. "Lasher is a symbol of female sexual fantasies," Rice emphasizes. "He can be a symbol of masturbation. The promise of Lasher down the hallway is the promise of a good orgasm."

Lasher does manage to incarnate into flesh, but his attempts to procreate with the witches kills most of them. Rowan is one of the few survivors, and she gives birth to his offspring. It turns out that he had been the spirit of a Taltos, a mythical creature that loves sexual pleasure for its own sake. The childlike Taltos suffer no guilt over their erotic appetites, making them the characters that most clearly embody Rice's ideal.

The witches must face the fact that they can give birth to these beings; it marks them as different from other humans. One of them, Mona, is the most powerful and precocious of any witch thus far. At the age of thirteen, she is a genius with a lusty appetite and the ambition of seducing all of the males in her family. Not only does she have a number of sexual encounters, but all involve some degree of incest.

"It's wonderful to write about Mona," Rice effuses. "She is my heroine for the nineties. I can go anywhere with her. She's like Lestat to me. The freedom derives from her intelligence—it's incredibly much fun to work with a brilliant character—and from her courage. She has a capacity for action that I personally lack. I adore being Mona."

Rice took some criticism for this character. Some people were upset that a child was depicted in such a sexually provocative manner. When questioned in a magazine interview, Rice admitted that she sympathized in her fiction "with incest and with people loving each other." The double layer of intimacy from the combination of sexuality and family bonding fascinated her.

A local newspaper, *The Times Picayune*, quoted her out of context, drawing a flurry of angry letters. Rice defended herself by explaining that she did not approve of actual incest; she had been speaking of what goes on in her fictional framework.

On the subject of age, she would not back down. She insisted there was nothing wrong with a thirteen-year-old wanting sex with an older man. "I am very much in support of women to choose partners whom they consider responsible and mature," she affirmed. "Today, by not acknowledging that teenagers have reached full physical maturity long before they reach legal maturity, we have created a class of young women of childbearing age who are encouraged to play at sex with young males of the same age who are by no stretch of the imagination ready to become fathers or husbands. This is a travesty. We must recognize that sexual maturity comes much earlier than it did in ages past, and we must stand up for the rights of young people and reexamine our laws. . . . We are letting down those young people who must be educated for the responsibilities that fall on their shoulders and who must be legally held accountable for their actions."

Rice allowed Mona not only to have sex with Michael Curry, thirty-five years her senior, but to have a baby. The child turns out to be a female Taltos who unites with the only existing male and runs off with him, potentially to renew the species. As a character, Mona continued to interest Rice, so she plotted adventures for a future novel.

"He was my best friend."

By the end of 1993, John Preston's health was deteriorating badly. He faced a winter in Maine feeling his weakest. Although he tried to write and maintain many of his other activities, he eventually had to give up and put himself under a nurse's care. Rice had already lost Bill Whitehead to AIDS and John Dodds to cancer. Her father, too, had recently passed away. Now she faced another ordeal with her best friend.

"We tried to provide solace and comfort," she says. "We shipped all manner of things to John, from a cashmere Brooks Brothers robe, to a recliner that looked like a wingback chair. He seemed to be in full charge and in good hands. He was incredibly strong mentally. He was productive throughout all but the last few months of his life. He was unafraid of death."

In April 1994, Preston called Rice one last time to tell her good-bye. Requesting stronger medication, he went to sleep. Preston never regained consciousness.

"The day he died was a sad, sad day in our house," says Rice. "People who had never met him wept with me for him. We all mourned his passing. He was my best friend, my witness, my consolation. We were working writers, always supporting each other, always exchanging stories of our ups and downs in publishing, and our various ambitions and dreams. I miss him."

"I hope my better novels are yet to come."

With the witch series, the experiment of the pseudonyms was clearly finished. Eventually as more Rice fans learned of them, the Roquelaure novels found a large and appreciative audience. Simon & Schuster purchased rights to the series for audiotape, and Rice was delighted to learn that Elizabeth Montgomery would read the last two novels. "I'm thrilled. I love her. That she's willing to do it is great!" By the end of 1994, all three books were available on tape.

However, the erotic quality of Rice's writing springs from her perspective on life. There is no doubt it will frame the novels to come. Rice is intrigued with various types of bonds, be they between Taltos and dwarf, vampire and mortal, or uncle and niece. Since sexuality and connection hold deep mystery for her, she will continue to explore and surrender to it. The fifth vampire novel moves into more transgressive territory, in both religion and sex. Rice also expects to write another book involving the lusty Mona and her equally sensual nineteen-year-old cousin, Mary Jane. These young girls stir something deep inside her and she wants to find ways to express it. Although she may never return to Beauty's world, it is likely that the erotic aspects of dominance and submission will retain their place in Rice's imagination.

PART II

A
ROQUELAURE
CONCORDANCE

In the entries below, these abbreviations are used:

CSB: *The Claiming of Sleeping Beauty*

BP: *Beauty's Punishment*

BR: *Beauty's Release*

The numerals that follow such references are page numbers.

A

Adornment. Items used to enhance a slave's naked body, such as jewels, gold chains, gold glitter, horse tails, ribbons, or flowers. For example, slaves might wear nothing except an arm bracelet, a pair of boots, or tinkling bells adorning their genitals.

The various adornments draw attention to specific areas of the body that arouse onlookers and make the slaves feel vulnerable. Some of the slaves think wearing such adornments is more humiliating than being completely nude because they feel more conspicuous: "Adorned and yet exposed; it was mystifying." (CSB 117)

Tristan realizes that the welts from his lashings are ornamentation as well. He watches Laurent being rubbed with golden oil, and sees the welts transform into rich decorations. (BP 222)

When Beauty is exhibited at a banquet, she feels she herself is actually used as an ornament. In preparation, the Sultan's grooms have decorated her body with pearls, gold glitter, and paint, then have stuffed her full of fruit and honey. It makes her feel less human. (BP 228–30).

See also BODY AWARENESS; EXPOSURE; NAKEDNESS; SLAVES; VULNERABILITY.

Affection. *See* LOVE.

Alexi, Prince. The first slave in the Queen's castle that Beauty knows by name.

When she is presented to the court in the Great Hall, she sees Alexi serving the royalty. He spills some wine and the Queen orders him to be hoisted high and spanked. Alexi bears this punishment well because his intent is to attract Beauty's attention. (CSB 55, 57)

Beauty is quite taken with Alexi's physical appearance. She loves his compact, muscular body, auburn hair, brown eyes, and olive skin. On her first night in the castle, Alexi is brought to the Prince's chamber, where Beauty learns that he is nineteen and has been in service to the Queen for two years. The Prince commands that Alexi give him pleasure and then be bound onto a stone phallus so that Beauty can witness his humiliation. After the Prince falls asleep, Beauty sneaks out to watch Alexi. To her disappointment and jealousy, she sees Squire Felix, the Page who attends him, giving him the pleasure he craves. (CSB 66–81)

The groom, Leon, whom Beauty shares with Alexi, describes him as a model of good behavior, though rebellious in his own way. Part of him, Leon explains, has not fully surrendered to his life there at the castle. This description intrigues Beauty. (CSB 91)

Whenever he can, Alexi assures her that he is watching out for her. The next night in the Queen's chamber, Alexi, as the Queen's valet, shows Beauty what it means to obey even the most difficult commands. He makes love to her later in secrecy. Alexi tells her that the secret of being a slave is to learn to accept her life and yield to those who command her. Then everything will be simple. He insists that he actually adores his tormentors. (CSB 165–75)

Drawing a comparison between "strugglers" and "yielders," Alexi explains how he himself finally achieved serenity. At first he resisted becoming a Tribute to the Queen and ran from his father's house. However, the Queen's soldiers caught him and brought him to the castle. He refused to obey any commands. The Queen only laughed at his rebellion and bound him to the wall in her chamber. Day and night, Alexi was forced to watch her. (CSB 176–78)

As he grew bored, he looked forward to seeing her and even to bearing her discipline. Anything was better than standing idly against the wall. Soon he grew excited at the prospect and began to love the very thing he hated. The experience gave him an appreciation for how the constant paddling made him crave more. When another slave, Prince Gerald, was punished in front of him, he became jealous. (CSB 183)

After the torment of watching Gerald's sex games with the Queen, Alexi decided to become obedient. However, he had little self-control, so the Queen sentenced him to the kitchen. There he became a plaything and an object of derision for the kitchen crew. Abusing him was their duty. They spanked him, raped him, decorated him with sticky concoctions, and hung him in the garbage pit. He felt less than human and, with no release in sight, learned to accept his fate by focusing only on the moment; he learned that he must do exactly what was expected of him. (CSB 186–89)

From the kitchen, Alexi was sent to the stables, which he preferred, despite the constant torment from the stable workers. One stable boy, tall and strong, was particularly keen to punish and rape him, but Alexi found himself longing for this boy's attention. (CSB 189–93)

Finally, the Queen called Alexi back to the castle and he felt born again. Eager to please her, he endured each of her punishments without needing restraints. She teased him with difficult games, but he performed well enough to become her favorite slave and she named him her personal valet. He belonged to her, body and soul. However, the Queen still wanted to test his limits, so she continued to punish him. The Queen, Alexi tells Beauty, "wanted to study me, to break me down and make of me a toy for her complete amusement." (CSB 206)

One task the Queen commanded was that Alexi pleasure her former valet, whom he despised. Then she made him run a gauntlet of six other princes, who spanked him and instructed him in the art of sucking their organs. Alexi felt weakened by all of this humiliation. "I was *lost* in my suffering, my struggles, my anxiousness to please." (CSB 210) After initial resistance, he eventually achieved a state of calm resignation in which his punishments became pleasing.

Yet the Queen was still not satisfied. She sent Alexi to the Special Punishment Hall, where for one full hour ten Princesses were allowed to do anything they pleased to him. There he encountered Princess Lynette, who led the others in an aggressive assault. When they had finished, Alexi was tied to a tree overnight and told he would perform the next day as a circus animal with Princess Lynette before the Queen. (CSB 211–26)

Made to go through a series of ignominious positions, Alexi decided that the only way to outshine Lynette was to obey her perfectly. She struggled to be inventive to throw off his performance and nearly won, but Alexi outsmarted her by performing every humiliating maneuver.

Despite his outstanding performance, the Slave Master Lord Gregory called him rebellious and raped him for it. However, the Queen was pleased. She allowed Alexi to make love to her, although she warned him that worse torment awaited him. She next commanded him to be paraded naked before the common village people, then shamefully displayed on a platform for their inspection. After this ordeal, he lost his fear of being a slave; he tells Beauty that he can now do anything commanded of him. (CSB 234–36)

Finishing the story, Alexi believes he has helped Beauty to understand what it means to yield. However, his subservience has diminished his allure: When Beauty had believed him rebellious, she was more attracted to him.

See also BEAUTY, PRINCESS; BOREDOM; ELEANOR, QUEEN; FELIX; GAMES; GERALD, PRINCE; GREGORY, LORD; HUMANITY; KITCHEN; LEON; LYNETTE, PRINCESS; PUNISHMENT; SPECIAL PUNISHMENT HALL; SLAVES; STRUGGLERS; SURRENDER; YIELDERS.

Andre, Grand Duke. One of the Queen's relatives. Princess Lynette is his personal slave. He is in attendance as Lynette performs with Alexi before the Queen. (CSB 222)

See also LYNETTE, PRINCESS.

Anticipation. An element of the pleasure/pain the slaves experience when they are punished. Rice felt this was a key element in heightening sexual arousal.

As Beauty is taken from her home, she experiences fearful anticipation every step of the way because she has no idea what lies ahead. It grows worse as the Prince presents her before the royal Court, makes her watch other slaves being punished, and commands punishments for her. She hears enough bits and pieces of information to realize that something is about to happen but not enough to know what to expect. She is afraid but curious, and both of these aspects of anticipation enhance the experience for her.

Alexi describes similar feelings early in his captivity. For him, anticipation increases his fear and resistance, so to counteract them he develops an attitude of acceptance. Anticipation plays a lesser role in his existence as he yields to the Queen's will and stops trying to figure out what may lie in his future.

See also ALEXI, PRINCE; BEAUTY, PRINCESS; EXPECTATION; PLEASURE; SLAVES.

Anxiety. *See* FEAR.

Approval. *See* MASTERS/MISTRESSES.

Attention. For the slaves, having personal attention from their Masters and Mistresses can be simultaneously negative and positive. It magnifies their torment but in the process of intensifying their experience also enhances their pleasure. It can yield a sense of identity and purpose.

The slave's goal in the castle is to get the attention of the nobility, particularly the Queen, who represents a godlike power.

However, sometimes the only way to get it is to act out and draw negative attention—in the form of discipline. For some slaves, punishment is preferable to being ignored. "The punishments of the castle had been voluptuous; it had been exciting to be the playthings of a rich Court, to be the object of relentless attention." (BP 7)

Tristan feels sorry for slaves about whom no one seems to care. He believes the master's attention creates order for the slave, refining him in an embracing womb. "I liked the barefoot run through the village," he tells Nicolas, "because you were driving me and you were watching me." (BP 171) Public punishment is excruciating for Tristan but also delicious in the way the attention of the audience makes him feel emptied of himself. "I collected all the crowd's frenzy to myself; and the crowd enlarged my punishment as they enjoyed it. . . . I yielded to their lust." (BP 173) Being in the village magnifies both his delight and agony, since there are more people to pay attention to him as well as more people to be indifferent. He is constantly aware of both poles. (BP 171, 179)

At the Sultan's Palace, attention from the Lord is even more treasured because there are so many slaves vying for it. To get noticed, they must distinguish themselves. "We are lost, you see, unless they notice us." (BR 49) So Lexius, the Sultan's Chief Steward of the Grooms, insists that the slaves in his care comport themselves perfectly, because through them he will be noticed.

See also BEAUTY, PRINCESS; DISCIPLINE; EXAMINATION; EXHIBITIONISM; GOD; LEXIUS; SLAVES; TRISTAN, PRINCE; VOYEURISM.

Auction. The way disobedient slaves from the castle are offered to the villagers. The Queen's village is the only one in the realm allowed the privilege.

The slaves are exhibited on a turntable while their qualities are announced to eager bidders; before a mob of people, their subservience is demonstrated. The villagers who can afford it save their money all year for the privilege of purchasing one of the castle slaves. Tristan and Beauty are both quickly sold to new Masters. (BP 17–27)

Another auction at Midsummer involves Lords and Ladies from the castle who wish to become slaves. "The prices are dizzying," Nicolas claims. (BP 184) Everyone expects that Tristan's former Master, Lord Stefan, will offer himself for this auction since he has proved to be a weak Master and likely desires to be a slave. (BP 184)

See also BEAUTY, PRINCESS; MIDSUMMER NIGHT; QUEEN'S VILLAGE; STEFAN, LORD; TRISTAN, PRINCE.

B

Beauty, Princess (Sleeping Beauty). A fifteen-year-old, blond, blue-eyed princess and one of the principal protagonists of the Roquelaure series. One hundred years earlier, she had pricked her finger on a spinning wheel and had fallen into a deep sleep. Her entire court slept along with her, enchanted by a spell that could only be broken by a Prince awakening Beauty with a kiss.

The image of Sleeping Beauty derives from a seventeenth-century fairy tale by Charles Perrault, and is commonly understood as the image of a woman with unconscious potential. According to the tale, Beauty pricks her finger on a witch's poisonous spindle, but enchantment saves her: Rather than die, she and her Court are destined to sleep for one hundred years until a Prince awakens her with a kiss. The problem is that poisonous vines growing around the castle kill off many would-be suitors. Eventually one Prince gets through and claims her.

In CSB, the Prince cuts the thick, poisonous vines that cover Beauty's castle, enters, and finds her asleep in an upper chamber. He makes love to her and awakens her at the moment of penetration. Although she is frightened of him, she is also intrigued. The Prince tells Beauty's parents that he intends to take her back to his own castle, where she will learn wisdom and self-control. Beauty's parents understand what this means, since they themselves had once served in the castle of the Prince's ancestor, King Heinrick. They reluctantly allow the Prince to take her.

He parades Beauty through the streets of a village and subjects her to punishment and humiliation, but she is more horrified to be taken nude in front of people of her own rank. It makes her feel more vulnerable. Although the Prince proclaims his great love for her, he treats her as his slave and subjects her to torment by spanking her, having others spank her, and withholding satisfaction and reward. Beauty grows increasingly confused, but also captivated.

At his mother's castle, the Prince presents Beauty to the Court during a banquet in the Great Hall. She sees other naked slaves—all Princes and Princesses like herself—serving the castle royalty. When one slave, Alexi, spills wine, Beauty is shocked by his humiliation in front of everyone, but he later confesses that he was trying to get her attention.

In the Prince's private chamber, Beauty learns more about what it means to be a slave in the Queen's castle. The Prince wants her to undress him with her teeth and to submit to constant paddling, whether she deserves it or not. He notices that punishment "softens" her and makes her yield more readily.

The next day, Beauty meets her personal groom, Leon, and sees various rooms where slaves endure harsh punishments, such as having their hands and feet bound together and being hung exposed in the air. Leon answers some of her questions, but Beauty's curiosity remains unsatisfied. She is warned several times about rebelliousness, yet she quickly earns the reputation of being high-spirited and unable to conceal her emotions. "There was something savage in her . . . something untouched, for all her seeming fragility." (BR 7)

Unlike many Princesses brought to the castle, Beauty is quite passionate. "You are awakened to the desires of your Master as you should be," she is told. (CSB 87) She does not need the devices they use with many of the other girls.

Because the Queen disapproves of the Prince's love for Beauty, she orders Beauty to be tested on the Bridle Path. Lady Juliana, one of castle nobility, decides to ride beside her. Beauty discovers that she must run next to Juliana's horse, laced up in boots with small horseshoes on the bottom, and smacked with a paddle the entire way. (CSB 119–36)

The Queen approves of Beauty's performance. She requests her presence in her private chamber. Beauty hates this cold, imperious woman, but there is no escape, so she strives to do what she is told. In the bedroom, Juliana devises a difficult game for her, and Beauty fears that she cannot be both graceful and obedient, but she manages. The Queen orders her bound in a closet.

During the night, Alexi, the Queen's valet, makes love to her. He then tells her the story of how he came to the castle and how he learned obedience and serenity. Beauty is enchanted with him but realizes she liked him better when she thought he had a rebellious core. She herself cannot bear the thought of doing the things Alexi describes or of simply accepting her life there as the Prince's personal slave. She loves the Prince, but she wants more excitement. Her greatest fear is her own mind and the memories she has of her mundane existence in the castle from which she came. She cannot bear the thought of routine.

Beauty hears about slaves being sent to the village, a place where discipline is even worse. The Prince describes it as sublime punishment, which deeply intrigues Beauty, so she decides to hurl herself downward into greater savagery than the Court could provide; she wants to go deeper into herself. She already knows what the castle rituals can do for her, and she has reached its limits; there is no more mystery. Beauty rebels and gets herself sent to the dreaded village. She is thrilled by the possibilities that lie ahead even as she fearfully anticipates them. (CSB 243–50)

In the cart full of slaves on their way to the village auction, Beauty meets Tristan, the disobedient slave of the Prince's cousin, Lord Stefan. Tristan assures her that they are going to an interesting place, but he seems afraid.

At the auction, Mistress Jennifer Lockley pays twenty-seven gold pieces for Beauty. She wants Beauty to work in her highly profitable inn. Lockley's chief boarder, the Captain of the Guard, takes a fancy to Beauty and claims her as his own, subjecting her to heated orgies with his soldiers. Beauty likes her new situation better than the castle because the punishments are harsher and her Mistress is more practical, but she continues to rebel. She thinks it would be more interesting to be bad, and she desires to find someone who can put her in her place.

Jennifer Lockley satisfies her by exacting harsh discipline. For Beauty, it is not the Master that matters but the relentlessness of the punishment. "I wanted to be cast down, lost among my punishments." (BP 207) The scenarios seem normal and familiar to her, as if she was born to it, and she begins to experience herself in a context that seems right. Thus, she accepts the will of her superiors: "She felt an odd contentment, unlike anything she'd known at the castle." (BP 55) Yet when Beauty talks with Tristan and hears how he describes his love for his Master, she feels that something is missing from her experience. She enjoys both her Master and Mistress, but she does not love them. She cannot imagine yielding her soul to another, yet the idea begins to haunt her.

When Beauty finds herself among the six prize slaves that a Sultan captures from the Queen, she meets Laurent, a slave who has the capacity to be both dominant and submissive. They become fascinated with each other, but have no chance to explore their mutual attraction.

At the Sultan's Palace, Beauty realizes she has moved into a place of greater refinement, albeit with less respect for her humanity. She is treated as an animal, an object to be used strictly for pleasure. Again, however, this treatment seems normal and right to her. She likes it.

The Chief Steward sends her into the royal harem where she discovers how the women have been treated. Inanna, the Sultana, takes a special interest in Beauty and lets her know that the Sultan's wives have all been genitally mutilated so that sexual pleasure is difficult for them. Enraged by this cruelty, Beauty teaches Inanna a way to achieve pleasure with women. (BR 99–103)

The Captain of the Guard then rescues Beauty from the Sultan's Palace and tells her she must return to her father's castle and get married. She rebels, hating the idea of putting on clothing, but there is nothing she can do. She must resign herself to her fate. (BR 166)

At home, she receives and rejects numerous suitors, waiting for the one who can properly master her. She inflicts suffering on some of the Princes who court her, but she is too jealous of it to consider being anyone's full-time dominatrix. She yearns for a man like Laurent, and he eventually arrives to claim her as his Queen. In the secret of their bedchamber, he will continue to enslave her heart with rituals and devices that will bring her the exquisite pleasure she had known in her service to the Queen. (BR 199–210, 235–38)

> *See also* ADORNMENT; ALEXI, PRINCE; ANTICIPATION; BEAUTY'S DREAM; *BEAUTY'S PUNISHMENT*; *BEAUTY'S RELEASE*; BODY AWARENESS; BRIDLE PATH; CAPTAIN OF THE GUARD; CASTLE (BEAUTY'S); *CLAIMING OF SLEEPING BEAUTY, THE*; BEAUTY'S DREAM; ELEANOR, QUEEN; HAREM OF BEAUTIFUL AND VIRTUOUS ROYAL WIVES, INANNA; JULIANA, LADY; LAURENT, PRINCE; LEON; PRINCE, THE; QUEEN'S CASTLE; QUEEN'S VILLAGE; SULTAN'S PALACE; SURRENDER; TRISTAN, PRINCE.

Beauty's dream. Early in Beauty's captivity, she dreams about her former life in her father's castle. In the dream, she sees an old woman with a spinning wheel, on which Beauty pricks her finger. It causes her to fall asleep for one hundred years. This long sleep seemed to her merely a "deepening of the ennui" that she had known as part of her life at court. (CSB 67) Although her experience at the Queen's castle frightens and upsets her, she finds it an exciting contrast, and memories of the dream help her to accept her new situation. (CSB 66–67)

> *See also* BEAUTY, PRINCESS.

Beauty's castle. *See* CASTLE (BEAUTY'S).

Beauty's Punishment. The second novel in the series, *The Erotic Adventures of Sleeping Beauty*. In this book, Beauty experiences the life of a slave in the Queen's village, and her experiences are interspersed with first-person reports from Tristan, the Prince whom Beauty meets in the cart.

Tristan and Beauty face the horror of being auctioned off in the village, but both end up with people who know how to properly master them. Mistress Jennifer Lockley buys Beauty and takes her home to her Inn, the Sign of the Lion. Beauty quickly becomes a favorite of an important boarder, The Captain of the Guard, and he delivers her over to his soldiers. She also becomes a favorite of the Mistress herself, experiencing both cruel discipline and ecstatic lovemaking. Two other slaves at the Inn, Prince Roger and Prince Richard, tell Beauty about their experiences in the village and their strong desire to remain there rather than return to the castle. They, along with Beauty, prefer stern handling over the pampering received at the castle. Beauty learns more about herself and the complexity of her own desires, even as she grows to love her Master and Mistress.

Tristan becomes the property of Nicolas, the Queen's Chronicler. Nicolas harnesses him as a pony to drive his coach, then turns him over to the harsh Whipping Master for public punishment in the village square. Surprisingly, however, Nicolas treats Tristan as an equal in bed, asking him intimate questions about being a slave and demanding detailed, honest answers. Tristan does his best, and as a result, Nicolas falls in love with him. Tristan loves Nicolas as well because Nicolas is strong and perceptive enough to be a real Master and make Tristan endure what he most needs to test his limits as a slave.

The Captain of the Guard takes Beauty to an encampment, where she first sees the rebellious Prince Laurent. While there, she also hears about the presence of raiders in the land. When Nicolas later hires her for Tristan's pleasure, she tells Tristan about the raiders. Nicolas overhears this information. He tries to take Beauty home, but the raiders invade the town and grab the slaves. Beauty, Laurent, and Tristan find themselves on board a ship with three other slaves—the pick of the lot—and they learn that they are now in the hands of a new Master from a foreign land. They are not allowed to speak and they are treated with less respect for their humanity than they had been at the village.

One of the Queen's emissaries boards the ship and tells them that they are on their way to become the slaves of the Sultan; there is nothing he can do about it. The Sultan will treat them more abjectly but will delight in their passion. On board, the slaves are examined, ornamented, and made to perform sexually. Tristan misses Nicolas, but Laurent insists that their new fate will be a great adventure.

Punishment; Queen's Village; Sadomasochism; Slave;
Sultan's Raiders; Tristan, Prince.

Beauty's Release. The third and last novel in the series, *The Erotic Adventures of Sleeping Beauty.* This book takes up the experiences that Beauty, Laurent, and Tristan have in the Sultan's Palace and ends with Beauty's return to her father's castle.

The six slaves picked for the Sultan spend fourteen days at sea. It gives them time to become acquainted, and Beauty and Laurent grow attracted to each other. The slaves are all bathed and ornamented to be presented to the Sultan as his rightful plunder. After being led through the marketplace as if they are animals, they meet Lexius, the Chief Steward of the Grooms. Lexius tells them that as sensual creatures, they are considered beings without high reason. As such, they are forbidden ever to talk in the Sultan's Palace, and they must strive to stand out in their compliance, passion, and beauty. He presents only the best and most eye-catching slaves to his lord.

Beauty is sent to the royal harem where she experiences pleasure at the hands of the women and finds out what it means to be made into a piece of living sculpture. She helps Inanna, one of the women who have been genitally mutilated, to experience pleasure, and they grow to love each other.

Laurent and Tristan are destined to become ornaments for the Sultan's garden, but Laurent rebels. Intent on chastising him, Lexius takes Laurent into his private chambers. However, Laurent spots Lexius' true nature, turns the tables, and becomes the master. At first Lexius resists, but soon he submits to Laurent's commanding air. Both find they enjoy their new positions, which indicates to Laurent that Lexius was born to be a slave. Fate handed him the wrong role.

Lexius then takes Laurent to the Sultan's garden where other Lords abuse him. The Sultan enters and chooses Tristan and Laurent to accompany him. In his bedroom, he pits them against one another. Tristan triumphs, but Laurent ends up with Lexius. Later Laurent calls Tristan into Lexius' chamber and together they teach Lexius what it means to be a slave. This activity calls forth Tristan's own masterly abilities. Then Laurent asks Tristan about his experience with the Sultan. Tristan describes the Sultanate as a sacrosanct realm of high order; the Sultan is not just a Master but a great sovereign, and he feels privileged to be part of this wonderful new place.

Soon thereafter, Nicolas and the Captain of the Guard enter the palace to rescue Beauty, Tristan, and Laurent. The slaves protest this new abduction, but they are given no choice. Laurent insists that Lexius come with them, and he eagerly complies.

Onboard ship, Laurent couples with Beauty and she again finds herself drawn to him. Tristan reunites with his former Master. However, when Nicolas fails to properly punish him for his resistance at the Palace, Tristan grows disenchanted. Upon arriving home, Tristan and Laurent are sentenced to serve for one year as ponies in the Public Pony Stables, while Lexius must serve two weeks in the castle kitchen as a plaything for the servants. Beauty gets dressed and returns to her parents.

Laurent finds he enjoys being a pony, but his memories of dominating Lexius prompt him to master the other stable slaves. Tristan also loves being a pony, but still yearns for a Master. Nicolas hires him out and punishes him mercilessly, then buys him outright. They rediscover their mutual love. At the castle, Lexius becomes an accomplished slave, one of the Queen's favorites.

Laurent's father dies, leaving the Kingdom to him. Hearing that Beauty has rejected all suitors, Laurent claims her as his Queen and they find happiness together living out their master/slave scenarios.

> *See also* BEAUTY, PRINCESS; *BEAUTY'S PUNISHMENT*; CAPTAIN
> OF THE GUARD; *CLAIMING OF SLEEPING BEAUTY, THE*;
> DECORATION; DMITRI, PRINCE; DOMINANCE/SUBMISSION;
> ELENA, PRINCESS; HUMANITY; INANNA; LAURENT, PRINCE;
> LEXIUS; MASTERS/MISTRESSES; NICOLAS; PONIES; ROSALYND,
> PRINCESS; SLAVES; SULTAN; SULTANATE; SULTAN'S PALACE;
> TRISTAN, PRINCE.

Blood. A signal in the Queen's castle and village to end any punishment in process. The rules demand that there be no cutting or other type of harm, and drawing blood while paddling a slave indicates that his or her skin has reached its limit. (CSB 75)

> *See also* PUNISHMENT; RULES.

Body awareness. Focusing on parts of the body in ways that otherwise remain neglected. As the slaves are initiated into Queen Eleanor's service, they become highly sensitized to the way their bodies experience degrees of pain and pleasure. Attention to their erogenous areas heightens their experience, as does any kind of adornment. "When a slave's been well used, really well worked, the body is enhanced in some way." (BR 141) This is a pervasive theme of Rice's work: to place priority on the flesh as the source of the greatest experiences of life and truth.

Tristan becomes acutely aware of a pleasure zone when he is anally "measured" with two phallus sizes; he experiences "the phallus seeming to enlarge inside me as if my body existed for no other purpose than to embrace it." (BP 76) He feels no pain, "only the intensification of feeling opened and rendered defenseless." (BP 71)

Similarly, wherever the slaves are smacked with a paddle or jewelry or gold touches their skin, wherever cool air caresses their nudity or hair brushes them, they focus on those spots. "It seemed her body was all concentrated then in its shameful and secret places." (CSB 50) In such moments, the mind is forced to inhabit the body wherein all pleasure and pain derive.

Thus, the Masters and Mistresses use a variety of devices to keep the slaves intensely aware of the erotic zones of their bodies. When Beauty's groom places clamps on her nipples or genitals, Beauty "felt parts of herself of which she had been unconscious." (CSB 112) Although many of these devices involve pain, there is also pleasure, and some slaves like Alexi come to crave these experiences.

See also ADORNMENT; PUNISHMENT; SKIN.

Boredom. The bane of a slave's existence.

Alexi describes this aspect of being at the castle to Beauty. He tells her that he was initially rebellious, and for this he was chained to a wall in the Queen's chamber and forced to watch her and other slaves. When there were many long hours of little or no activity, he soon grew bored, and only his occasional spankings and the Queen's activities relieved it. He looked forward to punishment, much as he had originally despised it, and he realized that the Queen had used boredom to break him down and make him crave exactly what he had resisted. Through boredom he recognized that there were worse things than performing for the Queen. To relieve his boredom, he finally became obedient. He also developed an attachment to the Page, Felix—despite the way Felix punished him—because he was interesting.

Beauty is also afraid of boredom, but her fear derives from memories of her past life at her father's castle, where she had to sit at endless dinners and do nothing. She does not wish to return to such a repetitive and empty life. (CSB 181, 185) For this reason, she trades life at the Queen's castle for even harsher discipline in the village.

See also ALEXI, PRINCE; BEAUTY, PRINCESS; BEAUTY'S DREAM.

Breaking a slave. The phrase that many of the masters use to describe the effect of their discipline. It refers to the practice of "breaking" horses to a harness or bridle. To speak about the slaves in such terms places them on the level of animals. (BP 120, 124)

See also HUMANITY; SLAVES; SOFTENING.

Bridle Path. An area outside the Queen's castle reserved for games involving mounted riders and slaves. Early in Beauty's initiation, the Queen sentences her to run on the Bridle Path. The Prince thinks the command too harsh, which makes Beauty afraid of what she faces. Her groom gives her a pair of boots on which small horseshoes are attached. He tells her she must lift her legs like a prancing horse and keep her hands behind her neck as she runs alongside Lady Juliana's horse.

Beauty watches other slaves in the line go out. Each runs with a mounted rider, who paddles him or her from behind. Some slaves seem to enjoy it, while others struggle. Each slave must run along a line of tables at which the nobility are feasting and watching, and all must stop in front of the Queen to hear whether she is pleased.

As Lady Juliana drives Beauty along, Beauty feels pain and

fear, but to her surprise, both eventually evolve into a relaxed sense of acceptance. She knows she cannot be saved, so she begins to enjoy the exercise. When she finishes the trek and meets with the Queen's approval, Leon tells Beauty that she has excellent form; she was born for the Bridle Path.

Lady Juliana thereafter exercises Beauty on the path in the mornings until Beauty leaves for the village. (CSB 125–38)

See also BEAUTY, PRINCESS; FESTIVAL NIGHT; JULIANA, LADY; PUNISHMENT.

C

Captain of the Guard. A chief officer of the Queen. This blond, green-eyed officer accompanies the Prince to Beauty's castle, then helps him escort her to the Queen's castle. At the first village through which they pass, the Prince commands the Captain to bind Beauty and stand guard to prevent anyone from touching her. (CSB 19)

The Captain also captures Alexi when Alexi resists being a Tribute, and brings him to the Queen over his saddle. One of his favorite slaves is Tristan, whom he personally prepares for the Queen, so when he sees Tristan disgraced in the village, he takes affront. However, the Captain is also pleased to see this slave again. (CSB 177, BP 122)

After Beauty comes to the village, she becomes the Captain's special slave. Her new Mistress owns the Inn where the Captain boards, so he claims Beauty as his own: He sleeps with her, commands her to clean his quarters, and when the mood strikes him, turns her over to his men. He likes her for her insolent spirit, and she likes him for his strict treatment of her. (BP 39, 49–50)

After the Sultan's raiders abduct Beauty, the Captain of the Guard rescues her. At first, she resists because she likes her experience at the palace, but then finds she enjoys being with him again. (BR 153) When she returns home, the Captain misses her and turns to Laurent for friendship.

See also ALEXI, PRINCE; BEAUTY, PRINCESS; QUEEN'S VILLAGE; SIGN OF THE LION; TRISTAN, PRINCE.

Captivity. The various states of imprisonment for the slaves. For some who relish forced consent, captivity is "voluptuous."

The Princes and Princesses must serve the Queen as pleasure slaves for a defined period of time. Although often fettered, they are expected to learn internal constraint through perfect surrender and obedience. When bound, the slaves struggle to convince themselves that they are completely helpless, but when they must endure punishment unfettered, their true submissive nature comes forth. For example, when Tristan is unshackled on the Public Turnstile, he exhibits inner strength as he strives to do what his Master commands. Although going without shackles is frightening because he must rely on his own control rather than the restraints, it is also more exhilarating. Powerlessness draws out secret powers of the self. One unable to perform without fetters risks being even more tightly bound. It is easier to submit to restraints but more terrifying. (BP 103, 172)

Their state of captivity worsens for six slaves when the Sultan's raiders grab them and cart them off to a foreign land. "We're true captives now," says Tristan, because they are no longer under the Queen's protection. The rules may change and there is no escape. (BP 221)

Beauty claims that the most hopeless of all forms of captivity is falling in love. She and Laurent experience this when they decide to marry and find themselves helpless to the feelings of love that overtake them. (BR 233, 238)

> See also DOMINANCE/SUBMISSION; LOVE;
> MASTERS/MISTRESSES; PUNISHMENT; QUEEN'S CASTLE;
> QUEEN'S VILLAGE; SELF-CONTROL; SLAVES; SURRENDER.

Castle (Beauty's). Where Beauty grew up and where the Prince awakens her and her Court from a sleep of one hundred years. He cuts through poisonous vines upon which other Princes have died to make his way to Beauty's sleeping chamber. He awakens her with a kiss (and a sexual embrace), then tells her parents, the King and Queen, that he plans to take her away to his mother's castle.

Although Beauty is afraid to leave with him, she later looks back on her life at this castle as dreary and repetitious. When forced to return home after her servitude, she is morose. Rejecting all suitors, Beauty remains unhappy until Laurent claims her as his Queen. (BR 237–38)

See also BEAUTY, PRINCESS; KING; PRINCE, THE.

Castle (Queen's). See QUEEN'S CASTLE.

Claiming of Sleeping Beauty, The. The first book in the series called *The Erotic Adventures of Sleeping Beauty.* Using the characters from the fairy tale, Rice explores what she calls a "wholesome" fantasy world of bondage and discipline.

A powerful and clever Prince awakens Beauty from her hundred-year sleep and takes her to his mother's castle for her "enhancement," during which time she is to serve as a love slave to him and others of the Court. Beauty is only fifteen and quite innocent, but she soon learns what is expected of her as she is probed, inspected, penetrated, and spanked. Humiliated by these things and embarrassed at her own excitement, she soon yearns for the disciplinary attention.

Forced to serve the Prince and obey his every command, she is first paraded naked through a village, then tied up in the castle to be properly displayed to the nobility. She sees other slaves like herself and feels a special attraction to one named Alexi, the Queen's favorite. Alexi also has eyes for her.

Although the Prince loves Beauty and declines to subject her to harsh discipline, the Queen has other plans. She wants to test Beauty right away, so after Beauty tours the slave quarters, she is prepared for the Bridle Path. One of the nobility, Lady Juliana, rides with her.

Beauty performs to the Queen's satisfaction, although she obeys mostly out of fear. She is intrigued by those slaves, such as Alexi, with reputations for rebellion, although he seems more a model of good behavior. When the Queen forces Beauty to perform meaningless and humiliating stunts, Beauty grows restless and angry. She cannot imagine living a life like this, merely for the amusement of the royalty. Her one advantage is that she is already quite passionate, despite her inexperience, and does not have to be trained to respond. Yet, she wants more satisfaction and excitement than life at the castle promises.

One night Alexi tells Beauty his story. She learns how he was broken down by the Queen until his rebellion evolved into obedience and serenity. Beauty is surprised. She had heard he had an inner core that never yielded, but he assures her that he yields to whatever is asked of him; he has endured the most humiliating experiences he could ever imagine and has triumphed. He finds strength in yielding and in living for the moment, accepting that this is his life. He desires only to serve the Queen.

Beauty soon finds herself being worked and trained to be the Prince's personal slave. The routines become boring until something else captures her interest: She hears about the village, where incorrigible slaves are condemned to serve and sees the beautiful Prince Tristan waiting to be sent there. Frightened but curious, Beauty disobeys the Prince and gets sentenced to the village. She gets on the cart with Tristan, ready for adventure.

> *See also* ALEXI, PRINCE; BEAUTY, PRINCESS; *BEAUTY'S PUNISHMENT; BEAUTY'S RELEASE*; BRIDLE PATH; ELEANOR, QUEEN; GREGORY, LORD; JULIANA, LADY; MASTERS/ MISTRESSES; PRINCE, THE; PUNISHMENT; QUEEN'S CASTLE; SLAVES; SURRENDER.

Claire, Princess. One of the slaves at the Queen's castle. She runs ahead of Beauty on the Bridle Path, and Beauty later comments to Alexi that Claire had suffered. Alexi tells her Claire has no depth or mystery. (CSB 172)

> *See also* BRIDLE PATH; SLAVES.

Crown Prince. *See* PRINCE, THE.

D

Decoration. How the slaves are used at the Sultan's Palace. They are placed in niches in the wall or in various positions in the garden. The Lords barely notice them. Tristan claims it is like being part of the pattern on the wall. (BR 34, 139)

> *See also* SLAVES; SULTAN'S PALACE.

Deferred satisfaction. One method for punishing the slaves in the Queen's castle, and of teaching them self-control. The slaves are kept in a constant state of sexual arousal but forbidden to touch themselves or seek any form of relief unless their Masters or Mistresses allow it.

Beauty first learns this lesson at an Inn where the Prince spanks her, arouses her, then leaves her to suffer from frustrated desire. This ritual introduces her to a new part of herself—her own intense passion—and she must learn about all of her secret desires in order to be able to fully surrender to them. When the Prince finally makes love to her, the release is all the greater for her having waited and suffered. (CSB 35)

> *See also* DISCIPLINE; ENHANCEMENT; PUNISHMENT; SELF-CONTROL; SLAVES; SUFFERING; SURRENDER.

Dildo. *See* PHALLUS.

Discipline. The practice of testing and punishing the slaves for the purpose of their improvement. Some of the slaves tolerate discipline best when it is harsh, relentless, and engulfing. (BP 171) Working a slave well enhances the body. (BR 141)

Lady Juliana tells Beauty she will teach her some discipline: She will present a task to test Beauty's will to please and help Beauty achieve self-control. She scatters roses on the floor of the Queen's chamber and tells Beauty she must gather them with her teeth, one at a time, on her hands and knees, quickly, before Juliana can paddle her too many times. She is to present the roses to the Queen. Beauty feels the threat of losing her grace, and the task proves humiliating. No matter how well she performs, she feels she has not pleased Lady Juliana, and there seems an endless number of roses to gather. Lady Juliana finally relents, ends the game, and kisses Beauty, which inspires Beauty to pick up a rose and give it to her tormentor. Beauty is confused by her own gesture; It seems she wants to please the one she despises, but it is a step toward accepting her position and yielding to her superiors. The discipline had its intended effect. (CSB 158)

Nicolas disciplines Tristan by subjecting him to ever-increasing debasement and humiliation. Each new experience frightens Tristan, but he grows to love this Master who knows exactly what he needs. The worse his punishment is, the more eagerly he serves. (BP 170)

> *See also* BEAUTY, PRINCESS; ENHANCEMENT; GAMES; HUMILIATION; QUEEN'S VILLAGE; PUNISHMENT; SELF-CONTROL; SLAVES; TRISTAN, PRINCE.

Disgrace. A state of supreme reproach, reserved for the most disobedient slaves. As the lowest of the low, they are made to wait on other slaves and be abused by them.

Alexi displeases the Queen and, in his disgrace, is made to endure whatever the kitchen crew and stable boys wish to do to him. He also must attend to other slaves' pleasure, letting them instruct and abuse him. (CSB 127, 208–12)

Disgraced slaves who are considered incorrigible are sent to the village for even harsher discipline. Both Beauty and Tristan are sentenced to this frightening form of exile. (CSB 253)

Laurent disgraces himself by running away from his Mistress. He is sent to the village and bound on a Punishment Cross, paraded through the village, and then displayed as a disobedient slave. (BP 199)

> *See also* ALEXI, PRINCE; BEAUTY, PRINCESS; DISOBEDIENCE; HUMILIATION; LAURENT, PRINCE; PUNISHMENT; PUNISHMENT CROSS; QUEEN'S VILLAGE; SLAVES; TRISTAN, PRINCE.

Disobedience. What slaves who behave according to their own will rather than the will of their Masters or Mistresses are guilty of. Disobedient willfulness is severely punished because, for their own good, the slaves must learn complete and perfect surrender.

When Beauty watches Prince Alexi, the Crown Prince whips her for it, and when Alexi rebels against the Queen, he is sent to be abused by the kitchen and stable help. The most disobedient slaves are sent to the village, where punishments are even worse. Royal slaves are rarely sent, but both Beauty and Tristan end up there on the auction block.

One of the most disobedient slaves is Laurent, who craves constant attention. As a result, he tends to provoke his Masters into continuous discipline. With Lexius, the Sultan's steward, Laurent switches positions, performing the supreme act of disobedience by grabbing the dominant role and treating his Master as a slave.

When Nicolas and the Queen's men attempt to rescue them from the Sultan's Palace, Laurent and Tristan are both disobedient. They are ordered to leave, but they resist. For this rebellion, the Queen sentences them to serve one year as ponies in the Public Pony Stables. (BR 176)

See also ALEXI, PRINCE; BEAUTY, PRINCESS; DISGRACE; LAURENT, PRINCE; PUNISHMENT; QUEEN'S VILLAGE; SLAVES; SURRENDER; TRISTAN, PRINCE.

Dmitri, Prince. A village slave. When Tristan first sees him, Dmitri is on the Public Turntable getting thoroughly whipped. With his black hair, he had been one of the most handsome princes at the castle. Although he had dedicated himself to pleasing and being contrite, he had repeatedly exhibited poor self-control. Thus, he had been sent to the village.

Dmitri ends up as one of the six slaves captured by the Sultan's raiders. His fate is to become decoration in the Sultan's garden, hung from a cross. When the other slaves are rescued, Dmitri is left behind. (BP 155, 221; BR 7, 71)

See also DECORATION; PUBLIC TURNTABLE; SLAVES; SULTAN'S GARDEN.

Dominance/submission. The desire to achieve intimacy or sexual satisfaction through rituals that involve one person being assertive while the other surrenders to what is demanded. In such relationships, there is a continuous exchange of power; the uses to which the power is put can range from sadomasochism to the mere exercise of control and subjugation. Dominant/submissive sex games can be a means of developing trust for fully exploring fantasies: The dominant partner finds pleasure in power, while the submissive desires to surrender responsibility and will. The scenarios they create together can move them toward a profoundly erotic experience and greater sensation or satisfaction. In the intensity of getting close to the most basic desires, psychological needs fuse with the body, and the flow of energy back and forth can expand or transform both parties.

In the Queen's realm, the dominant position is that of Master or Mistress, and the submissives are called slaves. "All her Masters and Mistresses had been strangers to [Beauty], defined perfectly in the instant she realized her helplessness and vulnerability." (BP 9) As it happens, however, some of those who find themselves formally in one position actually desire the opposite.

Princes from other countries who visit the Queen marvel that she can get her Princes and Princesses to serve as slaves. Yet these foreigners are attracted to the hierarchy, some yearning to serve and some to command, prompting the slave Laurent to wonder, "Do all beings have both inclinations at war within them?" (BR 11)

When Beauty gets to the village, she hears that one of her former Mistresses, Lady Juliana, had once been a slave. Surprised, Beauty chafes at how cruel and demanding Juliana had been to her: Someone who knew the slaves' lot should have been more tolerant. Beauty believes that if she were a Mistress, she would be less harsh, yet she herself feels like whipping Juliana good and hard for her behavior. Beauty only later realizes how much she needed a harsh and relentless Mistress. She does not desire to be one but if she was, she would be as cruel as Juliana. (BP 43–44; BR 209)

Tristan wants his tormentors to know that he needs a real master, although he is terrified of the incentive this knowledge gives them for more extreme punishments. He understands that there must be trust between Master and slave, as well as awareness of each other's ability to be in the dominant or submissive position. Tristan is a true submissive and he despises his first Master, Lord Stefan, for his inability to command. Stefan had been unable to master him, so he had run from the castle and ended up in the village.

There Nicolas buys him and Tristan finds in Nicolas a true Master who knows his deep need to be humiliated and punished. "I felt the undeniable urge to fall at my Master's feet," Tristan says, "to tell him silently that I understood my lot . . . and that I gave thanks from the depths of my being that he had seen fit to break me so thoroughly." (BP 120)

The slave has to love the Master or the punishment so that he will want to please, and the Master must know—and do—what the slave needs. Both exercise some form of control and some degree of submission to the other. To have a real Master is Tristan's only hope for a "deep love"—a loss of himself into someone who is good at what he does; he needs to be debilitated and absorbed. The stronger the Master, the deeper the submission, and the more the slave delights in being loved by the Master. Tristan views the Master as an anchor in the chaos, creating order and purpose. (BP 126)

Nicolas understands the psychology of the relationship. He knows that some Masters, such as Lord Stefan, have a temperament more suitable to slavery, and that "the best slaves sometimes make the best Masters." (BP 169) Tristan learns the truth of this statement when Laurent gives him the chance to discipline Lexius, their Master at the Sultanate. Tristan seems to transform from a submissive slave into a cruel and relentless Master—the kind of Master he had wanted Stefan to be. (BR 142)

Laurent knows the full power of his captors only when he feels completely helpless to them and thoroughly humiliated and punished. If he has not had enough, he will provoke his Masters into something more severe. This is his power, that "we who are bereft of all privileges may yet goad and guide our punishers into new realms of heat and loving attentiveness." (BR 15) Later he comes into his own, experiencing the other side of the Master/slave relationship when he forces Lexius to become submissive to him. "It was an ecstatic freedom to be whipping him. . . . It was merely the completion of a cycle." (BR 88) He realizes how much he loves being masterful, while Lexius seems to enjoy being placed in a subordinate position. Laurent hates Lexius for showing him this side of himself, yet also loves him. (BR 90)

Laurent is the slave who can best play out the opposing dominant and submissive positions: "It has never been one or the other for me. . . . In my dreams, I liked both parts of the drama. And when I saw the opportunity I became the Master. Moving back and forth only sharpens the whole experience somewhat." (BR 162) Instructing Lexius, Laurent tells him that a slave cannot pick whom he will serve. "You must give yourself over to the idea of service. . . . And each true Master or Mistress becomes all Masters and Mistresses." (BR 136)

When Laurent includes Tristan in a threesome with Lexius, the lines between dominant and submissive truly blur: Formally, he and Tristan were the slaves, Lexius the Master, yet each has the capacity to fill either position. When Tristan enters, Laurent claims, "Now I have two slaves . . . or you have two masters, Lexius. It's difficult to judge the situation one way or another." (BR 137) Following Laurent's lead, Tristan masters Lexius, but then Lexius asserts his position and tells them he will hang them both on the Punishment Crosses. The constant turnarounds are initially confusing to the participants, as are all transitional states, yet those who can adjust like Laurent settle easily into the position demanded by the situation at hand.

Laurent returns to the village to serve in one of the most degrading positions, as a pony to be rented out from the Public Pony Stables. Although he enjoys the subservience, he cannot resist the urge to master other slaves during recreation periods. He knows too well both sides of his nature. Eventually, his father dies and he returns to his Kingdom. He finds he likes being King and he readily takes charge, having grasped the nature of power from the perspective of one who is powerless.

See also BEAUTY, PRINCESS; LAURENT, PRINCE; LEXIUS; MASTERS/MISTRESSES; NICOLAS; SADOMASOCHISM; SLAVES; TRISTAN, PRINCE.

Doubling. A form of punishment for bad behavior in the Queen's castle. In the Hall of Punishments, slaves are handcuffed hand and foot, then hung from hooks so that their extremities are bound together, leaving their private parts exposed. Completely helpless to their tormentors in this position, they can be easily teased or spanked.

Beauty sees Princess Lizetta doubled for her misbehavior in the Maze. Although this form of punishment horrifies Beauty, she later learns that Lizetta actually enjoys it. (CSB 100)

See also HALL OF PUNISHMENTS; LIZETTA, PRINCESS; PUNISHMENT.

E

Eleanor, Queen. The Crown Prince's mother and the most powerful monarch in the realm. The other Kings and Queens send their children to her castle as Tributes. Queen Eleanor has learned this practice from the Sultan who lives across the sea, and from time to time, she allows him to capture some of her prize slaves.

A contradictory story states that Eleanor, known simply as "the Queen," is carrying on a long tradition from her ancestors of presiding over a sexual training program for captive princes and princesses.

The Queen's castle is on the other side of the forest from the castle where the Prince claims Beauty. Using punishment, humiliation, and other forms of discipline, the Queen believes she is developing these "love slaves" for their own enhancement and improving their ability to command when they return to their own Kingdoms. Her own favorite form of punishment is simply paddling a slave's backside with her bare hands, over her lap; it is the most intimate expression, like a parent to a child. "In this position alone all obedience and subjugation can be taught." (CSB 201)

The Prince brings Beauty to the Queen's castle and Beauty thinks of the black-haired, youthful Queen as a "light threatening to blind her." (CSB 146) Cold and regal, the Queen does as she pleases, with accountability to no one but herself. She seems quite large and strong. Beauty hates her and feels despised by her. The Queen thoroughly examines Beauty, then spanks her, and Beauty dislikes the feeling that she is a toy in the Queen's hands.

The Queen perceives at once that her son, the Prince, is in love with his new slave, although he has properly presented Beauty as a Tribute to her. She disapproves of this kind of bond between Master and slave, so she commands that Beauty go through several tests of obedience. The Prince wants to keep Beauty in his quarters; he tries to protect her from having a rigorous schedule too soon, but the Queen commands that Beauty be groomed, adorned, spanked, then run on the Bridle Path to see how well she performs. (CSB 122)

When Beauty pleases her, the Queen commands that Beauty be brought to her own private chamber, so that she can taste

Beauty's charms. Beauty is told that this is a great opportunity because it is a privilege to gain the Queen's attention. In the bedroom, the Queen instructs Lady Juliana to devise another test for Beauty. Lady Juliana proposes a difficult game but Beauty manages to please both her Mistresses despite her dislike of them. The Queen then commands that Beauty be bound in her dressing room, where Alexi rescues her and tells her how he managed to become the Queen's valet. (CSB 125–64)

Alexi describes how the Queen became fascinated with him because of his rebellious attitude and behavior, so she had him bound to a wall in her chambers to break him down. He watched her undress and thought her quite beautiful. When he finally became obedient, the Queen put him through several harsh trials, then declared him her favorite slave. (CSB 165–239)

> *See also* ALEXI, PRINCE; BEAUTY, PRINCESS; GERALD, PRINCE;
> JULIANA, LADY; MASTERS/MISTRESSES; PRINCE, THE;
> PUNISHMENT; QUEEN'S CASTLE; QUEEN'S CHAMBER; QUEEN'S
> VILLAGE; SLAVES; SULTAN; TRIBUTES.

Elena, Princess. One of the six slaves captured by the Sultan's raiders. Originally trained at the castle, she had run away on a lark and had been sentenced to go to the village. Elena served the Lord Mayor for a year as a farm slave.

Clever and insolent, she shows disdain for the Sultan's grooms; they punish her severely for talking after she has been commanded to remain silent. When Tristan, Laurent, and Beauty are rescued, Elena is left behind at the Sultan's Palace. (BP 222; BR 4, 6)

> *See also* FARM; RUNAWAY; SLAVES; SULTAN'S PALACE.

Elvera, Lady. Laurent's Mistress at the castle. Aloof and cold, with gray eyes and raven hair, she likes to embroider and to have Laurent whipped as she takes her breakfast. She also watches him couple on the lawn with various Princesses. Although he wants to please her and inspire warmth, he decides one day to run away in search of adventure and harsher discipline. In retaliation, Elvera sentences him to the village. (BP 191; BR 9)

> *See also* LAURENT, PRINCE; MASTERS/MISTRESSES.

Enhancement. The state of being intensified or improved.

When the Prince tells Beauty's parents that he intends to take her to his castle, they understand that her tenure there will be for her improvement. She will attain wisdom, understanding, and self-control. This is the goal of the Queen's program for her slaves, so that they will return to their lands and rule with a greater sense of who they are and what they can endure and achieve. "They're not so vain any longer," says Leon, a groom, "they have great self-control, and often a different view of the world, one which enables them to achieve great understanding." (CSB 90)

After all the torment and humiliation he endures, Alexi believes that he is much stronger and more confident. He claims he can now do anything asked of him, and this knowledge gives him a sense of calm and serenity that is the envy of the other slaves. (CSB 237) Tristan and Laurent report a similar experience, particularly as their discipline becomes harsher, more refined, and more degrading. (BP 178; BR 16–17)

See also DISCIPLINE; SELF-CONTROL; SLAVES; UNDERSTANDING; WISDOM.

Erotic. The state of excitement that most of the slaves experience in their captivity. They are required to keep themselves in sexual readiness at all times, which means for the males that they must be erect and vulnerable. Kept in ignorance about the outcome of many activities, they learn to match the force of thrill against the resistance of fear until they find a way to make the thrill dominate. This state of tension and unrelieved desire, with just a hint of anxiety, toughens them and gives them greater self-control. Stretching and testing through risk allows them to overcome limitations. They find challenge and renewal in the repetitions of discipline.

For some slaves, being under another's will is also erotic. They prefer the submissive role, and when ordered to do something, they grow greatly excited. "There is something undeniable in the true slave who worships those of unquestioned power. He or she longs for perfection even in the slave state, and perfection for a naked pleasure slave must be yielding to the most extreme punishments. The slave spiritualizes these ordeals, no matter how crude and painful." (BP 178)

For Beauty, however, it is anxious anticipation followed by the sight of other slaves—particularly those she believes to be rebellious—that keeps her aroused. When the Prince first awakens her from her sleep of innocence, she discovers the pleasures of sex. Her excitement is enhanced when he asks difficult tasks of her, humiliates her, and spanks her. She is embarrassed by her desire, but her groom assures her that the ability to be aroused over what she experiences is a great advantage. The Queen's program for the slaves depends on erotic tension, and some of the Princesses have to be taught to be aroused rather than coming by it naturally. (CSB 88)

Beauty also finds the erect state of the Princes around her quite erotic, and she risks punishment several times to feed her desire to look at them. (CSB 72, 80)

One of the most frequently employed means to increase erotic attention for the slaves is the use of adornments. When clamps are placed on sensitive areas, it draws the slave's attention there and enhances excitement. Jewelry serves the same purpose, making the slaves appear more exposed and vulnerable than if they wore no adornment at all. (CSB 117)

> *See also* ADORNMENT; ANTICIPATION; BODY AWARENESS; CAPTIVITY; DISCIPLINE; DOMINANCE/SUBMISSION; EXPOSURE; LOVE; NAKEDNESS; READINESS; SADOMASOCHISM; SLAVES.

Eugenia, Princess. A slave in the Queen's castle who loves Lord William. She has olive skin and long, rippling hair. Sentenced to serve two years, she does not wish to return to her own Kingdom after her service because she wants to stay with her Lord. (CSB 91)

> *See also* WILLIAM, LORD.

Examination. The process of checking slaves for their capacity to serve. Before slaves are chosen for the Queen, they are examined for beauty, strength, and psychological qualities.

Tristan recalls that he went through this process at his father's castle. "I remembered them ordering me to remove my clothes and how they touched me and watched me as I stood still for their probing fingers." (BP 176) This same procedure takes place for the Midsummer auction, in which Lords and Ladies volunteer to become slaves. Only the most appropriate to the position are chosen. (BP 183)

Other types of examinations continue to be part of the slaves' experience as they are freely touched and looked over by anyone who wants to do so. Beauty is treated to a humiliating (but arousing) examination in the Great Hall, and Nicolas allows three village boys to check over Tristan to their heart's delight and to Tristan's shame and discomfort. In more extreme situations, such as at the auction, the private parts of the slaves are handled or opened wide and exposed for all to see. (CSB 50; BP 20, 64–65, 176, 183)

The examinations at the village, on board the Sultan's ship, and at the Sultan's Palace all feel like tests to the slaves, the standards for which they do not know. They are evaluated for their levels of arousal and passion and for their compliance with humiliating postures and behaviors. Beauty is also examined by the women in the Sultan's harem because they are curious about her genitalia and her ability to be sexually aroused. (BP 218; BR 62)

Beauty turns this vulnerable position around when she is forced to return home and take a husband. She examines each suitor for his worthiness as a Master, but all fail the test. She physically explores one young Prince, then advises him, since he liked the experience so much, to deliver himself to the Queen, which he does. (BR 209)

See also AUCTION; EXPOSURE; SLAVES.

Exhibitionism. The act of displaying oneself for others to see. Being the focus of attention arouses some of the slaves to the point where they act out to get the stimulation of being publicly punished. Alexi mentions that he likes being watched, Tristan prefers a large audience when whipped, and Laurent loves being displayed on the Punishment Cross for all to see.

See also EXPOSURE; DOMINANCE/SUBMISSION; VOYEURISM.

Exposure. The experience of being naked and vulnerable, which the slaves both fear and desire. They are kept naked throughout their captivity and are commanded to keep themselves in a constant state of sexual readiness. The male slaves are more exposed than the females because readiness means staying erect at all times. Their desire is obvious, and this embarrassing exposure shames many of them. As slaves, they are always under scrutiny for their perfection, passion, and obedience.

A further step is the exposure demanded when a Master or Mistress commands the slaves to "open themselves," meaning to further expose their private parts. Their Masters may also command them to "open" themselves psychologically by confessing their feelings, such as when Nicolas questions Tristan. In both forms, the slaves are shocked; they feel emptied of self and vulnerable, yet also stronger for the experience. They have gone into their fears or humiliations and have yielded, and some feel enlarged by this. (BP 170, 173).

See also ADORNMENT; EXHIBITIONISM; NAKEDNESS; SLAVES; SURRENDER; VULNERABILITY.

Extraordinary slaves. Describes the status of being special or of standing out among the other beautiful slaves.

Beauty is one such nonpareil. The Prince adores her, but when she sees the other castle slaves, she fears she may become just one of many. Although she hates being on display, she also loves the attention, understanding that it singles her out. She longs to be special. (CSB 51–54)

When the Queen summons Beauty to her private chambers, Beauty is told this is a great opportunity; it is rare for a slave to get the Queen's notice. Alexi, too, has been noticed by the Queen. He stands out in virtue of his strength, beauty, and spirit. He soon realizes that he wants to be the Queen's favorite slave, so he becomes extraordinary in his obedience and submissive to her every whim. (CSB 237)

Tristan, too, is extraordinary enough to make his Master, Lord Stefan, fall in love with him. However, he rebels and gets sent to the village. There he wins the love of his new Master,

Nicolas, who bonds so strongly with him for his unique beauty and passion that he eventually buys Tristan outright from the Queen. (BR 221, 228)

Laurent is one of the most exceptional slaves. He can perform the most base subservience or take the role of Master—whatever the situation demands. He is larger and stronger than most of the other slaves, so he receives more attention as well as more abuse. However, he is happy to be noticed. (BR 226)

Beauty, Laurent, and Tristan are among the six slaves chosen by the Sultan's raiders as the prize slaves in the Queen's realm. The others are Elena, Dmitri, and Rosalynd. Lexius, the Sultan's Chief Steward, wants the captured slaves to shine without rivals in their compliance, passion, and beauty. Hundreds of grooms prepare slaves for the Sultan and, as Chief Steward, Lexius will present only the finest. "We are lost, you see, unless they notice us." (BR 48) He gets his wish when the Sultana bonds with Beauty and the Sultan brings Tristan and Laurent into his bedchamber. (BR 124–31, 222)

> *See also* ALEXI, PRINCE; ATTENTION; BEAUTY, PRINCESS;
> DMITRI, PRINCE; ELENA, PRINCESS; LAURENT, PRINCE;
> ROSALYND, PRINCESS; SLAVES; TRISTAN, PRINCE.

F

Failure. *See* DISOBEDIENCE; SHAME.

Farm. The home of the village's Lord Mayor.

On his first full day in the village, Tristan arrives at the Farm as part of a team of "ponies." With the other slaves, he collects apples for his Mistress, gets groomed, then discovers what it means to be the newest slave. He must give pleasure to the other ponies while forced to go without himself. "The one chosen must suffer," one pony tells him. (BP 84)

Before being captured for the Sultan, Princess Elena was one of the Lord Mayor's slaves at the Farm. She served there for a year. (BR 6)

> *See also* ELENA, PRINCESS; LORD MAYOR; PONIES; TRISTAN,
> PRINCE.

Fear. The experience of many of the slaves, particularly early in their captivity when they have no idea what to expect. This emotion is part of the Queen's discipline, because the more pressure fear exerts, the more pleasure can be gained. The training program is set up to maintain a balance between physical discomfort and mental joy. The Masters utilize emotional sources of arousal, including fear, while abiding by rules that keep the slaves safe.

The protective frame allows the slaves to find momentum for their pleasure. The fear they experience is not as extreme as terror in the face of real danger; they know they are capable of coping and they can use the punishments to test their resources. Some of them act out to contrive a situation that allows for maximum arousal without violating the safety zone. Others test the master to ensure he is maintaining the status quo.

In her initial experience at the castle, Beauty is frightened much of the time because she never knows what to anticipate. Although her groom Leon answers her questions, he leaves enough mystery to keep her in a constant state of dread. Lord Gregory tells Beauty that fear is merely indecision. If she realizes there is no escape and that she must submit to whatever is asked of her, she will be less anxious and more able to bear the punishments. In short, if she will just accept the conditions and understand that she is protected from harm, she can yield to the full measure of the experience. Thus, she will suffer no fear. (CSB 49)

The stable boy, Gareth, reiterates this with Laurent: "Fear is only good when you have a choice in things." (BR 187) Resignation results in a calm attitude and an ability to perform one's best.

Alexi comes to this conclusion after his ordeal in the kitchen and stable. He most fears boredom, so when abuse and discipline alleviate it, he comes to crave them and to accept his lot. He thinks only of the moment, which results in a state of calm and serenity. He tells Beauty that to reduce her fear, she must find her own understanding. (CSB 170–71)

Although Beauty fears the Queen's village, the idea of it also excites her. Thus, she rebels against the Prince, whose ability to frighten her has diminished, and gets herself sent there. When Beauty observes that, despite his poise, Tristan fears the village, her confidence wavers. As it turns out, they both find satisfaction. The harsh discipline alleviates Tristan's deepest fear that he will not find a Master to suit his needs. (BP 10, 125)

Laurent's greatest fear is intimacy. In the Sultan's bedchamber, he feels hot and excited, though dread consumes him regarding "this silence in the bedroom which precursed the rawest and most heartfelt disasters of the soul, the most thorough subjugation." (BR 123) When he becomes King of his realm, he experiences this fear again, as well as when he claims Beauty as his Queen. Falling in love, he feels panic, but decides to surrender to the full experience. (BR 238)

Laurent experiences fear of a Master only with Lexius, the Sultan's Chief Steward. He sees in Lexius the opportunity to know a hidden side of himself: being Master rather than slave. However, when he assumes this position with Lexius, Laurent discovers that he loves it. (BR 24)

> See also ALEXI, PRINCE; BEAUTY, PRINCESS; CAPTIVITY;
> DOMINANCE/SUBMISSION; LAURENT, PRINCE; LOVE;
> MASTERS/MISTRESSES; PUNISHMENT; SADOMASOCHISM;
> SLAVES; TRISTAN, PRINCE; VULNERABILITY.

Felix, Squire. One of the Queen's Pages. He is tall, young, and blond, and possesses arms strong enough to lift the slaves off their feet and hold them upside down. When Alexi spills wine in the Great Hall, Felix punishes him. Felix also brings Alexi to the Prince's quarters on Beauty's first night in the castle. Beauty despises Felix for his part in Alexi's humiliation, but when she later sneaks out to see Alexi impaled on a phallic statue, she watches Felix, at great risk, relieving Alexi's desire.

Alexi claims to like Felix because he is the most interesting Page, and that counts for quite a lot in the monotonous castle routine. The deeper nature of their relationship, however, remains secret. (CSB 68, 180)

> See also ALEXI, PRINCE; PAGES.

Festival Night. A special evening of high festivity for the nobility of the castle. They sit at tables along the Bridle Path and watch the slaves being driven along by mounted riders. The slaves are specially groomed and adorned because they must run before the Queen. Some of them adore Festival Night, while others fear it. Afterward, the slaves are bound to pillars in the midst of the feasting Lords and Ladies. (CSB 125)

See also BRIDLE PATH.

Forgiveness. The state of grace that the slaves crave. It is the most exquisite aspect of obedience.

The slaves desire to be absolved of their willful deeds, but often the gift of forgiveness comes only at the price of suffering. The Queen has an elaborate system of punishments for disobedience and she withholds her favor until a slave has performed to her satisfaction; he or she must show readiness to be perfectly obedient. Only then can they earn the favors that come with forgiveness. (CSB 71)

Lord Gregory, however, is not as easily satisfied. The slaves fear him more than they do the Queen. He disapproves of slaves who seem secretly rebellious and punishes them severely for their attitudes. Lord Gregory is an unforgiving Master. Alexi learns that he cannot be pleased. (CSB 237)

See also DISGRACE; DISOBEDIENCE; ELEANOR, QUEEN; GOD; GREGORY, LORD; PUNISHMENT; SLAVES; SUFFERING.

G

Games. Part of the disciplinary exercises used to work the slaves. With rules and commands that keep the slaves off-balance, the games serve as tests of obedience. The slaves are never quite certain how to please.

Lady Juliana plays such a game with Beauty. She commands her to use her teeth to gather a group of scattered roses; Beauty must crawl to them on her hands and knees, eluding Juliana who comes behind to spank her, and she must bring the roses, one by one, to the Queen. The task seems endless and graceless. Beauty hates Juliana for making her do it, but she performs well enough to please her, conquering yet one more hurdle in her education as a slave. (CSB 148, 158–61)

Alexi also describes several games. One of his experiences involves performing a series of humiliating behaviors, such as jumping through hoops, in an effort to outshine another slave. (CSB 218–20) In another game, he must gather gold grape-size balls and bring them to the Queen before the stable boy can whip him five times. The Queen shoves each ball into his anus and he must hold them there while he fetches more. "It made me feel softened with love and weak and totally possessed," he says. (CSB 197)

The Sultan also has games in mind for the new slaves, but before he can test their obedience and evaluate their performance, the Queen rescues them. (BR 144)

See also ALEXI, PRINCE; BEAUTY, PRINCESS; DISCIPLINE; HUMILIATION; OBEDIENCE.

Garden (Queen's castle). An area outside the castle used for festivities. In the garden, Beauty sees slaves bound high overhead, in various states of contortion from their exposure and suffering. They are either spread-eagle or affixed to wheels that turn slowly. Below them, the Lords and Ladies sit dressed in their finery, dining and enjoying the sights. (CSB 128)

See also FESTIVAL NIGHT; QUEEN'S CASTLE.

Garden (Sultan's). *See* SULTAN'S GARDEN.

Gareth (soldier). One of the two soldiers who whip Tristan daily as they bring him to the Queen's castle. He grows to love Tristan and misses him more than any other slave. (BP 123)

See also GEOFFREY; TRISTAN, PRINCE.

Gareth (groom). The stable boy at the Public Pony Stables who takes charge of Laurent and Tristan. A demanding Master, he is the best groom in the village. The slaves thrive under his strict discipline. Gareth favors Laurent and, in his stall, becomes his secret lover. (BR 180, 226)

See also LAURENT, PRINCE; PUBLIC PONY STABLES.

Gerald, Prince. The Queen's valet before Alexi acquires the coveted position. Gerald is sixteen years old.

One day while Alexi is bound to the wall in the Queen's chamber, the Queen uses Gerald to torment him. She plays sexual games with Gerald, who dislikes her attention to Alexi because he fears being replaced. What he does not know is that his tenure as a slave is nearly over and he is about to be sent home. (CSB 181)

See also ALEXI, PRINCE; ELEANOR, QUEEN; QUEEN'S CHAMBER.

Geoffrey. One of the two soldiers who has the daily duty of whipping Tristan as they take him to the Queen's castle. Geoffrey develops a deep affection for Tristan and misses him after he becomes a slave at the court. (BP 123)

See also GARETH; TRISTAN, PRINCE.

Gerhardt, Lord. One of the nobility at the Queen's castle. His female slave (possibly Princess Claire) chafes over the way he runs her on the Bridle Path: He likes to take it slow, savoring every moment, while she desires to run full out. Lord Gerhardt punishes her for this disobedient attitude. (CSB 130)

See also BRIDLE PATH.

God. The omnipotent creator of life, and source of absolution. The imagery and rituals surrounding the Queen and the Sultan convey the impression of Godlike authority and power.

The Queen has designed the hierarchy of the Master/slave relationship in her realm, and she doles out punishment and forgiveness as she sees fit. She is accountable to no one and nothing save the rules she herself sets up. The slaves crave her attention, and only those with sufficient spirit and obedience come into her special favor. Everyone answers to her, including the Crown Prince, and everyone fears her disapproval.

The Sultan seems even more imperious, and his presence is foreshadowed with biblical imagery: The Sultan's Chief Steward presents himself as part of a trinity, and the Sultan first appears in a lush garden, suggesting the garden of Eden; his grooms are described as angels, young and delicate of build, with perfect skin. (One chapter's title, "The Garden of Male Delights," is derived from Bosch's painting "The Garden of Earthly Delights," which depicts Eden.)

Tristan describes the Sultanate as a highly ordered, sacrosanct realm in which each thing has its place, and where the great privilege is to be noticed by the highest authority. The slaves feel less human, less significant here, but the refinement of the rituals surrounding obedience, guilt, perfection, and absolution provide a sense of participating in something sacred. The Sultan is not a mere Master; he is a sovereign. (BR 139–40)

See also ELEANOR, QUEEN; FORGIVENESS; SULTAN; SULTANATE.

Grace. An elegance of motion that the slaves want to achieve. They are seeking perfection in their performance and must sometimes sacrifice grace to speedy obedience. The ideal is to achieve both in the most exquisite balance. Lack of grace makes them self-conscious and inhibits their performance. (CSB 158)

See also PERFECTION.

Great Hall. The area of the castle where the Crown Prince presents Beauty to the Queen's court. Beauty sees the Queen here for the first time.

In this hall, the Queen commands that Beauty be bound on a table to be displayed for the Lords and Ladies. While the nobles inspect her, the slaves serve a banquet, and Beauty first spots Alexi, the Queen's valet. He spills wine and gets punished. This experience is Beauty's first exposure to what she can expect at the castle. (CSB 47)

After being rescued from the Sultan, Laurent and Tristan are presented to the Queen in the Great Hall. For their disobedience and resistance, she sentences them to a year at the Public Pony Stables. (BR 173)

See also ALEXI, PRINCE; BEAUTY, PRINCESS; EXAMINATION; LAURENT, PRINCE; QUEEN'S CASTLE; TRISTAN, PRINCE.

Gregory, Lord. The overseer of the Pages and slaves, the Master of Postulants, he is one of the Queen's principal servants. A tall, gray-haired man with gray eyes, Lord Gregory is cold and stern, wanting the slaves to be punished even more than they already are. He is harder to please than the Queen herself. Gregory dislikes rebelliousness, and he watches both Beauty and Alexi closely, believing they share the same incorrigible spirit of unyielding resistance.

Much as he disapproves of it, however, it also seems to arouse him. He is especially fascinated with Alexi. Even when the Queen believes Alexi has been perfect, Lord Gregory accuses him of rebelliousness and wants to subject him to more discipline. To show his scorn, Gregory rapes him, then warns him of further punishment. (CSB 230)

Lord Gregory also disapproves of the way the Prince protects Beauty from rigorous discipline. He thinks she should be thoroughly worked like the other slaves. When he catches her one night watching Felix tormenting Alexi, he lets her know he is keeping his eye on her. One false move and she will be properly disciplined—*his* way. As Beauty grows used to the castle and learns to perform, Lord Gregory accuses her of being infected with Alexi's rebellious spirit. He fears she will make a mockery of their rituals. What she needs, he believes, is a severe lesson in obedience and surrender. (CSB 250)

Beauty does not give him the chance, however, as she rebels enough to be considered incorrigible. She gets sent to the village, out of Gregory's grasp. (CSB 48, 81, 250–51)

See also ALEXI, PRINCE; BEAUTY, PRINCESS; MASTERS/
MISTRESSES; QUEEN'S CASTLE; PUNISHMENT; SLAVES.

H

Hall of Punishments. A room in the Queen's castle reserved for punishing disobedient slaves who please themselves instead of their Masters.

Beauty sees Princess Lizetta punished here. Leather cuffs are placed on Lizetta's ankles and wrists, and she is lifted into the air and "doubled": Her hands and feet are affixed together on a hook, leaving her secret parts exposed. Beauty is horrified but Lizetta actually enjoys this punishment. (CSB 99–108)

See also DOUBLING; LIZETTA, PRINCESS; PUNISHMENT; QUEEN'S
CASTLE; SLAVES.

Harem of Beautiful and Virtuous Royal Wives. The Sultan's collection of female slaves. Lexius takes Beauty to this room and
makes her crawl into a small opening to gain access to the
women. They seem alien, dangerous, and wildly licentious. Immediately, they examine and caress her, then impale her on the
phallus of a bronze statue.

A silent woman watches this sexual activity and Beauty believes her to be the Sultana. Later Beauty finds out that her
name is Inanna. Through her, Beauty discovers that all of the
Sultan's women have been mutilated; because the clitoris has
been removed, they cannot achieve their own pleasure without
great difficulty and can only give pleasure to the men. Beauty is
outraged by this cruelty, and she enthusiastically teaches Inanna
how to achieve an orgasm. (BR 59–65, 91–103)

See also BEAUTY, PRINCESS; INANNA; SULTAN'S PALACE.

Harm. Cutting, burning, or in any way injuring a slave. There is
a strict rule in the Queen's castle and village against harming
any slave. They are to be well treated and well fed, because the
goal of their punishment is enhancement, not injury. (CSB 90)

See also BLOOD; PUNISHMENT; RULES; SKIN; SLAVES.

Heinrick, King. The Prince's great-grandfather. Beauty's father
had served Heinrick as a pleasure slave. Then one hundred
years had passed while Beauty's Court fell into a deep sleep. For
that reason, Heinrick's great-grandson, the Prince, became
Beauty's contemporary when she awoke. (CSB 6)

See also PRINCE, THE.

Helplessness. *See* CAPTIVITY; SLAVES.

Humanity. A dimension of existence that the slaves feel they lose
as they descend into harsher punishments and deeper degradation. It is similar to the way an orgasm feels in its total loss of self

into a boundless experience: "The pleasure dissolved the humanity she had known." (BP 6)

Most of the slaves feel they are treated like animals to be used in some functional manner, such as pleasure or common labor. The Captain calls Beauty a partridge, the Queen refers to Alexi as her pet, and Tristan and Laurent are made to wear horses' tails and pull carts or carriages. Even worse, at the Sultan's Palace, they are tethered together like animals and led through the market on their way to captivity. Soon thereafter they become no more than objects, used as wall fixtures or garden decorations. The foreign tongue also has the effect of making them feel dismissed as insignificant, since the Lords make no effort to help them understand. In addition, the slaves are not allowed a human voice; their new captors believe that their extreme sensuality cannot coexist with the capacity for high reason. (BP 69; BR 33–34, 124)

Tristan actually enjoys the feeling of being merely part of the design; the Palace seems to him an ordered realm in which he has a clearly defined purpose even if it is merely as an object. He experiences this sense of fit again when he and Laurent are sentenced to serve at the Public Pony Stables, where they are muted, bitted, and harnessed for labor and display. Although their grooms engage in conversation with them, they are considered no more than animals. (BR 78–79, 179–99)

See also DECORATION; PONIES; PUBLIC PONY STABLES; SLAVES.

Humiliation. A deep sense of personal shame, or a decrease in pride and self-esteem.

Beauty experiences this feeling as soon as she awakens from her deep sleep. She discovers that she is naked and must remain in that state in front of her family and servants. When the Prince spanks her, the humiliation increases. "To be commanded by one so very young . . . is to feel one's helplessness." (CSB 12) To show her how he puts the lowliest person above her, the Prince allows a common cobbler to touch Beauty. She is mortified but knows her obedience is being tested.

As the Prince parades her naked in front of strangers, particularly people of her own rank, Beauty's shame worsens. "It was one thing to be shown to the rustics who praised her and would make a legend of her, but she could already hear the babble of haughty speech and laughter. This was unendurable." (CSB 45) He then commands her to crawl on hands and knees and allows her to be bound for display and the examination of her most private parts.

Beauty soon learns that humiliation is to be a constant companion at the castle. There are endless variations of it, and when she yields to it, she feels as if she has lost herself. (CSB 173) She witnesses other slaves in humiliating postures and learns that punishment inevitably involves some form of degradation. For example, slaves who are bound with hands and feet together so that their genitals are fully exposed must endure the slaps and taunts of any passerby. Beauty discovers that being perfectly obedient does not save her from such ordeals. (CSB 101–102)

Alexi tells Beauty his own story and she learns about ordeals even worse than she had imagined. Not only was he abused by lowly servants but his bodily secrets were put on a degrading display before the villagers. Having endured it, he feels stronger and more serene, but he still recalls the feeling of fear and shame from being so thoroughly abased. (CSB 237)

When sentenced to the Queen's village, Tristan reports on his own experience of deep shame. His new Master allows him to be thoroughly examined by rough village boys, then turns him over to the Whipping Master for public punishment. He must endure this beating without fetters; in other words, he cannot even have bindings to resist. He must exercise supreme self-control, even as he becomes the target of garbage throwing. At another time he must also pull a coach in a pony harness, with a horsetail phallus strapped into his anus. Although these degradations are worse than any he has experienced before, he tells his Master that he is grateful. "It was what I *needed*. . . . I had pride in it." (BP 170)

Laurent sums up the slave's humiliation as the result of their highborn status mingled with deprivation and the knowledge that their power will one day be reinstated. He is the equal of those who enjoy his nakedness and who punish him. Yet, defenseless against them, he has been stripped of all accouterments of privilege. (BR 10)

I

Inanna. The Sultana at the Sultan's palace. She is tall and stately, with dark hair and eyes. More richly dressed than the other wives, she is also more alluring.

When Beauty enters the royal harem, the women play with her, examine her, and caress her. Inanna stands apart, watching. Beauty thinks the Sultana seems conflicted over what she observes and carries an air of great sadness. Later, dressed as a man, Inanna frees Beauty from her fate as a statue in a niche in the wall and takes her to a secret chamber. Beauty discovers that Inanna is quite passionate. However, she has been mutilated to prevent sexual pleasure: There was "nothing left but the portal that the man might enjoy." (BR 99)

Beauty teaches her a way to become orgasmic without a clitoris, and they make love to each other. Beauty desires to remain with Inanna but is rescued instead by her former Master. She hopes that Inanna will now be able to use what she has learned and teach it to the other wives. (BR 75, 91–103)

Incorrigibles. Slaves whose rebellion is so out of control that extreme methods are needed to tame them. Some never fully surrender. The Queen sentences such slaves to the rigors of the village.

Beauty and Laurent are the two most resistant slaves, although Alexi has the reputation of having a core deep within him that never surrenders. Beauty rebels deliberately in order to get sent to the village, and even there she acts out in ways that invite the most frightening discipline. She speaks back to her Mistress and challenges her to do her worst. Beauty cannot fully surrender to this woman, however, nor to anyone else until she falls in love with Laurent.

Laurent displays a mischievous spirit, having the capacity to play the dual role of both Master and slave. When he grows bored at the castle, he runs away for adventure, and his consequent punishment is rather harsh. Yet he loves being bound to the Punishment Cross. In an even more brash display of ego, he turns the tables on his Master Lexius and makes Lexius perform as his slave.

See also BEAUTY, PRINCESS; DISGRACE; DISOBEDIENCE;
LAURENT, PRINCE; QUEEN'S VILLAGE; RESISTANCE;
SURRENDER.

Inn (Jennifer Lockley's). *See* SIGN OF THE LION.

Inn (before arrival at castle). The place where the Prince and Beauty stay overnight on their way to the Queen's castle. Here the Prince decides to further instruct Beauty in the ways of obedience. She must wait on his table on hands and knees, eat from the floor, and endure being spanked by the Innkeeper's daughter. The Prince tells Beauty that such pain will soften her. The Innkeeper's daughter then bathes her and tells her she behaved admirably. (CSB 23–43)

See also BEAUTY, PRINCESS; DISCIPLINE; HUMILIATION;
INNKEEPER'S DAUGHTER; SOFTENING.

Innkeeper's daughter. A young brunette at the Inn where the Prince stays with Beauty on his way to his mother's castle. At the Prince's command, this girl brings him a wooden paddle, then spanks Beauty with it herself. Afterward, she bathes Beauty and ties her to the four-poster bed to await the Prince's whim. (CSB 25–26)

See also BEAUTY, PRINCESS; INN (BEFORE ARRIVAL AT CASTLE).

J

Jerard, Prince. One of the human ponies harnessed with Tristan in the village. He loves pulling coaches, running hard, and being thrashed.

Because Jerard ran from the castle, he was sentenced to three years of hard labor in the village. Sold to the Public Pony Stables, he quickly became one of the best "ponies" in the village. He has already served two years, so he understands the slave hierarchy and has favorite Masters. He is proud that Nicolas frequently chooses him because Nicolas whips him freely and hard. Jerard loves a Master who does what he does well; it brings out the best in the slaves. (BP 84)

When Laurent becomes a pony in the stables, he takes a special interest in dominating Jerard, who eagerly responds. (BR 196–97)

See also PONIES; PUBLIC PONY STABLES; QUEEN'S VILLAGE.

Julia, Mistress. Wife to Nicolas, the Queen's Chronicler, and Tristan's Mistress. As the character most closely resembling Anne Rice, Julia is an educated petite brunette with long brown hair and small wrists. Unlike most other women, she can read and write.

When Nicolas purchases Tristan and brings him home, Julia insists that he be "measured." She uses two leather phalluses to evaluate his experience with anal surrender. One has a long horse's tail attached to it, and she makes him wear it.

Tristan accompanies her to the Public Tents so that Julia can watch him couple with a Princess for her own entertainment. However, Tristan's primary focus is Nicolas, his Master. (BP 67)

See also NICOLAS; PHALLUS; PUBLIC TENTS; TRISTAN, PRINCE; VOYEURISM.

Juliana, Lady. A lady of the Queen's Court. Juliana has long blond hair, which she keeps braided, and she dresses in the finest velvet and jewels. Beauty is jealous of Juliana's position over the slaves and hates her for her privilege.

Although Princess Lizetta is Juliana's slave, Juliana becomes fascinated with Beauty. She sympathizes with the Prince's infatuation with Beauty, but she wants to have a chance with the new love slave as well. When the Queen orders Beauty to run on the Bridle Path, Juliana accompanies her on horseback. Beauty performs well enough to be called into the Queen's chamber, where Juliana is allowed to do with her as she pleases. She devises a difficult game of discipline and humiliation, which Beauty performs perfectly, despite her antagonistic feelings toward Lady Juliana. To her own surprise, after the game Beauty offers a rose to Juliana, as if she loves this woman, her tormentor. (CSB 158–62)

As Beauty falls into a routine, Juliana spends a great deal of time with her, running her on the Bridle Path and sitting with her in the garden. Eventually Beauty tires of it all and behaves badly enough to be sent to the village. Lady Juliana is deeply grieved to see her go. (CSB 252)

To Beauty's surprise, she learns that Juliana had once been a slave. She had liked the entire experience so much, and had come into such strong favor with the Queen, that she returned to the castle after her servitude as one of the nobility. She had wanted Roger to be her slave and had promised to be a wicked Mistress, but Roger had run away instead. Beauty reacts adversely to the report of this role reversal, annoyed that Juliana could be such a cruel Mistress. However, Beauty herself finds she wants to punish Juliana in just the way Juliana punishes her slaves. (BP 42–44)

See also BEAUTY, PRINCESS; BRIDLE PATH; DOMINANCE/ SUBMISSION; GAMES; MASTERS/MISTRESSES; ROGER, PRINCE.

K

Kitchen. One of the Queen's favorite places to discipline her slaves. She sentences both Alexi and Lexius to become playthings of the kitchen staff. They then realize, by contrast, what a privilege it is to be playthings of the royalty. (CSB 186; BR 175)

See also ALEXI, PRINCE; LEXIUS; QUEEN'S CASTLE.

King. Beauty's father. Along with his Court, he slept for one hundred years after Beauty pricked her finger on a witch's spindle. When the Prince wakes her with a kiss, the King wakes as well and acknowledges the Prince's right to take his daughter to the Queen's castle as a Tribute. He understands what Beauty will learn, because he himself once served as a slave to the Prince's forebear, King Heinrick. (CSB 6–7)

When the king hears that Beauty was kidnapped by the Sultan, he demands that the Queen rescue her and send her home. He urges Beauty to marry, but to his chagrin, she rejects all suitors. Finally, Laurent arrives to claim her. The King is overjoyed when Beauty gladly accepts him. (BR 234)

See also BEAUTY, PRINCESS; HEINRICK, KING.

King Heinrick. *See* HEINRICK, KING.

King Lysius. *See* LYSIUS, KING.

L

Laurent, Prince. Lady Elvera's personal slave at the castle, the Prince with whom Beauty falls in love, and the hero of the third Roquelaure novel, *Beauty's Release.* He has brown hair and eyes, and he tells his own story.

High-spirited and defiant, Laurent's air of power derives from being heavily muscled, taller than most of the other slaves, and able to play equally the parts of both Master and slave. Laurent loves adventure and constantly gets himself into complex situations to get attention. He had served in the castle for a year, attaining a degree of perfection that had finally bored him, so he had finally decided to run away. The slave side of him loved being caught and condemned because it gave him a feeling for the power of his Masters. "I must be the emblem of the worst punishment," he claims. (BR 16)

The Queen's soldiers had flushed him out of the woods near the village. To teach him his place, the Captain of the Guard anally impales Laurent on a Punishment Cross and parades him through the village. The Queen refuses to see him, but sentences him to four years of village labor. However, the Sultan's raiders capture him first and take him to the Sultan's Palace.

The Sultan's Chief Steward, Lexius, becomes attracted to Laurent's spirit. They develop a relationship in which Laurent can practice being a Master because Lexius desires to be subservient. Laurent enjoys the feeling: "The moments in which my soul yielded, in which everything formed a complete pattern, were moments when I was in command." (BR 222) After returning to the village and becoming a pony at the stables, he continues to dominate others. The slaves he punishes most are the ones he most loves. Able to endure disciplinary measures heretofore unimaginable, Laurent's soul gains peace as he resigns himself to his fate. (BR 217)

His father's death ends his service to the Queen; he is ready to become King. He fully understands the nature of power from both sides, and he can exercise authority clearly and decisively. His subjects love him for it, and with his new air of command, he claims Beauty as his Queen. She is delighted because she has found no other suitor who can master her or who understands the depth of her desire to be a slave. (BR 222, 230, 237–38)

> *See also* ATTENTION; BEAUTY, PRINCESS; *BEAUTY'S PUNISHMENT*; *BEAUTY'S RELEASE*; DOMINANCE/SUBMISSION; ELVERA, LADY; LEXIUS; LEXIUS' CHAMBER; LOVE; MASTERS/MISTRESSES; QUEEN'S VILLAGE; PONIES; PUBLIC PONY STABLES; PUNISHMENT CROSS; RUNAWAYS; SADOMASOCHISM; SLAVES; SULTAN; SULTAN'S GARDEN; TRISTAN, PRINCE.

Leon. The personal groom at the Queen's castle for Beauty and Alexi. He is fair-haired with hazel eyes.

Leon gently bathes and attends to Beauty, answering her questions and giving instructions that will make her ordeals a bit more tolerable. He tells her he will punish her only if he is ordered to do so. Beauty enjoys Leon's attention but dislikes the way he adorns her to present her to the Queen. She is also annoyed when he fails to answer questions about the Bridle Path.

Beauty asks Leon about Alexi and he tells her that although Alexi is a model of good behavior, he possesses a rebellious core. When Beauty later reports this perception to Alexi, it confuses him because he claims to be perfectly obedient to the Queen. (CSB 84, 222)

> *See also* ALEXI, PRINCE; BEAUTY, PRINCESS; SLAVES' HALL.

Lexius. The Sultan's Chief Steward of the Grooms. He arrives as part of a group of three, signifying the Trinity, and he is one of the few foreigners who can speak the language of the Queen's realm. Tall, delicate, and elegant, he has dark hair and eyes and a melodious voice. He seems at once both ferocious and innocent.

Lexius understands that the slaves can speak and reason, although such things are forbidden in the Sultanate. In private, he carries on a dialogue with them. He takes a special interest in Laurent's defiant spirit, because it seems to hold possibilities for him. When they are alone, Laurent takes advantage of Lexius' desire to be mastered by commanding him to become a slave. Initially confused, Lexius wants to repeat the experience, even as he publicly masters Laurent. Lexius, however, was born to be a slave, despite his apparent fate as Master. To give him even more experience in being submissive, Laurent arranges for Tristan to master Lexius as well. The chief groom responds fully and deeply to the harsh discipline. When it is over, he lies between Laurent and Tristan in an aura of love. (BR 81–90, 133–44)

When the Queen's people arrive to rescue Tristan and Laurent, Laurent orders Lexius to come with them. He complies, ready to be a slave in the fullest sense. At the castle, he throws himself at the Queen's mercy. She tells him she chooses her own slaves but still sentences him to two weeks in the kitchen. Lexius soon becomes a happy and accomplished slave, serving the Queen daily on the Bridle Path. (BR 37–51, 81–90, 155, 175, 222)

> *See also* BEAUTY'S RELEASE; DOMINANCE/SUBMISSION; KITCHEN; LAURENT, PRINCE; LEXIUS' CHAMBERS; MASTERS/MISTRESSES; SLAVES; SULTANATE; SULTAN'S PALACE.

Lexius' chamber. The room in the Sultan's Palace where Lexius takes Laurent for discipline and ends up as Laurent's slave. Laurent finds the room warm and quiet; the bed linens are made of red silk, and there are hanging lamps all around. Because Laurent has guessed what he truly wants and has invited Tristan to help make it happen, in the privacy of this chamber Lexius becomes the submissive he truly is. (BR 81–90, 133–44)

> *See also* DOMINANCE/SUBMISSION; LAURENT, PRINCE; LEXIUS; SULTAN'S PALACE; TRISTAN, PRINCE.

Lizetta, Princess. Lady Juliana's personal slave.

Beauty first sees Princess Lizetta in the Hall of Punishments. The black-haired slave is being disciplined for petulance in the Maze and for failing to provide good sport. To Beauty's horror, Lizetta is "doubled," hung up with her hands and feet bound together and her private parts exposed. Beauty later learns that Lizetta purposely misbehaves when she grows bored and endures her Mistress's displeasure to get this treatment. She is a valuable slave because she is resigned to her fate, but she loves to struggle within the boundaries of that acceptance. (CSB 99)

See also DOUBLING; HALL OF PUNISHMENTS; JULIANA, LADY; SLAVES; STRUGGLERS; YIELDERS.

Lockley, Jennifer. The Innkeeper of the Sign of the Lion who purchases Beauty at auction for twenty-seven gold pieces. Mistress Lockley is practical but harsh. She specializes in taming rebellious spirits. Tall, with black hair, she is cold, unforgiving, and commanding.

She makes Beauty wash the floors with the scrub brush in her teeth and thrashes her soundly for the least imperfection. On the other hand, she also favors Beauty and brings her into her private chamber for a lovemaking session. Beauty loves this Mistress more than she had loved the Prince, although neither completely wins her heart. (BP 27)

See also DOMINANCE/SUBMISSION; MASTERS/MISTRESSES; QUEEN'S VILLAGE; SIGN OF THE LION.

Lord Mayor. A stern Master who runs the Queen's village. He lives on a farm and goes around in a coach pulled by twelve Princesses. Princess Elena was one of his slaves. (BP 182)

See also ELENA, PRINCESS; FARM; QUEEN'S VILLAGE.

Love. Deep affection for another person. When love occurs between Master or Mistress and slave, it makes the relationship both more simple and more difficult. For example, the Prince falls in love with Beauty when he claims her as his slave, and although he does not spare her from spankings and other forms of humiliation, he wants to protect her from some of the disciplinary ordeals other slaves must endure. His mother, the Queen, disapproves of his attachment, so she orders Beauty to go right into training. The Prince protests, but his pleas have no effect.

The other Master/slave couple who love each other in the castle are Tristan and Lord Stefan. When Tristan misbehaves because he considers Stefan weak, Stefan sentences him to the village, then deeply regrets it. They both mourn their separation, as the Prince does his from Beauty when she likewise gets herself sent to the village. (CSB 173, 252)

Tristan tells Beauty about his relationship with Stefan and later with his new Master, Nicolas, whom he truly loves. One must love the Master or Mistress, he claims, and he can only love one who can meet his needs for strict, unrelenting punishment. Slaves take pleasure in serving such Masters because they are "enfolded in a womb of relentless attention and pleasure." (BP 179)

Beauty sympathizes, but she feels that as long as she loves the punishments, she does not have to yield her soul to a Master or Mistress. She believes that perhaps she has not found the right Master, and she begins to long for something that she may be missing. Only when she meets Laurent does she feel the stirrings of love. Despite his position as a slave, he has the proper masterly spirit to tame her. Laurent and Beauty both fear how love masters them internally, but when they agree to marry, they decide to resign themselves to it. (BR 7, 163, 169, 233) "It shall be the worst and most hopeless captivity of all," Beauty sighs. (BR 238)

> *See also* ATTENTION; BEAUTY, PRINCESS; CAPTIVITY; LAURENT, PRINCE; LOVE SLAVE; MASTERS/MISTRESSES; NICOLAS; SLAVES; STEFAN, LORD; TENDERNESS; TRISTAN, PRINCE.

Love slave. A term for the slaves at the Queen's castle. Some are actually loved by their Master or Mistress, as the Prince loves Beauty, but this term actually describes their role as pleasure slaves. (CSB 47)

> *See also* LOVE; SLAVES; TRIBUTES.

Lynette, Princess. One of the ten Princesses allowed to torment Alexi in the Special Punishment Hall. Blond with blue eyes, Lynette is the personal slave of the Grand Duke Andre, and she takes the lead in abusing Alexi.

Princess Lynette exhibits unusual spirit. She shows such a flair for dominance that the Queen hears about it and commands a repeat performance of what Lynette did with Alexi. Lynette is clever and plans to outshine Alexi. She guesses that he will try to upstage her, so she immediately takes the upper hand by commanding him to obey, then quickly tests his best behavior. When he has come through perfectly on each of her commands, she asks of him an act so embarrassing and degrading that he can barely perform. "I want to see your buttocks move," she insists. "I want to see them dance while your feet remain still." (CSB 227) When he hesitates, she forces him to begin with her own hands. Alexi dislikes her bravado, and even when he finally believes he can endure anything asked of him at the castle, he still feels anxious about Princess Lynette. (CSB 218, 237)

Lynette runs from the castle and escapes to freedom in King Lysius' realm. Her success causes much consternation among the soldiers. Few slaves ever reach the border because most of them actually wish to be caught. It is confusing to the Queen's Court that a slave with Lynette's spirit wants to leave. (BP 191)

See also ALEXI, PRINCE; HUMILIATION; OBEDIENCE; RUNAWAYS; SLAVES; SPECIAL PUNISHMENT HALL.

Lysius, King. The monarch who provides asylum for slaves who escape the Queen's castle or village. (BP 177)

See also RUNAWAYS.

M

Masochism. *See* SADOMASOCHISM.

Masters/Mistresses. The people in power at the Queen's castle, in the village, and at the Sultan's Palace. They must be firm but loving. They are free to do with the slaves whatever they like, short of harming them. The true Master knows that the source of a slave's suffering lies in primitive patterns that form the soul; slaves use suffering to discover their own inner truths. The slaves that a Master punishes most mercilessly are those he most possesses; even their private parts belong to him. Slaves can hide nothing from the Master, and if they resist or withhold instead of yielding, they must be harshly punished.

A firm Master is best, because an ambivalent person makes the ordeal for the slaves harder to bear. To be good, the Master must be willing to be hated, because his power is directly related to how much tolerance he has for a slave's antipathy. Paradoxically, such a Master can best be loved by the slave for that very power.

Masters who fall in love with their slaves have a more difficult time; they may become ambivalent about exercises meant to enhance the slave's wisdom and self-control. To be an excellent Master, they must know their slave's deepest need for punishment and abasement and work hard to fulfill it. Otherwise the slave will be disappointed or unable to trust.

Beauty's first Master is the Prince, until he sends her to the village, where she becomes a slave for Jennifer Lockley. She appreciates this woman's strength of command, but withholds her soul. Beauty also prefers being mastered by the Captain of the Guard over the Prince. He punishes better and loves more tenderly.

Tristan escapes his weak Master Lord Stefan and acquires a Master he can love in Nicolas, the Queen's Chronicler. Nicolas asks Tristan to describe his impressions of being a slave, and he explains that the slave needs a Master who can create order; he "lifts the slave out of the engulfing chaos of abuse" (BP 178) and refines and perfects him in ways that random punishment can never achieve. A true Master is Tristan's only hope "for a deep love, a loss of myself to someone . . . who is sublimely cruel, sublimely good at mastering . . . and loves me also." (BP 171) Because the Master retrieves the slave from chaos, he is an irresistible figure at the core of the whole mystery of the slave's existence.

Tristan believes the slave must be flexible and respond to the will of all Masters, many of whom are as capable of cruelty as kindness and warmth. The slave who can yield under these conditions exhibits an awesome depth of submission. (BP 119) For example, Nicolas allows Tristan to make love to Beauty because it pleases him; the next day, it might please him equally to have Tristan whipped through the streets, "And very possibly he thinks that the one will enhance the torment of the other." (BP 205)

Although they are ostensibly in the dominant position, some Masters prefer their slaves to be commanding, reversing the roles, while some slaves are really Masters at heart. For example, Laurent is a slave who understands the Master's power. Given the opportunity to turn the tables on his Master Lexius, he finds he likes the position of commanding a slave (particularly one who had been his Master) and he does well with the responsibility. (Lexius, for his part, loves being dominated, despite his formal position as Master.) Upon Laurent's return to the life of a slave, he looks for opportunities to master the slaves around him. (BR 234)

> *See also* BEAUTY, PRINCESS; CAPTAIN OF THE GUARD; DOMINANCE/SUBMISSION; ELEANOR, QUEEN; ELVERA, LADY; GERHARDT, LORD; JULIA, LADY; JULIANA, LADY; LAURENT, PRINCE; LEXIUS; LOCKLEY, JENNIFER; LORD MAYOR; LOVE; NICOLAS; PRINCE, THE; QUEEN'S CASTLE; QUEEN'S VILLAGE; SADOMASOCHISM; SLAVES; STEFAN, LORD; SULTAN; SULTAN'S PALACE; TRISTAN, PRINCE; WILLIAM, LORD.

Maze. An area of the Queen's castle used to work the slaves. It is not described, but when Princess Lizetta is punished for being petulant in the Maze, it is clear that the slaves are meant to provide some sort of sport there for the nobility. (CSB 100)

> *See also* LIZETTA, PRINCESS; QUEEN'S CASTLE.

Measuring. *See* PHALLUS.

Midsummer Night. The night when an unusual ritual is enacted in the village and castle. Those of the royalty or from the village who wish to offer themselves as slaves for a year are examined for suitability and placed on auction. Only a small fraction of volunteers are accepted—only the strongest, most beautiful, and most aristocratic—and the names are announced at midnight. The new slaves are immediately stripped and prepared for service. The villagers chosen for this honor go serve in the lowliest positions at the castle, while the Lords and Ladies command very high prices in the village. "Of course there is dread, regret, abject fright at the wish being violently fulfilled." (BP 183)

Nicolas describes this ritual to Tristan and tells him that everyone believes that Lord Stefan will offer himself this year, and that the Queen, who is disappointed in his performance as a Master, will accept him. (BP 184)

See also Auction; Stefan, Lord.

Mortification. *See* Humiliation.

N

Nakedness. The state in which the slaves are kept in the castle, the village, and the palace. It is a symbol of the exposed self. Not only does this nakedness set the slaves apart from their fully clothed Masters and Mistresses and strip them of all accouterments of power and prestige but it also keeps them vulnerable and ever in a state of readiness for pleasure.

Beauty is quite disturbed by this aspect of her captivity. She tries to hide and shield herself, but the Prince commands her to remain exposed. Initially she dislikes the experience of being naked in front of others, particularly people of her own rank, but she soon grows used to it. (CSB 46)

When Beauty first sees other naked slaves in the castle, she is pleased by the fact that the males are equally naked with the females. However, she feels sorry for them because they seem more vulnerable to abuse and humiliation. (CSB 53)

Beauty's service to the Queen comes to a premature ending, and she must once again don clothing. Finally accustomed to the freedom of her nakedness, she feels as if she is being forced into a new kind of bondage. (BR 168)

See also Body Awareness; Humiliation; Readiness; Slaves; Skin; Vulnerability.

Nicolas. The Queen's Chronicler and Chief Historian in the village, and Tristan's Master. He is young, but his white hair distinguishes him. Tall and slender, with a serene, impenetrable face, he has "blue eyes full of darkness at the very centers." (BP 60)

Nicolas lives in a fine house with his wife, Mistress Julia, and owns an incalculable wealth of books. He pays twenty-five gold pieces for Tristan and immediately shows his fitness to be Master by ordering a series of humiliations and punishments. He harnesses Tristan with a team of other human ponies and drives him as if he is no more than an animal.

After all this, Nicolas soothes and kisses Tristan and takes him into his bed to make love as equals. He falls in love with Tristan and treats him tenderly in private but continues to punish him in public because he needs it. Tristan appreciates this treatment and soon loves his Master. "You illuminate the punishments," Tristan tells Nicolas. (BP 172)

On Tristan's second night, Nicolas asks him about his experience as a slave, and they talk together. Tristan confesses his deepest feelings to Nicolas and later tells Beauty he is fully satisfied with his situation. He hopes Nicolas will eventually buy him outright. (BP 165–79)

After the Sultan's raiders kidnap Tristan, Nicolas accompanies the rescue party. When he fails to punish Tristan for his resistance, Tristan becomes disenchanted with him. However, Nicolas comes to watch Tristan at the stables where he is hired out as a pony. Nicolas then hires Tristan to pull a cart, punishes him harshly, chronicles his experiences, and takes him for secret trysts until Tristan falls back in love with him. When Tristan finishes serving his time at the stables, Nicolas is allowed to buy him as a permanent slave. (BR 153, 218–22)

> See also BEAUTY'S PUNISHMENT; BEAUTY'S RELEASE; DISCIPLINE; DOMINANCE/SUBMISSION; JULIA, LADY; LOVE; MASTERS/ MISTRESSES; PUNISHMENT; QUEEN'S VILLAGE; TRISTAN, PRINCE.

Nobility. *See* MASTERS/MISTRESSES.

Nothingness. How some of the slaves describe the experience of losing themselves into a harsh punishment, a loving Master, a larger scheme, or just plain pleasure. "In this place we are *nothing* but our bodies," says Tristan of the Sultan's Palace, "*nothing* but the pleasure we give, *nothing* but our capacity for evincing feeling. All else is gone." (BR 139) Their very nothingness connects the slaves to each other. To achieve a state of being nothing is akin to union with God, or perfection.

See also GOD; PERFECTION.

O

Obedience. Compliance with a command. The primary task of the slaves is to learn perfect and immediate obedience; it shows that their will is not their own. They must yield to a will outside themselves. Obedience gives a slave's life clarity and simplicity. Surrender is the path to greater enhancement, even though it means greater vulnerability and the loss of self.

When the Prince tells Beauty she must obey, he asks of her certain behaviors that strip her of dignity and pride. She is commanded to parade naked in front of strangers, eat off the floor, undress him with her teeth, submit to his whims and passions, and allow herself to be spanked for his pleasure. Other people, such as the Queen, also issue commands that she must obey, and she realizes that obedience does not necessarily bring reward or avoid punishment. Nevertheless, Alexi assures her that accepting her part of the relationship will enhance her understanding and result in serenity and grace. (CSB 237)

Beauty learns that disobedient slaves considered incorrigible in the castle are sentenced to serve in the Queen's village. She decides to bring this fate upon herself and meets Tristan, another slave from the castle, on his way to the village. They discuss the question of obedience. Beauty feels that since they are already bad slaves, why should they obey in the village? Tristan thinks it will go easier for them if they do. To disobey is to experience the anguish of their Masters' displeasure and to be corrected and humiliated. Yet both crave such punishment, so the question continues to nag them. (BP 5–10)

Beauty takes a stab at disobeying her new Mistress, Jennifer Lockley, and discovers how harsh the consequences are. Obedience looks a little more attractive. (BP 62)

When Tristan and Laurent fail to obey the Queen's men sent to rescue them from the Sultan, they draw a year's sentence in one of the most degrading positions in the village: ponies for hire from the public stables. Although they feel humiliated, they also discover that disobedience has its rewards: They love being ponies. (BR 176)

See also DISGRACE; DISOBEDIENCE; PUNISHMENT; SLAVES.

Openness. *See* BODY AWARENESS; EXPOSURE; VULNERABILITY.

Ornamentation. *See* ADORNMENT.

P

Page. A type of servant in the Queen's castle. Pages are chosen for their height and strength because they are required, if the need arises, to lift slaves into the air, hold them upside down, and paddle them. (CSB 68)

Squire Felix, the only Page named, is fond of Alexi, who thinks him the most interesting Page in the castle. When the Prince commands Felix to punish Alexi, Felix disobeys the Prince to relieve Alexi of some of his misery. (CSB 80)

See also FELIX.

Pain. *See* DISCIPLINE; PUNISHMENT; SADOMASOCHISM; SLAVES; SUFFERING.

Paradox. A contradictory state. This is an aspect of the slaves' experience that confuses them but also deepens their self-knowledge. Being punished toward the goal of improving themselves involves complex emotions that often result in paradoxical sensations. They can be calm while excited, proud to be humble, rebellious in their submission. They may grow to love and hate their tormentors and to experience excruciating pleasure. The same hand can be violent or gentle, or have cold fingers that burn. "I love it," Alexi tells Beauty about his punishment at the castle. "I loathe it. . . . I am humiliated by it, and recreated by it. And yielding means to feel all those things at once and yet to be of one mind and one spirit." (CSB 239)

Such contradictory feelings are possible when the slaves gain license to seek total arousal in scenarios that involve pain or humiliation but keep it contained and safe. Because they can get close to what is usually frightening and uncomfortable, they can find enjoyment in the stimulation without the consequent anxiety that accompanies real danger. Thus, suffering or shame can be both terrible and delicious.

In the village, Beauty and Tristan find their existence to be a delirium of abasement; it is "horribly luxurious" and "deliciously terrible" to be tormented, a momentous loss of pride and soul. Yet they love it. (BP 205–206)

The Sultan's Palace is no exception to contradiction. Laurent exclaims that there can be "nothing but the highest quality [of slave] for this utter abasement." (BR 11) Within this paradoxical realm, he can be both Master and slave.

See also DOMINANCE/SUBMISSION.

Parlor. A room in the Queen's castle. Beauty is adorned with jewels and bells and presented here to Lady Juliana and the Queen. As she serves them wine, she smarts from the humiliation of their remarks about her and becomes aware of herself as having no significance. It is in this room that the Queen decides Beauty's initial discipline. (CSB 118)

See also ADORNMENT; BEAUTY, PRINCESS; QUEEN'S CASTLE.

Passion. *See* EROTIC; PLEASURE.

Patience. One of the traits that the slaves develop as a by-product of their discipline. They are forced to endure much pain and humiliation toward the goal of losing their own wills and becoming obedient. Many of the tasks are frustrating, futile, or seemingly endless, and the slaves must learn to endure long hours of such activities to prove their obedience.

See also DISCIPLINE; ENHANCEMENT; GAMES; PUNISHMENT.

Perfection. The ultimate state toward which the slaves must aspire. Some slaves interpret perfection as the feeling of being emptied, becoming "nothing," or of feeling unified with a Master or a form of punishment. "Perfection for the naked pleasure slave must be yielding to the most extreme punishments." (BP 178) All discipline has this goal: The good slave realizes the triumph in doing things perfectly, no matter what is asked. (BP 12) Some Masters, such as the Crown Prince, cannot tolerate even the slightest imperfection, and they see their personal slave's performance as a reflection of their own ability to command.

See also DISCIPLINE; ENHANCEMENT; NOTHINGNESS; PURIFICATION; SLAVES; SUFFERING.

Phallus. A penis-shaped implement used to discipline, humiliate, and pleasure the slaves. Phalluses are made of various materials, such as stone, wood, and leather. The slaves acting as village ponies must wear phalluses with horses' tails attached, both as "adornment" and for "discipline." Tristan's mistress measures him with several sizes to determine which he can wear. Special harnesses keep the phalluses in place while the ponies are marching. (BP 69, 74)

See also ADORNMENT; DISCIPLINE; PONIES; SLAVES.

Place of Public Punishment. The arena in the village where slaves are publicly punished for the villagers' amusement. The atmosphere is that of a fair, with bets being placed and slaves on display in every manner of humiliation. Some slaves are spanked by a Whipping Master on the Public Turntable, then pelted with garbage, or tied to a high wooden pole and forced to march in a circle while being paddled by four attendants. Others are hung upside down on an iron carousel. In the surrounding area slaves are available for rent in the Public Tents.

Beauty and Tristan both witness this place, and Tristan's

Master has him whipped here "for his good looks." (BP 42, 101–102)

> *See also* PUBLIC TENTS; PUBLIC TURNTABLE; PUNISHMENT;
> QUEEN'S VILLAGE; TRISTAN, PRINCE; WHIPPING MASTER.

Pleasure. The result of erotic stimulation. The slaves—also known as "pleasure slaves"—are required to defer their own pleasure and to please their Masters and Mistresses at all times. Only their Master's whim allows them full release from the tension of their constant sexual readiness. The Masters get great pleasure from dominating and humiliating slaves, while the slaves enjoy pleasing their Masters.

Suffering can also have a pleasurable dimension if the stimulation from the torment is done under the auspices of protection, that is, following the rules that the slaves come to no harm.

> *See also* BODY AWARENESS; DEFERRED SATISFACTION;
> DOMINANCE/SUBMISSION; EROTIC; PARADOX;
> SADOMASOCHISM; SLAVES; SUFFERING.

Ponies. The position to which the Queen sentences some of the slaves in the village. It is believed to be the most degrading of all punishments. The slaves are rented out as ponies for pulling carriages, carts, or other loads. They wear anal plugs to which horsetails are attached, bits, harnesses, and boots with horseshoes. The ponies are forbidden to speak, and some are fitted with blinders.

Nicolas harnesses Tristan with a team of ponies to pull his carriage out to the Lord Mayor's Farm. It is Tristan's first experience as a pony, and it both horrifies and soothes him to be thus treated. The "ponies" are fed, stroked, and treated as animals. One slave, Jerard, claims he is proud to be a pony. (BP 75–79)

Tristan and Laurent are both sentenced to a year at the Public Pony Stables because they had tried to thwart the Queen's rescue of them. Laurent discovers he feels safe in a harness because he fears the intimacy of a lone Master. He can take the abuse as long as he is confined in his appointed role; he wants to be used for constantly changing tasks. He also likes the way the group mentality of the ponies draws them all together, rather than isolating them as individual slaves; they amplify each others' pleasures and pains. The pony life simplifies things for the slaves and harnesses their strengths. (BR 182, 217)

> *See also* JERARD, PRINCE; LAURENT, PRINCE; "PONY BLOOD";
> PUBLIC PONY STABLES; TRISTAN, PRINCE.

"Pony blood." The term the groom Gareth uses to describe the will and strength a slave may show to be a perfect pony. He thinks it applies perfectly to Laurent's spirit. (BR 182)

> *See also* GARETH (GROOM); LAURENT, PRINCE; PONIES.

Pony Stables. *See* PUBLIC PONY STABLES.

Possession. Taking over the will of another, as Masters do with their slaves. "When you enter my kingdom," the Prince tells Beauty, "you shall be mine more completely than ever." (CSB 45) She soon grows to love the experience and claims, "It was worth any humiliation, that, to be possessed by another." (BR 23) In suffering someone else's will, she discovers her true submissive self.

Nicolas and Tristan possess one another in the bond of love between Master and slave. Laurent and Beauty possess each other because they both understand the other's secrets.

> *See also* CAPTIVITY; DOMINANCE/SUBMISSION; LOVE;
> MASTERS/MISTRESSES; OBEDIENCE; SURRENDER; WILL.

Power. *See* DOMINANCE/SUBMISSION; MASTERS/MISTRESSES; SADO-MASOCHISM.

Powerlessness. *See* DOMINANCE/SUBMISSION; SADOMASOCHISM; SLAVES; SURRENDER.

Pride. Self-admiration or conceit. It is a trait that the slaves must purge in order to truly serve their Masters and Mistresses.

When Beauty struggles against being shown naked to the townspeople, the Prince accuses her of pride. He wants her to be proud of her beauty but not vain, not thinking she can place her own will or desires above his. (CSB 22)

> *See also* SURRENDER.

Prince, The. The eighteen-year-old aristocrat who succeeds in entering Beauty's castle and claiming her as his own. Tall, with black hair, he has a commanding presence, but he is mysteriously restless, cold, and dissatisfied. "He liked to think of himself as a sword—light, straight, and very deft, and utterly dangerous." (CSB 5) He knows Beauty's story. When he sees how other Princes have died on the poisonous vines of her castle, he cuts the vines at the roots and enters unscathed. (CSB 1–2)

Waking Beauty, the Prince takes her to his castle, teaching her what will be expected of her in terms of perfect obedience. She must refer to him as her Prince or Master, and answer all questions respectfully. She is to go without clothes, always be sexually ready for him, and do everything he asks, quickly and perfectly. He is now her Lord and his will is hers. The Prince loathes the sight of any imperfection in her. He punishes her mercilessly for the slightest clumsiness or flaw. (CSB 12)

Beauty is the Prince's first slave, and he falls in love with her, to his mother's disapproval. He wants to keep Beauty for himself and have her sleep in his chambers, but the Queen first wants to test Beauty's obedience. The Prince realizes he must curb his love so that she can be properly trained to gain all the benefits the castle offers. (CSB 119–22)

Although the Prince finally wins the privilege of having Beauty in his chamber, she rebels against him, so he sentences her to the village. He himself had inspired her rebellion when he had called the village "sublime punishment." The Prince is deeply grieved to lose her. (CSB 250; BP 8)

> *See also* BEAUTY, PRINCESS; BEAUTY'S CASTLE; ELEANOR, QUEEN; LOVE; MASTERS/MISTRESSES; PRINCE'S CHAMBER.

Princes and Princesses. *See* individual entries arranged alphabetically by given name (e.g., for Prince Alexi, see ALEXI, PRINCE). *See also* SLAVES; TRIBUTES.

Public Pony Stables. Where slaves in the village can be rented for pulling carts or carriages, or used for draught work. The place has a mud floor covered with straw, and the walls are filled with harnesses. Feeding troughs and beams over which the slaves must lean for rest frame the stalls. A recreation pen allows them to play with one another for an hour a day, and although they have grooms, they get no attention from an individual Master.

Nicolas takes Tristan here for a day and commands him to show such spirit on the track that he is hired out immediately. Later the Queen sentences Tristan, along with Laurent, to spend a year as a pony here, for his disobedience. (BR 176, 179)

See also LAURENT, PRINCE; PONIES; QUEEN'S VILLAGE; TRISTAN, PRINCE.

Public Tents. Individual tents set up at the Place of Public Punishment, where villagers can rent a slave. In one such tent, Mistress Julia buys a Princess for Tristan, then watches while he takes her. (BP 57, 150–55)

See also PLACE OF PUBLIC PUNISHMENT; QUEEN'S VILLAGE; VOYEURISM.

Public Turntable. Where slaves are publicly whipped at the Place of Public Punishment in the Queen's village. The slave places his head on a headrest, and the crowd cheers and jeers, then throws garbage. Afterward, they toss money to show their degree of satisfaction, and these coins are collected and stuffed into the slave's mouth to give to his or her Master. "Buy out the slave's whipping and the Master will bring him back all the sooner." (BP 106)

Nicolas subjects Tristan to this abuse, without fetters, and Tristan claims that "nothing had so seared me and emptied me." (BP 105)

See also PLACE OF PUBLIC PUNISHMENT; QUEEN'S VILLAGE; TRISTAN, PRINCE; WHIPPING MASTER.

Punishment. The various forms of chastisement for reproval, correction, and perfection that Masters and Mistresses inflict on slaves. It is intended for the slaves' enhancement and takes the form of spanking, paddling, whipping, friction against rough surfaces (like a jewel-encrusted bedcover), slapping, teasing, binding in vulnerable positions, difficult tasks, disciplinary games, and various forms of humiliation.

The slaves are at the mercy of their Masters and Mistresses. To discipline the slaves and keep them off guard, punishment can happen at any time, last for any duration, and be ordered whether or not the slave has been obedient. It can be a matter of random whim—whatever pleases the Master—or a matter of what the Master believes the slave needs. Physical pain "softens" the slaves, making them more malleable, particularly if they surrender to it rather than resist. Whatever torment they experience comes from the simultaneous pain and pleasure, wherein they are "caught between struggle and surrender." (CSB 96) They often learn to associate the paddle with sources of pleasure. (CSB 183)

That slaves bear the pain is also enjoyable for the Masters, whom they desire to please. Punishment becomes a connection between them; the slaves belong to their tormentors. (CSB 26, 34)

Tristan tells Nicolas what his punishment means to him. Although he fears it and initially had begged for mercy, he is glad that Nicolas forced him to be harnessed as a pony and publicly whipped. "And though I wept more desperately when I thought of it, and my cock swelled in the lacings, and I marched harder, trying to squirm away from the snapping thrash, it gave a strange luster to my surroundings." (BP 119–20) He describes how the attention of the crowd to his misery at the Public Turntable had enlarged him and made him feel unified with his punishment. He loves his Master for knowing what he needed. The experience empties and enlarges him, like orgasm; he yields to it rather than attempting to triumph over it, and takes genuine delight in bearing whatever a strong Master can dish out. (BP 173–74)

During extreme forms of punishment, Laurent feels the "coming of tranquility, a quiet place in the very center of frenzy, in which I could surrender all the parts of my being." (BR 190) Other slaves describe the experience as being emptied or becoming nothing but their sensations.

The slaves also find opportunities to punish each other, as when Laurent dominates other ponies. The Masters sometimes order it, as when the Queen commands a gauntlet of princes to paddle Alexi. (BR 212–14)

See also ATTENTION; DISCIPLINE; DOMINANCE/SUBMISSION; ENHANCEMENT; EXPOSURE; MASTERS/MISTRESSES; NOTHINGNESS; PARADOX; PERFECTION; PLACE OF PUBLIC PUNISHMENT; PLEASURE; POSSESSION; PUNISHMENT CROSS; PUNISHMENT SHOP; SADOMASOCHISM; SELF-CONTROL; SLAVES; SOFTENING; SUFFERING; SURRENDER; WILL; WISDOM.

Punishment Cross. The form of punishment Laurent must endure when he is captured as a runaway. It is "a rude wooden cross . . . [with] a short, stubby phallus sticking up from where the two beams were fitted together . . . jutting up and forward at a slight angle." (BP 190) The soldiers bind Laurent to the cross-beams, impaling him anally, then parade him through town on a cart pulled by human ponies.

The Sultan's garden also contains Punishment Crosses. Slaves are mounted as decoration for the Lords who dine there. Laurent admits that he loves these crosses, although he also fears being mounted on them. "I suppose that's why I love it." (BR 145)

See also LAURENT, PRINCE; SULTAN'S GARDEN.

Punishment Shop. Where villagers can send their slaves to be spanked; those who own many slaves and cannot paddle them all every day often make use of this shop.

Beauty's Mistress, Jennifer Lockley, sends her slaves to the Punishment Shop on a regular basis. The slaves are spanked individually by a Master who takes them over his lap for the entertainment of the customers who dine there; they can pay extra for extra paddling. The atmosphere is more intimate than the Place of Public Punishment. (BP 141)

See also LOCKLEY, JENNIFER; PUNISHMENT; QUEEN'S VILLAGE.

Purification. Cleansing the slaves as part of the disciplinary ritual. They are regularly bathed and given douches and enemas to purge them and ready them for their Masters and Mistresses. At the Sultan's Palace, the faces and legs of the male slaves are also shaved. The loss of privacy and the helpless feeling of being possessed by the Master inside and out, are humiliating. (BP 216; BR 54)

See also HUMILIATION; PERFECTION; POSSESSION; SLAVES.

Q

Queen (Beauty's mother). Along with her Court, this woman slept for one hundred years until the Prince woke Beauty, her daughter. Having served as a slave in King Heinrick's castle, the Queen knows what lies ahead for Beauty. She requests that the Prince not parade Beauty naked but accepts his decision about what will be best for her daughter. (CSB 16)

See also BEAUTY, PRINCESS; BEAUTY'S CASTLE; HEINRICK, KING.

Queen Eleanor. *See* ELEANOR, QUEEN.

Queen's castle. The place where the Crown Prince takes Beauty as a Tribute to his mother, the Queen. Across the mountains, it is larger than the castle where Beauty grew up. Princes and Princesses from across the land are sent here as Tributes to the Queen, and they serve for a specified period of time, not to exceed five years, as naked slaves for the pleasure of the royalty.

There are many rooms at the palace. Each has a specific function in the Master/slave structure of the Queen's overall program of discipline. The slaves are groomed in the Slave's Hall and punished in the Hall of Punishments or the Special Punishment Hall. For extreme discipline, they are sent to be the playthings of the kitchen and stable staff. In the Training Hall, female slaves learn how to experience pleasure while males are trained to associate discipline with pleasure. Each of the nobility has his or her own chambers, and Beauty sees the inside of the Prince's and the Queen's chambers. She also experiences what it is like to be on display in the Great Hall and in the Parlor. Slaves make their initial entrance in the Great Hall and are received here again for their reward upon their departure.

Outside the palace are special areas for working the slaves, such as the gardens and banquet area, a maze, and recreation areas like the Bridle Path.

> *See also* BRIDLE PATH; ELEANOR, QUEEN; GREAT HALL; HALL
> OF PUNISHMENTS; KITCHEN; MAZE; PARLOR; PRINCE'S
> CHAMBER; QUEEN'S CHAMBER; SLAVES; SLAVES' HALL;
> SPECIAL PUNISHMENT HALL; STABLE (QUEEN'S); TRAINING
> HALL.

Queen's chamber. The bedroom for her Royal Majesty, Queen Eleanor. She brings her favorite slaves here for her pleasure.

During Beauty's first days, the Queen wants her in her chamber, so Beauty gets an insider's view of the grand room. Surrounded by dozens of candles, the bed has tapestried draperies. Beauty plays a game of discipline with Lady Juliana here, watches Alexi undress the Queen, and gets bound to a wall in the dressing room. (CSB 140–65)

Alexi, too, has a story to tell about this room. It is where he learned to become an obedient slave and where he now serves as the Queen's valet. (CSB 179)

> *See also* ALEXI, PRINCE; BEAUTY, PRINCESS; ELEANOR, QUEEN;
> GAMES; JULIANA, LADY; QUEEN'S CASTLE.

Queen's Chronicler. *See* NICOLAS.

Queen's emissary. The tall, gray-haired Lord who boards the Sultan's ship to see which slaves were captured in the raid. He tells the slaves that he has exacted a high price for them on the Queen's behalf, but he can do nothing to change their fate. They will serve the Sultan for the next two years. (BP 222)

> *See also* SULTAN.

Queen's soldiers. The men who guard the Queen's realm, retrieve the Tributes, and patrol the borders. If they catch a runaway, they are allowed to take their pleasure with him or her, and while they transport a slave to the castle, they begin the slave's training with their own methods. Tristan grows to love the two soldiers who regularly torment him, as well as the Captain of the Guard. They all miss Tristan when they turn him over to the Queen. (BP 191)

See also CAPTAIN OF THE GUARD; GARETH (SOLDIER); GEOFFREY.

Queen's village. The village near the castle where many of the Queen's merchants and servants live. Run by a stern mayor, it is the largest, loveliest, and most prosperous in the country. Royal slaves who have been seriously disobedient and who are in need of dire punishment are sent here, and the villagers enjoy the special privilege of buying the slaves at auction for the summer months. "Everywhere these people looked they saw some delectable bit of naked flesh, punished or positioned or harnessed for their pleasure." (BP 119) Many of the slaves are used for common labor in the fields as well as for pleasure.

The village enjoys the reputation among the castle slaves as being a much worse place than the castle: If the slaves realized the true terrors of the village, they would never dare to get themselves into trouble and risk the Queen's displeasure. Lord Gregory uses this reputation to warn Beauty to be obedient; he tells her that being sent there would be more than she could bear. The village is for incorrigibles, and no favorite slave of the Crown has ever been sent there. The Prince takes Beauty to see these disgraced slaves so that she will understand what a terrible punishment it is. (CSB 104, 246)

Beauty and Tristan both get themselves sent to the village for disobedience. They soon discover that the punishments tendered here are more humiliating and cruel, but they appreciate the severity. The terror for Tristan is that "we were true slaves here. Not playthings in a palace of pleasure . . . but real naked slaves in a real town, and we would suffer at every turn from common men." (BP 66) The slaves are publicly disciplined and never coddled by being told repeatedly what is expected. As a result, because much more is required in terms of surrender and endurance, they experience a level of their own powers not available to them at the castle. "We were the groaning underbelly of a place so vast and vital and overwhelming it made the castle seem a monstrous confection." (BP 75)

Of significance to the slaves are the Place of Public Punishment, the Punishment Shop, the Public Turntable, the Public Tents, and the Public Stables, as well as the houses of their Masters and Mistresses. The villagers tolerate no disobedience because they work for the Queen. Each time they punish a slave, they are doing what the Queen wants them to do. They love to examine and humiliate the slaves as well. The Masters in the village can sell their slaves at any time for any sum of money.

All slaves are sent once a week to a central grooming hall where they are properly fed and rested. Just as in the castle, no one may do real harm to any slave, but "the slaves should at all times exhibit evidence of sound whipping." (BP 18)

The Queen believes that being sentenced to the village is the worst possible fate for a slave, particularly to serve in the stables as a rental pony. She reserves this punishment for Tristan and Laurent upon their return from the Sultan's Palace because they disobeyed the men she had dispatched to rescue them.

> *See also* BEAUTY, PRINCESS; *BEAUTY'S PUNISHMENT*; FARM; JULIA, LADY; LOCKLEY, JENNIFER; LORD MAYOR; MASTERS/ MISTRESSES; NICOLAS; PLACE OF PUBLIC PUNISHMENT; PONIES; PUBLIC PONY STABLES; PUBLIC TENTS; PUNISHMENT SHOP; SIGN OF THE LION; TRISTAN, PRINCE; VOYEURISM; WHIPPING MASTER.

R

Raiders. *See* SULTAN'S RAIDERS.

Readiness. The state in which the slaves are expected to be at all times for their Masters. Any slave who gains sexual release or loses control is severely punished. (CSB 69, 88)

> *See also* EROTIC; SLAVES; SUFFERING.

Rebellion. *See* DISOBEDIENCE; RESISTANCE; SURRENDER.

Resignation. *See* SURRENDER.

Resistance. What the Masters and Mistresses punish in their slaves. A slave who resists surrendering his or her will to the master is viewed as willful and disobedient; it is considered better for the slaves to allow the Master to understand their needs and guide their behavior through disciplinary channels. Slaves who continue to resist despite being disciplined are considered incorrigible and sent to the Queen's village for more extreme measures. (CSB 244, 250)

> *See also* DISCIPLINE; DISGRACE; DISOBEDIENCE; INCORRIGIBLES; QUEEN'S VILLAGE; SLAVES; SURRENDER; WILL.

Respect. The deferential attitude required of the slaves toward their Masters and Mistresses. This is one of the Prince's first commands to Beauty: She must address him with respect at all times with her posture and her voice. She can also demonstrate respect by kissing his boot, keeping her eyes down, being immediately and perfectly obedient, and crawling on her hands and knees. She must also show respect to anyone who is part of the Prince's Court, including the servants. "To the lowliest scullery maid you owe this respect," Lord Gregory explains. Part of this attitude of respect requires that Beauty voice no complaints about how she is treated. (CSB 84–86)

> *See also* DOMINANCE/SUBMISSION; MASTERS/MISTRESSES; OBEDIENCE; SLAVES; SURRENDER.

Restraints. *See* CAPTIVITY.

Richard, Prince. An aristocratic, red-haired prince who has served in the village for one year. Beauty meets him at the Sign of the Lion. Previously he had been at the castle for six months, but he was unable to control himself. He needed direct commands and hard discipline, and he does well at Mistress Lockley's Inn. Richard is about to be sent back to the castle, a fate he fears, and he hopes he brings in enough money for the Inn to inspire Jennifer Lockley to buy him. (BP 92, 144)

> *See also* LOCKLEY, JENNIFER; SIGN OF THE LION.

Roger, Prince. A slave at the Sign of the Lion. He bathes Beauty her first day there. He was sent to the village for sneaking off with a slave whom he reveals to have been Lady Juliana. Later, Juliana became one of the castle nobility and asked for Roger to be her slave, but he ran from her. He has been at the village for several years because Mistress Lockley will not let him go. (BP 37, 41–44)

See also JULIANA, LADY; SIGN OF THE LION.

Roquelaure, A. N. The pseudonym Anne Rice used to write *The Erotic Adventures of Sleeping Beauty* so that she could freely create extreme masochistic fantasies.

A *roquelaure* is a cloak. Rice had seen this word in a story by L. Sheridan Le Fanu, "Master Justice Harbottle."

See also BEAUTY'S PUNISHMENT; BEAUTY'S RELEASE; CLAIMING OF SLEEPING BEAUTY, THE.

Roquelaure, S. T. The person to whom Anne Rice dedicates the Sleeping Beauty series. The initials refer to the name of her husband, Stanley Travis Rice.

Rosalynd, Princess. One of the slaves captured by the Sultan's raiders. A natural slave, she has curly black hair and dedicates herself to pleasing. However, since she has poor self-control except when tightly bound, she has ended up serving in the village to purge her fears. (BP 222; BR 7)

Rosalynd is one of the six slaves who makes it as far as the Sultan's Palace, and she is left behind when three of them are rescued.

See also SLAVES; SULTAN'S PALACE.

Roses. *See* GAMES; JULIANA, LADY.

Royal Wives of the Harem. *See* HAREM OF BEAUTIFUL AND VIRTUOUS ROYAL WIVES.

Rules. The basis for the system that regulates the behavior of both the slaves and the Masters. Essentially, the Masters and Mistresses must observe the rule that no slave can be injured or harmed: The skin cannot be cut, burned, wounded, or broken. Otherwise, they can do with the slaves as they like. This rule holds in the village as well. There is also an unspoken rule that guides the quality of conduct for the Masters: that they perceive what the slave needs and deliver it without ambivalence or hesitation. The slave will judge whether or not the Master is good at his position.

Rules for the slaves are numerous:

1. Keep eyes down; never look into the Master's face.

2. Remain in a position of subservience, such as a squat, with hands behind the neck.

3. Obey the Master or Mistress at all times, no matter what is asked.

4. Speak only when granted permission, and answer with respect, in such words as "Only if it pleases you, my Prince."

5. Never complain or plead.

6. Keep passion under control; only the Master decides when release may occur.

7. Show no interest in other slaves.

8. Remain on hands and knees at all times, unless commanded by the Master to do otherwise.

9. Remain naked and exposed at all times, except when adorned for the Master's pleasure or sport.

10. Be ever in a state of readiness for the Master's pleasure.

11. Use hands for a task only when a task cannot be otherwise completed; slaves must rely on their teeth and mouths.

12. Work fast when commanded, yet gracefully.

13. Be correct in one's behavior, but artful.

14. Surrender fully to the Master's will; note what pleases him or her.

Alexi adds another rule for Beauty's guidance: Think only of the present, and forget about one's former life or what might be in the future. He tells her that this will aid her in achieving serenity and acceptance. (CSB 172)

In the village, slaves may not speak unless allowed to by the Master, and in the Sultanate, they are not allowed a voice under any circumstances. (BP 14)

Breaking any of the rules is swiftly punished, but slaves might be punished even if they obey perfectly. Discipline is performed at the Master's whim. (CSB 8, 112)

See also BLOOD; DISCIPLINE; DOMINANCE/SUBMISSION;
MASTERS/MISTRESSES; NAKEDNESS; OBEDIENCE;
PUNISHMENT; QUEEN'S CASTLE; QUEEN'S VILLAGE; RESPECT;
SAFETY; SKIN; SLAVES.

Runaways. Slaves who attempt to leave the Queen's realm. If they get to the borders of King Lysius' realm, they receive safe passage, although they are then faced with the disgrace of explaining themselves to their parents and of passing up their reward of gold and finery.

To avoid the Queen's service, Alexi had run from his father's castle, but the Queen's soldiers had captured him. The Queen worked hard to break down his rebellious attitude. She sent him to be the plaything of the lowliest and roughest servants in the castle and exposed him to other forms of humiliation until she "broke" him into obedience.

Jerard had run from the Queen's castle after serving time as a slave, and had nearly made it to the next Kingdom, but he, too, had been captured. "The great difficulty," he says, "is reaching the border." (BP 84) His punishment is to serve time as a pony in the village.

Beauty thinks about running away and wonders why so few slaves attempt it. She believes she would, but only in order to be captured and punished and to avoid ever returning to the castle. Shortly after she arrives in the village, she learns that a Princess has escaped. The Captain of the Guard is concerned when this Princess is not quickly found. The runaway turns out to be Princess Lynette, who had performed so admirably with Alexi, and she evidently succeeds in her escape. (BP 190, 207)

Nicolas tells Tristan that runaways are rare because the Princes and Princesses have been examined for their suitability for slavery; if they run away, chances are good they actually wish to be caught. "Defiance is the motive, boredom the incentive." (BP 176) Only those slaves who take time to steal their Master's garments are successful.

When Laurent had run from the castle for adventure, he had felt vulnerable and exposed; unable to conceal himself, he was like an animal giving sport. Because his soul belonged to the world of power and submission, he regretted attempting to escape. He was soon caught and sentenced to four years in the village. (BP 190; BR 13)

Some slaves feel it is better to submit to the ordeals of slavery than to run because flight indicates fear, which is humiliating to admit. Others just wish to avoid explaining to anyone that service at the castle is intolerable. (BP 149)

See also ALEXI, PRINCE; JERARD, PRINCE; LAURENT, PRINCE; LYNETTE, PRINCESS.

S

Sadomasochism. The most extreme form of dominance and submission, in the Queen's realm and the Sultanate it involves consensual symbolic violence. One partner, the Master, inflicts pain or humiliation to help the other, the slave, gain emotional catharsis. Both enjoy their parts in the scenario, and both desire to achieve ever greater feelings of authenticity. The rituals make the fantasy concrete and the presence of a partner makes it real and immediate. Sadomasochism eroticizes mental and physical pain by synthesizing body, mind, and spirit. The stronger the passion, the more intense the ritual. For the masochist, the violent loss of control translates into psychic orgasm and the obliteration of self. Participants understand that transgressive sex is forbidden and the forbidden is frightening, so fear becomes part of the fullest exploration of sexuality. Taking the risk can produce a radical transformation of the body into a sense of openness to a fuller existence. In the Queen's realm, sado-masochistic relationships are built on the recognition that cruelty must be balanced with tenderness. What starts in fear ends in love, satisfying both parties.

Most people have a definite preference for dominating or submitting. Tristan, Beauty, Alexi, and Lexius all crave the slave's position and thus embody the masochist perspective. The Queen's slaves are examined for their capacity to surrender, although only some are true slaves psychologically. The slave Juliana actually returns to the castle as a wicked Mistress. Those slaves with deeper needs than the castle can meet, run away to get themselves sent to the harsher demands of the village. A true slave seeks not mere pleasure and pain, but agony and ecstasy.

Masochists strive for the completion of the soul, satisfying an inner god that demands attention and shedding the smaller self. The goal is oblivion, ridding oneself of conflict and limitation. Slaves wish to contact unknown dimensions of themselves, because touching the unknown is tantamount to touching God, the source of energy and life. To view the experience as people wanting pain for the sake of pain is a superficial understanding; masochists reach for deeper psychological ground by spiritual-izing the ordeal. They want to come to terms with the inner paradoxes of pain and desire. Obedience, suffering, shame, and surrender to achieve transcendence form the heart of maso-chism just as they do religion. "I wished I could remain so for-ever, a permanent symbol of baseness, worthy only of scorn," says Laurent. (BR 17)

The pride of masochists is that no one can outdo them in the extremity of their suffering. The goal is to experience men-tal purging and extend one's psychological space. Although Beauty describes the delicious suffering and initiates readers into this world, Alexi, Tristan, and Laurent give the most com-prehensive descriptions of the experience.

When the Queen uses boredom to break down his rebellion, Alexi discovers a powerful attraction toward pain. Since he finds boredom unendurable, he begins to view punishment as pleasur-able. As the Queen's disciplinary measures increase in frequency and intensity, Alexi grows to love his tormentors, particularly the ones who hurt him most (such as the stable boy). Accepting the abuse makes him feel stronger and in greater control of himself, and this attitude yields a state of serenity. (CSB 176–237)

Tristan expresses the masochistic desire to be thoroughly punished and disciplined and to become an abject slave to a strong will. Although he trembles at the thought of what such a Master can do, he also appreciates one who knows his needs and who can take charge. When Nicolas has him publicly whipped on the block, he leans into the strokes in "a gesture of total recognition of the whipping." (BP 125) He is grateful for the pain: "I gave thanks from the depths of my being that he had seen fit to break me so thoroughly." (BP 120) It is his only hope "for a loss of myself to someone . . . who is sublimely cruel, sublimely good at mastering." (BP 171) Nothing in the castle had been so effective; "nothing had so seared and emptied me." (BP 105)

Laurent has the unusual capacity to be both Master and slave; as such he knows how to push himself into the most extreme moments of sensation. He runs from the castle and draws quick and harsh punishment. "How it titillated my soul to know there was not the slightest hope of mercy for me," he says about being impaled on the Punishment Cross. (BR 15) At such moments, he knows the full power of his captors, and his greatest desire is to be cruelly chastised. "I love those crosses!" he later admits, even though they also terrify him. (BR 145) About a sound beating, he insists, "It was good, the whipping. It was the thick leather strap that I had craved ever since we left the village, the sound, punishing strap that I needed. It was the beating I had dreamed of." (BR 107) However, Laurent also exhibits the traits of a Master and is not a pure masochistic type. He grows to love both sides of the scenario and to play out each position with the full knowledge and experience of the other. Laurent is the most sexually integrated of any of the slaves or Masters and might best capture the actual complexity of the human soul.

See also ALEXI, PRINCE; BEAUTY, PRINCESS; BODY AWARENESS; DISCIPLINE; DOMINANCE/SUBMISSION; EROTIC; JULIANA, LADY; LAURENT, PRINCE; MASTERS/MISTRESSES; SLAVES; STABLE BOY; SUFFERING; SURRENDER; TRISTAN, PRINCE.

Safety. The condition of being protected from harmful risk or danger. The Queen's system of discipline operates within the parameters of safety. Erotic pleasure can be enhanced within a protective frame because the people involved can get close to the stimulation produced by risk and negative emotions without real danger.

The Queen ensures safety by setting up various rules to guide the behavior of both the Masters and the slaves, primarily, that the master should never inflict real injury. Because of this protection, love and trust can develop between Master and slave, as it does with Tristan and Nicolas: Tristan trusts that Nicolas will take him to the most profound state of the experience of punishment and humiliation without physical or emotional danger, while Nicolas trusts that Tristan will yield to it and not try to run away. (BP 186)

The slaves also feel safe when they feel confident of what they can endure. When some form of punishment reveals resources they did not recognize before, they can face new and more harsh forms of punishment with the belief that they can bear whatever is asked. (CSB 237; BP 170–71)

Alexi discovers safety in an attitude of acceptance: To think only of the present moment results in serenity and the belief that he can endure the punishments meted. (CSB 172)

If slaves desire a safer setup, they may manipulate conditions to achieve it. Psychologically, Tristan feels unsafe with Lord Stefan, a weak Master, so he runs away in order to be sent to the village. He hopes to find a stronger Master who understands what he needs in terms of the full measure of the masochistic experience, and he meets such a person in Nicolas. As he is put through brutally humiliating exercises and whippings, he realizes that this is a Master with whom he can feel emotionally safe. (BP 170–72)

See also DOMINANCE/SUBMISSION; QUEEN'S CASTLE; RULES; SADOMASOCHISM; TRUST.

Self-control. What the slaves must acquire during their training and service. Learning to control themselves, particularly their passion, is one of the goals of discipline. A well-trained slave will have superior self-control, and all the slaves are heavily worked toward that end. Those who need extra attention are sent to the Training Hall or to the village. (CSB 96, 176)

> *See also* Discipline; Enhancement; Queen's Village;
> Readiness; Slaves; Training Hall.

Shame. *See* Humiliation.

Sign of the Lion. The largest and most prosperous Inn at the village. Three stories high, with leaded windows, it sits on a public square with other Inns.

Jennifer Lockley, who owns many slaves, runs the Sign of the Lion. She purchases Beauty at the village auction to be one of her slaves. Beauty soon learns what it means to work for this relentless Mistress. Her first task is to take a scrub brush in her teeth and clean the floors. She meets Prince Richard and Prince Roger at this Inn, and they tell her more about the castle and the village. (BP 27)

The Captain of the Guard is the Inn's chief lodger, and he claims Beauty as his personal slave. She becomes a prize at one of the orgies he has there for his soldiers.

> *See also* Beauty, Princess; Captain of the Guard; Lockley,
> Jennifer; Queen's Village; Richard, Prince; Roger,
> Prince.

Skin. The point of focus for both Master and slave in the experience of discipline. The slaves are always naked, and the Masters want to see red welts on their skin from the whippings. The skin toughens from being worked, giving the slaves greater sensation and endurance. However, it also indicates when to stop: The drawing of blood means that it is time to quit and let the slave recover. (CSB 75)

> *See also* Blood; Body Awareness; Discipline; Nakedness;
> Punishment; Slaves.

Slaves. What the Princes and Princesses are called whom Queen Eleanor's allies offer to her as Tributes. There are over one thousand slaves in the castle. They are well fed and well treated until such time as the Queen returns them to their Kingdoms, enhanced and rewarded with wealth. In the castle, they are considered love slaves, used for pleasure, while in the village, they may be further employed for common labor. Their service is usually for a defined period of time, such as two years, but no one serves more than five. It may happen that a slave loves the castle life so much that he or she returns as one of the nobility, as Juliana did. Most, however, return to their homes wiser, more virtuous, wealthier, and with greater self-knowledge and self-control.

When it comes a slave's time to leave the Court, he or she is dressed splendidly and everyone assembles in the Great Hall to bid farewell. Some slaves are relieved that their service is over; others are disappointed, having found the experience to be exactly what they needed to feel alive and to gain the most from their inner resources.

Even though the Tributes are carefully examined for their physical and psychological suitability, not all of them find harmony with their fate. (BP 176) Some, such as Princess Lynette, run away to King Lysius, who offers them safe passage, while others suffer it out but find little pleasure. Some of the females have to be taught what their own pleasure means. Beauty learns that she is not to complain about her lot and that "to beg to be released would be a terrible thing." (CSB 90)

The true slave finds that "the rigors of the castle and the village become a great adventure." (BP 178) The Captain of the Guard, who sees them all, claims that "out of the batch of a hundred thousand timid and anxious little slaves, there are those who have invited the punishment, needing the rigors not to purify their faults but to tame their boundless appetites." (BP 126) Beauty learns that her primary goal as a slave is to please her Master. "The highest thing that you can do is please, so you sought to do it . . . of your own will." (CSB 171)

Having once been privileged and understanding its nature, these slaves worship those Masters of great power. "We who are bereft of all privileges may yet goad and guide our punishers into new realms of heat and loving attentiveness." (BR 15) They desire a harsh and unrelenting person of authority who is strong enough to command both himself and his slave. They long for the perfect

Master, one who can guide them through the engulfing chaos of punishment and offer purpose and clarity so that they can perfectly yield to the most extreme punishments and trust the experience. Otherwise they are lost, because the experience of punishment empties them. "Something in me was being absolutely annihilated," says Tristan of being publicly whipped. (BP 76)

Tristan feels utterly bereft in someone else's power, enduring their whims and eccentricities, so he spiritualizes the experience to get through it; for him, being part of a larger scheme gives his ordeal a purpose, as "all torments become an endless current of excitement." (BP 178). Yet submission is the goal of all discipline: that the slave learn to yield completely to the will of the Master. "We had been opened up and inalterably changed by our servitude," says Laurent, (BR 8) who describes himself as swimming in erotic torment.

Different slaves have different arousal needs. Beauty craves harsh and relentless punishment, Tristan wants to lose himself in a strong Master, and Laurent alternately seeks the viewpoints of slave and Master. Slaves who run away seek more excitement than those who opt to remain safe. Some slaves need to be taught their capacity for pleasure, while others yield to it at once. Some are happiest when deeply humiliated.

However, what the slaves believe they want from their Masters can turn out to be much worse than they had imagined. Beauty speaks out of turn to Mistress Lockley to get punished, but comes to regret it when the results are more severe than she had anticipated. (BP 200) At the Sultan's Palace, the punishment seems more refined, but the slaves are not allowed to speak, a treatment which makes them feel less human than had any procedure in the castle or village. (BR 47)

There are also Masters out of harmony with their position who prefer to be slaves. Some of the villagers and nobility want to experience the life of a slave, so each year at Midsummer they offer themselves for service. Lord Stefan is an example. They are carefully examined, and only a small percentage are chosen for the auction. (BP 183) Another Master who makes the switch is Lexius. After experiencing Laurent's domination, he allows himself to be taken to the castle to serve as a slave, at which he excels. (BR 154, 175)

Every few years, the Sultan captures the best slaves. They are the ones who have been disobedient in the castle because they wanted more stimulation. The village provides this, but the Sultan's Palace proves even more alluring. In the village, the slaves are treated as animals, but at the palace, they lose even more of their humanity: They become mere objects of decor. Tristan describes the palace as a sacred place with a true sovereign. It makes the abasement more harsh and indifferently applied but also more bearable. (BR 138)

See also ADORNMENT; ALEXI, PRINCE; ATTENTION; BEAUTY, PRINCESS; *BEAUTY'S PUNISHMENT*; *BEAUTY'S RELEASE*; *CLAIMING OF SLEEPING BEAUTY, THE*; CLAIRE, PRINCESS; DISCIPLINE; DMITRI, PRINCE; DOMINANCE/SUBMISSION; ELENA, PRINCESS; ENHANCEMENT; EROTIC; EUGENIA, PRINCESS; GERALD, PRINCE; JERARD, PRINCE; JULIANA, LADY; LAURENT, PRINCE; LEXIUS; LIZETTA, PRINCESS; LOVE; LOVE SLAVE; LYNETTE, PRINCESS; MASTERS/MISTRESSES; NOTHINGNESS; PERFECTION; PLEASURE; POSSESSION; PUNISHMENT; QUEEN'S CASTLE; QUEEN'S VILLAGE; READINESS; RICHARD, PRINCE; ROGER, PRINCE; RUNAWAYS; SADOMASOCHISM; SELF-CONTROL; SOFTENING; STRUGGLERS; SUFFERING; SULTAN'S PALACE; SURRENDER; TRIBUTE; TRISTAN, PRINCE; TRUST; VULNERABILITY; WILL; WISDOM; YIELDERS.

Slaves' Hall. The room in the Queen's castle where the slaves are groomed and where those slaves not chosen for one of the private bedchambers sleep on pallets. Lord Gregory takes Beauty to the Slaves' Hall to be groomed for the Prince, and she meets her groom, Leon, there. (CSB 82–93)

See also LEON; QUEEN'S CASTLE.

Softening. The term used for making a slave submissive, pliant, and subservient, body and soul. The Masters and Mistresses alternate humiliation and punishment with affection to achieve this effect.

Tristan and Beauty both think the villagers do a better job with this softening process because there is no pampering or permissiveness. A true slave needs a harsh Master before he or she can fully yield and trust that such a Master knows his or her needs. Tristan softens only under the most excessive humiliation, with the hope of appreciation and abiding love. (CSB 34; BP 120)

> *See also* DISCIPLINE; ENHANCEMENT; QUEEN'S VILLAGE; PUNISHMENT; SLAVES; SOUL; SURRENDER; WILL.

Soul. The innermost part of the self, comprised of the will and spirit. It is the locus of the greatest freedom and intimacy and "the only thing a slave can truly possess." (BP 208) The goal of discipline is to "soften" the slaves, to encourage them to yield this part of themselves to their Masters, along with their bodies. They are to surrender more and more deeply from within the dissolution of self into the will of another.

Alexi has the reputation of keeping part of his soul closed off, although he believes he is yielding totally. Beauty, too, gains this reputation from her rebellious spirit. She believes she only gives herself to the harshest punishments and belongs to no one, but she envies Tristan's surrender of his soul to his Master, Nicolas. Tristan's soul transforms into a sense of peace when he trusts his Master and feels in harmony with the punishments. (BP 170, 206–207)

Beauty ultimately yields her soul to Laurent, who becomes her Master. (BR 237–38)

> *See also* ALEXI, PRINCE; BEAUTY, PRINCESS; DOMINANCE/ SUBMISSION; LAURENT, PRINCE; LOVE; SAFETY; SURRENDER; TRISTAN, PRINCE; TRUST; WILL.

Spanking. The primary means of punishing or humiliating the slaves, either with a paddle or the bare hand.

The Queen prefers turning a slave over her knee and using her hand because it is more intimate; her slaves become her children. However, the Prince uses several types of paddles with Beauty, and she notices that all of the slaves' buttocks are reddened with welts, as if they have been paddled nonstop. Only when there is the threat of breaking the skin does the spanking subside. (CSB 75, 201)

Alexi helps Beauty to see the positive side of being paddled: It gains attention. Many slaves purposely disobey in order to be punished because it means they are being thought about by their Lords. For Alexi, being spanked means a break in the endless boredom he had once experienced at the castle.

Spanking is used in the public punishments at the village as well. Slaves are paddled on a turntable, on a carousel, on a pole, and at the Punishment Shop (BP 51–58)

See also ATTENTION; DISCIPLINE; PUNISHMENT; SOFTENING.

Special Punishment Hall. An area of the Queen's castle reserved for unusual forms of discipline.

The Queen sends Alexi here to increase his competence as a slave; she is angry at his seeming ineptitude. He wears a sign that describes him as clumsy and willful and gets turned over to ten Princesses who, for one hour, are allowed to do with him as they like. Princess Lynette takes the lead and torments him so skillfully that the two of them are ordered to do a repeat performance the next day for the Queen. (CSB 211)

See also ALEXI, PRINCE; LYNETTE, PRINCESS; QUEEN'S CASTLE.

Stefan, Lord. The Prince's favorite cousin and one of the Lords at the castle. Blond, with gray eyes, he suffers from an "excessive love" for his personal slave, Tristan. They had been lovers briefly before Tristan became a slave.

Lord Stefan is inferior to Tristan in every way and, having been bested by him, admires him. The Queen perceives the nature of their relationship and orders Stefan to become Tristan's Master. Although he tries, Stefan is hesitant and weak in his commands and too kind and approving. Tristan cannot please him because Stefan does not know how to be pleased. Finally, Tristan tires of him and misbehaves. Stefan sentences Tristan to serve in the village, an order he later regrets, but nothing can change it. Stefan mourns deeply over losing the slave he loves. (CSB 82, 243; BP 169)

In the village, Nicolas tells Tristan that all are certain that Stefan will ask to become a slave on the next Midsummer's Night, when people can request to be examined for such service. The Queen knows he is not the Master he should be and will accept him into the position. The idea amuses Tristan. (BP 183–84)

See also DOMINANCE/SUBMISSION; LOVE; MASTERS/
MISTRESSES; MIDSUMMER NIGHT; SLAVES; TRISTAN, PRINCE.

Stable (public). *See* PUBLIC PONY STABLES.

Stable (castle). One of the places the Queen uses to discipline disobedient slaves. It is part of Alexi's punishment for rebellion, but he finds he prefers it to the torments of the kitchen. Although the stable boys are rough, they seem like royalty compared to the kitchen crew. (CSB 189–91)

See also ALEXI; PRINCE; DISCIPLINE; QUEEN'S CASTLE; STABLE BOY.

Stable boy. The Queen's servant who takes a special interest in Alexi. This tall, strong young man torments Alexi endlessly, yet Alexi wants to stay with him to avoid going back to the kitchen. The stable boy paddles Alexi for the Queen, to her delight. (CSB 191)

See also ALEXI, PRINCE; STABLE (QUEEN'S).

Strugglers. A term coined by Alexi to describe slaves who are resigned but who continue to struggle to get attention. Princess Lizetta is an example. She misbehaves to provoke her Master and get more excitement. (CSB 173)

See also LIZETTA, PRINCESS; SLAVES; YIELDERS.

Submission. *See* DOMINANCE/SUBMISSION; SURRENDER.

Suffering. Deep misery from physical or emotional torment, it is the essential element of the slaves' experience. Suffering may push them into deeply spiritual feelings, test limits, and aid transformation. True slaves crave pain for its magnifying qualities and attempt to manipulate their Masters to make it more frequent and intense. They also enjoy watching other slaves suffer, as Beauty thrills to watch Alexi spanked. (CSB 56)

See also PUNISHMENT; SADOMASOCHISM.

Sultan. The sovereign of a foreign realm who taught the Queen the pleasure of owning and working slaves. (In another version of the same story, the Queen is carrying on a tradition long practiced by her ancestors.) He had sent the first slaves to her and had educated her in their proper care. From time to time, the Sultan sends raiders into her land to capture her best slaves. Thus, he becomes the new Master for Tristan, Beauty, and Laurent. The Queen initially surrenders them to the Sultan for a period of two years. (BP 223)

Laurent describes the Sultan as a delicate young man with short black hair, wearing purple robes. He exudes a radiance, a presence that is good-natured rather than forbidding. He seems a deity who accidentally bears human resemblance. All the slaves want him to notice them, and the grooms gain his attention for themselves when he notices their slaves. Yet it is "unforgivable to look up at him." (BR 119)

He selects Tristan and Laurent, pitting them against each other in his bedroom. Laurent guesses the secret of his eroticism: "He wanted the fluids of other men." (BR 131) Tristan wins the Sultan's favor and is allowed to remain with him. Later, Tristan tells Laurent that this man is more than a Master, he is a sovereign. Punishment has its fullest meaning only if it pleases him. (BR 138)

The Sultan loses these slaves when some of the Queen's men secretly take them back to the Queen's realm. (BR 152–53)

See also GOD; LAURENT, PRINCE; LEXIUS;
MASTERS/MISTRESSES; SULTANATE; SULTAN'S CHAMBER;
SULTAN'S GARDEN; SULTAN'S GROOMS; SULTAN'S PALACE;
SULTAN'S RAIDERS; TRISTAN, PRINCE.

Sultana. *See* INANNA.

Sultanate. The Sultan's realm, which includes the village through which the new slaves are paraded and the palace where they serve. It is larger than the Queen's village and more refined; individual slaves have less significance. They must stand out in some way to get noticed. The dominance/submission scheme is more fully realized here than in the Queen's realm, because the Sultan originated it. (BR 118)

Tristan views the Sultanate as a finer and more sacrosanct order. He feels less lost there. It is more engulfing, as the suffering is offered up to the Lord (whether he acknowledges it or not). Tristan considers it sublime, an advance to a higher stage of understanding and endurance. The slaves are reduced to their capacity to evince feeling and nothing more. They are not allowed to speak because their function is strictly to arouse and give pleasure. They are collectively connected in their nothingness, "joined in the indifference of the Master." (BR 139) This seems to Tristan to offer a great sense of organization and continuum. (BR 138–39)

See also GOD; SULTAN; SULTAN'S PALACE.

Sultan's chamber. The grand bedroom where the Sultan brings slaves that he wants to try. Tristan and Laurent are selected for this honor and Laurent describes the room: Beautiful slaves decorate the chamber as statues in niches on the wall, while others are bound to the bedposts or stand in a circle around a fountain. The bed, with white and purple veils, is on a dais that reminds Laurent of an altar. (BR 121)

See also SULTAN; SULTAN'S PALACE.

Sultan's garden. The area at the palace where the Lords dine and the Sultan chooses the male slaves he wants to try. It is a symbol of the Garden of Eden where God walked.

Tristan and Laurent are both hung on Punishment Crosses in this garden, along with other male slaves, then taken down and used by the Lords for their pleasure. Laurent realizes that the slaves serve merely as decoration unless singled out by the Sultan. He and Tristan both gain this honor. (BR 70)

See also GOD; SULTAN; SULTAN'S PALACE.

Sultan's grooms. Servants at the palace who care for the slaves. Beauty thinks they look like angels. Each is desperate for his own slaves to shine because only when the Sultan notices the slaves does the groom get his attention. These grooms instruct the new slaves to refrain from talking, to behave perfectly, and to look beautiful. Lexius is their Chief Steward. (BR 28)

See also LEXIUS; SULTAN.

Sultan's Palace. The central governing force of the Sultanate and the home of the Sultan. It is a realm of more refined pleasures and manners than the Queen's castle, although slaves are treated as having even less humanity. Many slaves stand in niches in the walls, blending into the patterns and serving as mere decoration.

Forbidden to speak, the slaves are denied the power of high reason. Their value is merely that of amusement or aesthetics. (BP 224; BR 54, 139)

See also SLAVES; SULTAN; SULTANATE.

Sultan's raiders. The people who sneak into the Queen's land one night and make off with six of the finest slaves from the village. They take Beauty, Tristan, Laurent, Dmitri, Rosalynd, and Elena on board a ship and place them in golden cages. After negotiating with one of the Queen's emissaries, the raiders take these slaves to the Sultan for a two-year period of service. (BP 195)

See also SULTAN.

Surrender. The giving over of one's soul to one's fate. The goal for the slaves is to eventually yield their wills totally to the will of their Masters. Surrender allows the slaves to discover deeper dimensions of pleasure, so that the torment they endure can be "deliciously terrible." (BP 205) They must learn to accept whatever they are asked to do, without tension or struggle, but with serenity, grace, and composure.

"You must resign yourself," Lord Gregory instructs Beauty. "You must accept. It is the hardest lesson, compared to which the pain is really nothing." (CSB 52)

Alexi describes himself as a "yielder" in contrast to Princess Lizetta, who is a "struggler"; she is resigned to her lot but craves more attention. Alexi himself practices perfect, graceful obedience. He learned this from having been broken after initially resisting the Queen's will. He feels strong in his emptiness, able to endure anything. He both loves and loathes his position yet is re-created by the very thing that humiliates him. Yielding means to carry paradoxical feelings, yet be of one mind and spirit. Although he views himself as a perfect model of surrender, Leon and Lord Gregory both describe Alexi as rebellious; there is part of him that will never yield. (CSB 172–237)

Beauty is attracted to Alexi for this trait, but when he shows her no evidence of it and urges her to accept and surrender as he has done, her desire recedes. Seeking other rebels like herself, she gets sent to the village, where she urges Tristan to follow her example and be disobedient. The few times she tries this, however, her punishment is severe, and she finds herself surrendering more and more to her new Master and Mistress, because she loves what they do to her. (BP 207)

Tristan, too, must love his Master to yield to him totally, and he can only love the one who will be firm with him and subject him to the severity of punishment that he needs. Lord Stefan was unable to be such a Master because he was weaker in body and soul than Tristan, but Nicolas proves worthy. Tristan is only too happy to yield to the agonizing things that Nicolas demands. "I have found my Master," he says, "the one who brings me into harmony with all punishments." (BP 206) Yet the experience is still one of deep mortification.

The Masters must also surrender to their fates. Many of them do, but some are actually masochists and would relish being dominated. Both Lord Stefan and Lexius desire this. There is talk that Stefan will offer himself as a slave during the Midsummer auction, while Lexius learns the joys of powerlessness under Laurent's firm hand. He also surrenders himself to the Queen for abasement and discipline. (BP 184, BR 175)

See also ALEXI, PRINCE; BEAUTY, PRINCESS; CAPTIVITY; DISCIPLINE; DOMINANCE/SUBMISSION; ENHANCEMENT; LEXIUS; LOVE; MASTERS/MISTRESSES; PARADOX; POSSESSION; PUNISHMENT; RESISTANCE; SADOMASOCHISM; SLAVES; SOUL; STRUGGLERS; TRISTAN, PRINCE; TRUST; WILL; YIELDERS.

T

Tears. Evidence that the slaves are really suffering. The object is to break down their wills and thoroughly debase them. Both pain and mortification can make them cry, and the males weep as easily as the females. They also cry from joy, as tears become a symbol of how pleasure and pain mingle.

See also SADOMASOCHISM; SUFFERING.

Tenderness. The finishing touch to discipline. Knowing the right balance between affection and cruelty bonds Master and slave.

The Captain of the Guard knows this as well as anyone. After whipping Tristan, he caresses his face and kisses his eyelids. "The last knot in me broke," says Tristan. (BP 125) Nicolas also knows how to be tender at the right moments, and for this he wins a place in Tristan's heart. Beauty finds the same treatment with Mistress Lockley.

See also DOMINANCE/SUBMISSION; LOVE; MASTERS/
MISTRESSES; SADOMASOCHISM.

Torment. *See* DISCIPLINE; PUNISHMENT.

Training Hall. A room in the Queen's castle where slaves are taught how to be ready and willing to receive pleasure.

Lord Gregory takes Beauty here to see the training in progress, although she herself does not need it since she already fully experiences her capacity for sexual pleasure. However, those Princesses who repress it must learn how to awaken and yield. Because they do not know this experience as a natural part of their lives, they are taught what they can feel. Paddled simultaneously with receiving pleasure, they are brought to the point of release but not allowed to go all the way. Beauty sees some Princesses straddling leather phalluses as they work themselves into an orgasmic state. They must learn to submit without shame, but also to control their pleasure, since their ecstasy belongs to their Masters or Mistresses.

There are also male slaves in the Training Hall learning better self-control; they must be able to remain erect under discipline. (CSB 94–98)

See also PLEASURE; QUEEN'S CASTLE; READINESS; SLAVES.

Transcendence. The experience of expansion that some of the slaves report when they fully submit to a will they deem greater than their own. During extreme forms of punishment or humiliation, a slave may feel emptied of self. In that moment, he or she may describe the sense of transcending limits or boundaries. Transcendence can result from greater self-knowledge, loss of a limited self-perception, or the ability to merge the self into another. Yielding to the will of a Master gives slaves more freedom to go into the excesses of their own experiences than if they are anchored in the limits of their own egos.

Alexi and Tristan both claim to have endured things they believed they could never bear. Doing so, they sense that they have expanded their resources for facing the next ordeal. When he is on the Public Turntable in the village, Tristan has a vision of a great scheme in which he is part. "My soul broke open," he says, (BP 207) and he understood his existence as an "entreaty to be used like the warmth of a fire is used." (BP 207) His purpose is to be dissolved in the will of others as a renunciation of self. He claims that the crowd's enthusiastic attention fed his experience and he left his body and became one with the punishment. (BP 173)

See also ENHANCEMENT; EROTIC; PLEASURE; PUNISHMENT;
SADOMASOCHISM.

Tributes. How the Queen refers to the slaves. The Queen's allies send their sons and daughters to her castle as Tributes, and the Queen trains them as pleasure slaves. This education offers them enhancement in the form of self-control, self-knowledge, and wisdom, and they are returned to their Kingdoms after a defined period—never more than five years—better able to command others. (CSB 47)

See also ELEANOR, QUEEN; QUEEN'S CASTLE; SLAVES.

Tristan, Prince. The slave who leaves Lord Stefan at the castle and finds a better Master in Nicolas, the Queen's Chronicler, in the village. His strongest desire is to find a place and purpose in an organized environment and to have his soul plundered. Reputed to be incomparable in his dignity, serenity, and ability to yield, this blond slave with the violet-blue eyes has been personally trained for the Queen's Court by the Captain of the Guard. He quickly becomes a favorite of all who torment him.

The dilemma for Tristan is that he and his first Master, Lord Stefan, have met previously at a tournament where they had become lovers. Tristan had bested Stefan in every event, even in bed, and Stefan finds it difficult to be a Master to him. Disappointed in his experience as a slave, Tristan disobeys Stefan and gets himself sent to the village. "I could not bear Stefan's love, his tentativeness, his inability to govern me. And for his weakness in our predestined bond, I despised him." (BP 125)

In the village, he meets his next Master, Nicolas, who buys him for twenty-five gold pieces and then subjects him to one humiliation after another. Nicolas puts Tristan into a harness and adorns him with a horse's tail so he can pull a carriage. Then Nicolas has Tristan punished on the Public Turntable for "his good looks." (BP 101) Tristan cannot believe the degradation he feels, as if something in him is being annihilated. Yet he also feels expanded by it all and grows to love his master, as Nicolas also loves him.

Alone in the bedroom together, Nicolas makes Tristan confess his secrets and describe what he desires in a Master. Tristan then yields his soul to Nicolas and feels transformed, in harmony with his fate and with the entire scheme of which he is part. They make love in Nicolas' bed as equals, no matter what kind of subjugation lies in store for Tristan in the daylight hours. (CSB 173, 246; BP 108–31)

Tristan is one of the six slaves captured by the Sultan's raiders, and he resists being kidnapped. He mourns his lost Master and Beauty has to remind him of his desire to obliterate himself: He can transfer his visions to the Sultanate. Pitted against Laurent in the Sultan's bedchamber, he triumphs and is allowed to remain with his Highness. Viewing the Sultan as a supreme sovereign and not just a Master, Tristan finds contentment. He loves the immensity of the place, with its high degree of order. (BR 139)

Laurent violates this order somewhat when he gives Tristan the opportunity to play Master. At first hesitantly, but then with gusto, Tristan dominates their Master, Lexius. Laurent thinks Tristan "seemed the very opposite of the weak Master he had once had." (BR 142) However, Tristan still prefers to be a slave. (BR 138)

When Nicolas comes to rescue Tristan from the Sultan, Tristan rebels again. Nicolas fails to take him in hand, so Tristan becomes disenchanted with his former Master, and Nicolas must work hard to win him back. The Queen sentences Tristan to a year of service at the Public Pony Stables, and Nicolas rents him out to pull his carriage. With enough harshness, balanced by love, Nicolas finally woos Tristan. Soon Tristan becomes his personal slave again when Nicolas buys him from the Queen. (BR 228)

> *See also* DOMINANCE/SUBMISSION; BEAUTY, PRINCESS; *BEAUTY'S
> PUNISHMENT*; *BEAUTY'S RELEASE*; JULIA, LADY; LAURENT, PRINCE;
> LEXIUS; LOVE; MASTERS/MISTRESSES; NICOLAS; PONIES;
> PUBLIC PONY STABLES; PUBLIC TURNTABLE; SADOMASOCHISM;
> SLAVES; SOUL; STEFAN, LORD; SULTANATE; SULTAN'S PALACE;
> SURRENDER; TENDERNESS; TRANSCENDENCE; TRUST;
> WHIPPING MASTER.

Trust. What the slaves must feel in order to yield fully to the commands of their Masters and Mistresses, and what the Master must feel to be able to treat a slave with affection and love.

Tristan finds the Master he wants in Nicolas, so he allows Nicolas to discipline and abuse him in whatever manner he chooses; as a good Master, Nicolas knows what Tristan needs even if Tristan balks at obeying a frightening command. Nicolas then provides Tristan with the opportunity to escape. Because this demonstrates Nicolas' trust, Tristan feels even more loyal. In such trust, they can transform the Master/slave relationship onto a higher plane, based on a genuine bond. (BP 186)

> *See also* LOVE; NICOLAS; SURRENDER; TRISTAN, PRINCE.

U

Uncertainty. A psychological dimension of the slaves' experience that increases their physical sensations. They can perform whatever is asked of them, and do it perfectly, yet still be uncertain that they have pleased their Masters. This causes constant self-evaluation and guilt, which leads to greater effort, body awareness, and self-knowledge.

There is also constant uncertainty over what will happen next, since, as captives, they are completely at someone else's mercy. Beauty is anxious as the Prince takes her to the Queen's castle. She never knows what to expect there, and each new experience carries the fear of losing control. (CSB 29)

For all of the slaves, going to the Sultan's Palace has the dimension of uncertainty, although Laurent views it as an adventure. Because the Sultan's rules and treatment of slaves is unknown, they cannot predict what may happen to them. (BP 226)

See also ANTICIPATION; CAPTIVITY; FEAR; PUNISHMENT; SLAVES; SULTANATE.

Understanding. One of the intended benefits for the slaves. The further they are pushed with their course of discipline, the more familiar they grow with their own inner resources—their ability to endure discomfort and humiliation. As a result, by the time their servitude is over, they have increased their self-understanding and their knowledge of human nature. As such, they are better fit to command their people than they had been in their ignorance.

See also DISCIPLINE; ENHANCEMENT; SELF-CONTROL; SLAVES; WISDOM.

V

Village. *See* QUEEN'S VILLAGE.

Villagers. The people who live in the Queen's village. All year they save their money for purchasing slaves sent down from the castle for the summer labor. Some of the wealthier villagers, such as Nicolas and Jennifer Lockley, purchase the slaves for longer periods of time—sometimes permanently. Those who cannot afford slaves can rent them, or at the very least, they can have fun humiliating them in public. (BP 3)

It is the duty of the villagers to torment the slaves; as a result the slaves are under constant scrutiny. The more people there are, the more the slaves feel under the watchful eye of a godlike awareness. "In the village, someone is always watching. . . . Someone always sees, comes to punish." (BP 171)

> *See also* AUCTION; LOCKLEY, JENNIFER; NICOLAS; PUNISHMENT; QUEEN'S VILLAGE.

Violence. *See* SADOMASOCHISM.

Voyeurism. Watching someone else in an explicitly erotic act. Some of the Masters and Mistresses get pleasure from watching their slaves have sex with other slaves; the slaves have no choice but to obey and perform perfectly. Even the fact that they are naked, their private parts exposed and examined, gives them the feeling that they are always watched. However, some slaves like this attention—particularly for its humiliation—and they go out of their way to put on a show.

Lady Julia subjects Tristan to this treatment. She rents a Princess in the Public Tents, encourages him to get his pleasure of her, and stands watching the entire time. He feels self-conscious but too deep in lust to let it bother him. He also enjoys being studied. (BP 152–53)

Lady Elvera does the same with Laurent. She likes doing her embroidery while watching Laurent capture and couple with Princesses. (BR 10)

At Tristan's request, Nicolas purchases Beauty for a night, then watches their lovemaking and listens to their conversation. Beauty finds this scrutiny disconcerting, particularly when he overhears her say something she knows to be a secret. (BP 210)

> *See also* ELVERA, LADY; EXHIBITIONISM; JULIA, LADY; NAKEDNESS; NICOLAS; PUBLIC TENTS; VULNERABILITY.

Vulnerability. The essential state of being a slave. At all times, they are commanded according to someone else's agenda. Defenseless in their exposure, and always at a disadvantage, they must endure having their legs opened, their private parts prodded, and their minds and bodies violated. Slaves are kept naked and on their knees, often with their hands bound or placed behind them. Beauty thinks the Princes are more vulnerable than the Princesses because their genitals are so exposed and so easily slapped in passing. (CSB 53)

She herself experiences this vulnerability immediately upon her enslavement, as the Prince parades her naked through a village on her way to the Queen's castle. Her own passion is evident, making her feel ashamed, but even in this state there is some degree of strength: "There was in her, even in her helplessness, a sense of power." (CSB 32) She knows that the Prince and the people watching all desire her. Still, she is not allowed to have a will of her own.

The constant voyeurism is another aspect of the slaves' vulnerability. For example, Julia rents a Princess for Tristan, then watches him have sex with the girl. He claims being watched adds an element of fear and pleasure to the experience, but he has no choice but to perform. There is no privacy for any of the slaves unless they grab it against the rules. (BP 152)

See also ANTICIPATION; CAPTIVITY; EXPOSURE; NAKEDNESS; PARADOX; READINESS; SLAVES; SURRENDER; VOYEURISM.

W

Whipping Master. A strong, shaggy-haired man in the village who whips the slaves at the Public Turntable for the amusement of the villagers. He especially delights in large, powerful slaves like Tristan; the more he can get out of a slave, the more he satisfies his audience. (BP 103)

See also PLACE OF PUBLIC PUNISHMENT; PUBLIC TURNTABLE; TRISTAN, PRINCE.

Will. The pivotal force in the power struggle between Master and slave. The slaves, who were once of a privileged class and who commanded others, must learn to surrender their wills to the wishes and commands of their Masters. It comes easily to some who desire to be subservient, but rebellious slaves are never quite tamed; they hold back until they find exactly the right person to whom to yield and lose themselves.

When he finds the right Master in Nicolas, Tristan describes this process. The Queen's Chronicler punishes him severely and subjects him to extreme degradation, but Tristan realizes he needs this and loves his Master for knowing and acting on it. After one such experience, Tristan says, "I felt emptied like a sack, light and without will." (BP 78)

Laurent realizes that people are willing to give up their power to the one who can take full control and exert clear, unhesitant, and definitive authority. The people of his own realm are relieved when he takes over after his father's death. They are like slaves who find the right Master: They willingly accept their fates if the Master understands and meets their needs. (BR 232)

See also SADOMASOCHISM; SLAVES; SOUL; SURRENDER.

William, Lord. The Queen's cousin and Princess Eugenia's Master. The Princess is in love with him and wants to remain at the castle to be near him, even if it means she remains in captivity as his slave. (CSB 91)

See also EUGENIA, PRINCESS.

Wisdom. One of the benefits of discipline for the slaves. If they can endure their punishments and humiliation, and surrender to the will of their tormentors, they may increase their understanding, self-knowledge, and ability to command the people of their lands. The point of their captivity is their betterment. (CSB 176)

See also ENHANCEMENT; SELF-CONTROL; SLAVES; UNDERSTANDING.

Y

Yielders. Slaves who learn to accept their position and resign themselves easily to the torment and discipline. They refrain from struggling the way Princess Lizetta does. Alexi describes himself as a "yielder," although there are those in the castle who believe otherwise about him. He names Prince Tristan as an example of yielding and urges Beauty to do the same. Because she has depth and mystery, she will suffer, and yielding can resolve her inner conflict. "That shall be your way, exquisite and personal devotion. Great calm, great serenity." (CSB 173)

See also ALEXI, PRINCE; LIZETTA, PRINCESS; STRUGGLERS; SURRENDER.

Yielding. *See* SURRENDER.

PART III

ROQUELAURE
TRIVIA

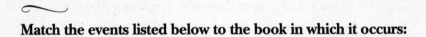

Match the events listed below to the book in which it occurs:

A. *The Claiming of Sleeping Beauty*
B. *Beauty's Punishment*
C. *Beauty's Release*
D. Did not occur

____ 1. Beauty recalls a dream from her life in her father's castle.

____ 2. Lord Stefan kisses Tristan good-bye.

____ 3. Beauty learns that Lady Juliana was once a slave.

____ 4. Lexius is wrapped in a rug.

____ 5. Laurent chooses Prince Geoffrey as his favorite pony.

____ 6. Elena is doubled.

____ 7. The Prince allows a cobbler to touch Beauty.

____ 8. Lord Gregory rapes Alexi for rebelliousness.

____ 9. The Captain of the Guard bows before Princess Beauty.

____ 10. Alexi runs away from his father's castle.

_____ 11. The Captain's soldiers play with Beauty.

_____ 12. Tristan is taught how to march properly.

_____ 13. Tristan and Laurent are sentenced to be hung on Punishment Crosses.

_____ 14. Geoffrey falls in love with Tristan.

_____ 15. Rosalynd succeeds in escaping the Sultan's Palace.

_____ 16. Richard describes the Punishment Shop.

_____ 17. Lady Julia rents a Princess for Tristan's pleasure.

_____ 18. The Queen sentences Laurent and Tristan to the Public Pony Stables.

_____ 19. Tristan and Laurent are pitted against one another.

_____ 20. Felix describes how he loves to serve his Master.

_____ 21. The Lord Mayor purchases Lord Stefan.

_____ 22. Tristan gathers apples for Lady Julia.

_____ 23. Beauty puts on her clothes.

_____ 24. Beauty disciplines a young Prince.

_____ 25. Tristan confesses his need for a strong Master.

Short answers #1:

WHO

1. caught Beauty watching Felix pleasure Alexi?

2. served as the Queen's valet before Alexi?

3. brought Alexi to the Queen after he ran from his father's castle?

4. gave runaway slaves safe passage?

5. drove his slave too slowly on the Bridle Path for the slave's taste?

6. caught Laurent's eye in the paddock at the Public Pony Stables?

7. successfully escaped from the castle?

8. ran just before Beauty on the Bridle Path?

9. asked the Innkeeper's daughter to paddle Beauty?

10. told Beauty she had mystery and depth?

11. told Beauty about Lady Juliana's past?

12. was auctioned off in the village before Beauty?

13. did Tristan see in the Lord Mayor's coach?

14. told Tristan the best slaves make the best Masters?

15. loves to embroider as she watches her slave?

16. does Alexi find most interesting in the castle?

17. likes to use her bare hands to spank her slaves?

18. specializes in taming rebellious slaves in the village?

19. does Alexi describe as a "struggler"?

20. shows Tristan what it means to be "measured"?

WHERE

1. does Beauty first see Laurent?

2. does the Queen send Alexi for his first taste of discipline ordered by someone besides herself?

3. does Alexi make love to Beauty?

4. does Tristan first see Dmitri?

5. does Nicolas take Tristan for a whipping?

6. does Beauty tell Tristan about the soldiers' concerns about invaders?

7. does Jerard tell Tristan what it means to be a pony?

8. does Lady Juliana make Beauty gather roses?

9. does Laurent propose marriage to Beauty?

10. does Laurent stand for the Sultan's inspection?

11. does Lexius learn what it means to have a Master?

12. does Beauty meet Inanna?

13. do the castle slaves sleep when they are not with their Masters?

14. does Jennifer Lockley threaten to send Beauty for discipline?

15. does Nicolas learn Tristan's name?

16. does Tristan feel the most frightened of his punishment?

17. does Lexius have his first slave experience at the castle?

18. does Nicolas treat Tristan as his equal?

19. does Alexi experience his worst humiliation?

20. does Elena serve as a slave before the Sultan kidnaps her?

WHAT

1. objects does the Queen use in her lawn game with Alexi?

2. does Leon use to adorn Beauty before she is presented in the Queen's parlor?

3. kind of spice do the Sultan's grooms use on Beauty?

4. does Beauty fear about returning to her father's castle?

5. problem do the Prince and Lord Stefan have in common?

6. is Beauty's first offense against the Prince?

7. does the Prince find outside Beauty's castle that might have deterred him?

8. phrase does the Prince teach Beauty to use to let him know her desires?

9. does Beauty do during her presentation to the Court that arouses the Prince's jealousy?

10. is Beauty's observation concerning the difference between male and female slaves?

11. color is Alexi's hair?

12. does Juliana ask Beauty to do with the roses?

13. does Nicolas tell the Public Whipping Master about the reason for Tristan's punishment?

14. does Leon tell Beauty about Alexi?

15. are the three benefits that Leon describes for the slaves?

16. color is the horse's tail that Tristan wears for Nicolas?

17. covers the case holding the two phalluses that Nicolas uses for Tristan?

18. do people drink at the Punishment Shop as they watch the slaves getting spanked?

19. did the Queen's emissaries do at Tristan's father's castle before selecting Tristan as a slave?

20. does Beauty compare to an altar?

Match the specific locations to one of the following:

A. Queen's castle C. Sultan's Palace
B. Queen's village D. None of the above

____ 1. Training Hall

____ 2. Auction

____ 3. Hall of Mirrors

____ 4. Special Punishment Hall

____ 5. Great Hall

____ 6. Kitchen

____ 7. Public Pony Stables

____ 8. Bridle Path

____ 9. Maze

____ 10. Sign of the Lion

____ 11. Harem of Beautiful and Virtuous Royal Wives

____ 12. Lexius' chamber

____ 13. Parlor

____ 14. Punishment Shop

____ 15. Slaves' Hall

____ 16. Public Tents

____ 17. Lion's Den

____ 18. Farm

____ 19. Garden of Male Delights

____ 20. Inanna's Fudge Shop

Fill in the blanks:

1. Beauty discovers _____ on the bottom of the boots she wears on the Bridle Path.

2. Princess Lizetta is punished for acting out in the _____.

3. Princess Lizetta's punishment is to be _____.

4. In contrast to Princess Lizetta, Alexi describes himself as a "_____."

5. Alexi is chained to a wall in _____.

6. Alexi began to respond to the Queen's discipline because of his desire to escape _____.

7. The Princesses were allowed to torment Alexi in the _____ Hall.

8. _____ makes love to Beauty in the cart on the way to the village.

9. The moment at which Beauty decides to rebel against the Prince, _____ is with him.

10. Beauty discovers Lady Juliana was once a _____.

11. Lord Stefan is related to the Prince as his _____.

12. _____ perceives that Beauty is like Alexi in her rebelliousness.

13. Alexi spills _____ to draw Beauty's attention to him.

14. Jennifer Lockley uses a white _____ to torment Beauty.

15. The Captain of the Guard uses a _____ to give Beauty pleasure when they make love in his room.

16. _____ first introduced the Queen to pleasure slaves.

17. On board ship, the slaves sleep in golden _____.

18. _____ are the Queen's closest allies.

19. Roger had slipped away with Princess _____ in the castle.

20. Inanna's official position is that of _____.

21. The slaves at the _____ auction at the village command the highest prices.

22. _____ escorts Beauty to Nicolas' house.

23. Tristan's eye color is _____.

24. Jerard has already served _____ years in the village.

25. Beauty runs the Bridle Path for the first time on _____ Night.

$\backsim$

Match the numbers with the appropriate item (some letters may be used more than once):

$\backsim$

A. 15   ____ 1. Minimum sentence in the village, in months

B. 25   ____ 2. Number of days it took the ship to arrive at the Sultanate

C. 27   ____ 3. Number of slaves the Sultan kidnapped

D. 6   ____ 4. Number of gold pieces paid for Beauty

E. 2   ____ 5. Number of years Laurent was sentenced to the stables

F. 14   ____ 6. Number of years Beauty slept

G. 1   ____ 7. Number of nights that Tristan and Stefan were lovers

H. 3   ____ 8. Number of years of Alexi's service to the Queen

I. 5   ____ 9. Number of months Tristan was in the castle

J. 100   ____ 10. Number of gold pieces paid for Tristan

K. 4   ____ 11. Number of years Laurent was sentenced to the village after running away

L. 10   ____ 12. Number of Princesses who tormented Alexi

M. 19   ____ 13. Beauty's age

N. 16   ____ 14. The Prince's age

O. 18   ____ 15. Number of years Laurent was in the
                      castle

P. 12   ____ 16. Number of years since Sultan's raiders
                      last invaded the village

               ____ 17. Number of village youths who examined
                      Tristan

               ____ 18. Alexi's age

               ____ 19. Number of Princes in the gauntlet the
                      Queen ordered for Alexi

               ____ 20. Gerald's age

               ____ 21. Number of years of Eugenia's servitude

               ____ 22. Number of years Elena was in the village

               ____ 23. Number of Princesses who pulled the
                      Lord Mayor's coach

               ____ 24. Number of times the stable boy was to
                      try to spank Alexi before he could finish
                      his task in the lawn game

               ____ 25. Number of years Jerard was sentenced
                      to serve in the village

Match the slave to the master:

____ 1. Alexi   A. Grand Duke Andre

____ 2. Beauty   B. Lord William

____ 3. Tristan   C. Lady Juliana

____ 4. Laurent   D. Nicolas

____ 5. Elena   E. Lady Elvera

____ 6. Lynette   F. The Prince

____ 7. Lizetta   G. Queen Eleanor

_____ 8. Claire   H. Lord Mayor

_____ 9. Eugenia   I. Laurent

_____ 10. Lexius   J. Lord Gerhardt

~~~~~

Match the trait with the slave:
~~~~~

_____ 1. Alexi   A. Red-haired male

_____ 2. Beauty   B. Intends to be disobedient

_____ 3. Laurent   C. Cannot control his lust

_____ 4. Tristan   D. Genitally mutilated

_____ 5. Rosalynd   E. Serene

_____ 6. Roger   F. Suffers on the Bridle Path

_____ 7. Richard   G. Bathes Beauty at the Inn

_____ 8. Dmitri   H. Refuses to give good sport

_____ 9. Lynette   I. Humiliates Alexi

_____ 10. Jerard   J. Wants to lose self in love

_____ 11. Inanna   K. Slender giant of a man

_____ 12. Claire   L. Runs away for adventure

_____ 13. Lizetta   M. Anxious if not run hard

_____ 14. Lexius   N. Jealous of Queen's attention to Alexi

_____ 15. Gerald   O. No control without tight shackles

Match the trait with the Master:

____ 1. Queen Eleanor | A. A village woman who can write

____ 2. The Prince | B. Wears braids

____ 3. Lord Stefan | C. Restless and moody

____ 4. Lord Gregory | D. Curious about slave experience

____ 5. Lady Julia | E. Able to be equally Master and slave

____ 6. Lady Juliana | F. Owns a farm in the village

____ 7. Captain of Guard | G. Secret lover of Laurent

____ 8. Gareth (groom) | H. Boyish innocence

____ 9. The Sultan | I. Weak as a Master

____ 10. Lexius | J. Queen's ancestor

____ 11. Jennifer Lockley | K. Chief lodger at Sign of the Lion

____ 12. Nicolas | L. Practical and unforgiving

____ 13. Heinrick | M. Chief Steward

____ 14. Laurent | N. Dislikes love between Master and slave

____ 15. Lord Mayor | O. Hard, gray eyes

Short answers #2:

BEAUTY'S STORY

1. How does the Prince first awaken Beauty?

2. What kind of vines cover Beauty's castle?

3. Where does the Prince find Beauty in the castle?

4. How was Beauty enchanted into a deep sleep?

5. How do Beauty's parents realize what the Prince had in mind for her?

6. Where does the Prince feed Beauty at the inn?

7. What does the Innkeeper's daughter use to tie Beauty to the bed?

8. To what animal does the Prince refer to describe Beauty?

9. Why is it worse for Beauty to walk naked in front of the nobility at the castle than in front of the villagers?

10. Why is the Queen displeased about her son's first slave?

11. To what does Beauty liken her long enchanted sleep?

12. How does Beauty feel about Lady Juliana when she first sees her?

13. What initial instructions in respect does Leon give to Beauty?

14. What most annoys Beauty about the way Leon prepares her to go before the Queen?

15. When did Beauty decide to rebel at the castle?

16. Why did Beauty resist Alexi's example?

17. What discipline did Beauty most dread?

18. How was Beauty used at the Sultan's Palace?

19. Who told Beauty she had to return home?

20. Why did Beauty refuse all suitors at her father's castle?

ALEXI'S STORY

1. What does the Prince use to punish Alexi all night for Beauty's benefit?

2. How is Alexi's torment diminished?

3. Which Princess does Alexi most fear?

4. How does Alexi first attract the Queen's special attention?

5. Who does the Queen first use to arouse Alexi?

6. What do the Princes lining the gauntlet teach Alexi?

7. Why does the Queen send Alexi away from her after he has decided to obey?

8. What lesson does Alexi learn in the kitchen?

9. Where do the kitchen staff bind him at night?

10. Who does Alexi favor during his disciplinary period in the kitchen and stables?

11. How does Alexi outshine Lynette when they perform before the Queen?

12. What is the worst task Lynette commands him to perform?

13. How does the Queen reward him?

14. In what position is Alexi displayed before the villagers?

15. How many times does Alexi make love to Beauty before he tells her his story?

16. What advice does Alexi give Beauty?

17. What secret thing does Alexi do to Beauty in the Prince's bedchamber?

18. What did the Prince command Alexi to put on him?

19. What did Alexi refuse to do for three days in the kitchen?

20. What did Lord Gregory hang around Alexi's neck before sending him in to the Princesses for abuse?

TRISTAN'S STORY

1. Where does Beauty first see Tristan?

2. Why did Tristan rebel against his Master at the castle?

3. What does Alexi say about Tristan's behavior?

4. What does Tristan believe he and Beauty must do in the village?

5. What does the auctioneer point out about Tristan?

6. What surprises Tristan about his new Mistress, Julia?

7. What does Julia do that frightens Tristan?

8. Who explains to Tristan what it means to be a pony?

9. How does Nicolas surprise Tristan?

10. What does Nicolas say to the Whipping Master that makes Tristan cringe in fear?

11. What does Tristan confess about this experience to Nicolas?

12. What special favor does Tristan ask of Nicolas?

13. What does Tristan learn about being the new pony?

14. How does Tristan become the means by which Nicolas gains information about the Sultan's raiders?

15. What is the essential difference between Tristan and Beauty?

16. Why does Tristan resist being taken to the Sultanate?

17. With whom do the Sultan's grooms couple Tristan for their entertainment?

18. What happens to Tristan in the Sultan's bedchamber?

19. Why does he resist being rescued from the Sultanate?

20. What causes the estrangement between Nicolas and Tristan?

LAURENT'S STORY

1. How did Laurent entertain his Mistress at the castle?

2. Why did Laurent run away?

3. How does the Captain of the Guard punish him when he gets caught?

4. How many times is Laurent sentenced to the Public Turntable on his first day in the village?

5. How does Laurent view the experience of being kidnapped?

6. In which of the other slaves does Laurent take a special interest?

7. How does Laurent provoke Lexius into coupling with him?

8. What does Lexius do that gives Laurent this advantage?

9. What does Laurent think of the Sultan?

10. What does Laurent teach Tristan in Lexius' chamber?

11. What does Laurent teach Lexius?

12. What disciplinary measure does the Queen take to punish Laurent for resisting rescue?

13. What does Laurent love about being a pony?

14. What does he dread about it?

15. How does the groom treat him?

16. Why does Laurent look forward to the hour of rest and recreation in the paddock?

17. What does Laurent do to earn himself a stinging phallus?

18. What terminates Laurent's service to the Queen?

19. What does Laurent put on Beauty when he claims her as his wife?

20. What does Laurent most fear?

___

Multiple choice #1:

____ 1. Beauty experiences her first full examination

    A. at the inn   C. in the Great Hall

    B. in her bedroom   D. in the kitchen

____ 2. Beauty meets her groom Leon in

    A. the Slaves' Hall   C. the kitchen

    B. the Queen's chamber   D. the Special Punishment Hall

____ 3. The Queen's first disciplinary sentence for Beauty sends her to

    A. the Bridle Path   C. the Parlor

    B. the Sign of the Lion   D. the Training Hall

____ 4. Lord Gregory shows Beauty how some of the Princesses are taught to experience pleasure in

    A. the Prince's chamber   C. the Slaves' Hall

    B. the Punishment Shop   D. the Training Hall

____ 5. When punishing Beauty, Mistress Lockley sends her other slaves to

    A. the Punishment Shop   C. the Bridle Path

    B. the Public Turntable   D. the Sign of the Lion

____ 6. The Whipping Master works at

    A. the Punishment Shop   C. the Public Turntable

    B. the Slaves' Hall   D. the Public Pony Stables

____ 7. Soldiers' night takes place at

   A. the Public Pony Stables   C. Nicolas' house

   B. the Sign of the Lion   D. the Garden of Male
                                      Delights

____ 8. All but the following are Inns on the village square
       except

   A. the Sign of the Lion   C. the Sign of the Plow

   B. the Sign of the Bear   D. the Sign of the Cross

____ 9. Alexi and Lexius share the experience of being
       disciplined in

   A. the Slaves' Hall   C. the Queen's stable

   B. the kitchen   D. the Prince's chamber

____ 10. Richard tells Beauty about his experience in

   A. the Punishment Shop   C. the Stables

   B. the Hall of Punishments   D. the Public Tents

____ 11. Tristan sees the most evidence for a larger order and
        purpose to his existence in

   A. the Queen's chamber   C. the Sultan's Palace

   B. the harem   D. the Sign of the Lion

____ 12. Nicolas humiliates and frightens Tristan

   A. in the Public Pony   C. at the Farm
      Stables

   B. on the Public Turntable   D. in the Sultan's Palace

____ 13. Laurent decides he likes being a Master from his
        experiences in

   A. the kitchen   C. the Sultan's ship

   B. the Sign of the Lion   D. Lexius' chamber

____ 14. Beauty first learns to undress another person with her
        teeth in

   A. the Queen's chamber   C. the Prince's chamber

   B. the Hall of Punishments   D. an Inn on the road

_____ 15. The slaves receive a reward at the end of their service in

    A. the Queen's chamber   C. the village

    B. the Great Hall   D. the Parlor

Short answers #3:

FORMS OF DISCIPLINE

1. What posture does the Prince instruct Beauty to assume while at the castle?

2. What term from working with horses is used to describe the process of transforming a slave's will?

3. What did the kitchen staff do to Alexi that drew the Page's pity?

4. Why does the Prince allow a village cobbler to touch Beauty's naked body?

5. What happens to Beauty right after she runs the Bridle Path?

6. What does Beauty fear about Lady Juliana's game of discipline with the roses?

7. How does Alexi feel under Princess Lynette's command?

8. Why is Lord Gregory displeased with Alexi even when the Queen is satisfied?

9. Which Princess spanks harder than the Queen?

10. What special benefit comes to a slave's Master from putting the slave on the Public Turntable?

11. What startling sight does Beauty see outside the Sign of the Lion?

12. What posture must Beauty adopt while scrubbing the floor of the Inn?

13. What happens to slaves in the Public Tents?

14. Why does Tristan like a large audience when he is being punished?

15. What function does the Special Punishment Hall serve?

16. How does the Punishment Shop benefit the slave Masters?

17. What is Beauty's first task at the Inn?

18. What do the Sultan's grooms put on the slaves on board ship that annoys them?

19. What are the slaves strictly forbidden to do while at the Sultan's Palace?

20. How are the slaves predominantly used at the Palace?

21. What does the Queen view as the most degrading position for slaves at the village?

22. How do the villagers serve the Queen's program?

23. How does Beauty test her suitors?

24. When a pony is punished, what letter of the alphabet is drawn on his chest?

25. What ingredients are used to draw this letter?

Multiple choice #2:

WHO SAID THE FOLLOWING?

____ 1. "To be commanded by one so young is to feel one's helplessness."

    A. Laurent   C. Alexi

    B. Beauty   D. Felix

_____ 2. "Surely you will allow Beauty some clothing . . . until she reaches the border of your Kingdom."

A. Beauty's father   C. Beauty's mother

B. the Innkeeper's daughter   D. the Captain of the Guard

_____ 3. "I liked the barefoot run through the village because you were driving me and you were watching me."

A. Tristan to Nicolas   C. Laurent to Jerard

B. Beauty to the Prince   D. Tristan to Lexius

_____ 4. "He did not know how to command. I was always distracted by other Lords."

A. Laurent about Lexius   C. Beauty about the Prince

B. Tristan about Nicolas   D. Tristan about Stefan

_____ 5. "I am becoming my punishments."

A. Laurent   C. Leon

B. Jerard   D. Tristan

_____ 6. "Stop admiring the male slaves so very much. . . . Don't revel in all I show you to frighten you."

A. Lord Gregory to Beauty   C. Nicolas to Tristan

B. Queen Eleanor to Tristan   D. Lynette to Alexi

_____ 7. "You shall run fast to gather each one in your teeth and place in the lap of your Sovereign."

A. Felix to Lynette   C. Lord Gregory to Laurent

B. Juliana to Beauty   D. Beauty to the Prince

_____ 8. "I feel ashamed when I give in, I feel as if I have truly lost myself."

A. Elena   C. Beauty

B. Lord Stefan   D. Alexi

____ 9. "Now I have two slaves. . . . Or you have two Masters, Lexius. It's difficult to judge the situation one way or the other."

    A. Laurent   C. the Sultan

    B. Tristan   D. Beauty

____ 10. "Tell me what you felt when you were made to march, after you were properly harnessed."

    A. Julia to Tristan   C. Lynette to Alexi

    B. the Captain of the   D. Nicolas to Tristan
       Guard to Laurent

Bonus Questions:

1. How does the Prince manage to enter Beauty's castle?

2. What two physical attributes must the Queen's Pages possess to fulfill their duties?

3. In what way is Beauty distinct from many of the Princesses brought to serve at the castle?

4. Where must each slave stop on the Bridle Path?

5. What disturbs Beauty about her relationship to Lady Juliana?

6. Why is a slave's fate considered to be worse in the village than at the castle?

7. What term describes how a slave begins to yield and become pliant to a Master?

8. What special privilege does the Queen's village enjoy over other villages in the realm?

9. What do the villagers desire to do to supplement this privilege?

10. In what phase was the moon when the Sultan's raiders invaded the village?

11. Who does Tristan see at the Square of the Inns that causes him dread?

12. What will Lord Stefan do on Midsummer Night?

13. After the cart drops off the slaves, in what manner are they taken into the village?

14. What first attracts the Captain of the Guard to Beauty?

15. What religious image does Beauty use to describe the Sultan's grooms?

16. The Princes and Princesses were called love slaves or _____ to the Queen.

17. The maximum length of a slave's service is _____ years.

18. The Sultan is allowed to keep kidnapped slaves for a period of _____ years.

19. _____ is the slave who wants to remain at the castle because she is in love with her Master.

20. In the Place of Public Punishment, Beauty is tethered to the _____.

21. Nicolas uses a _____ to watch Beauty and Tristan.

22. The color of the Sultan's bedlinens is _____.

23. Inanna is dressed as a _____ when she frees Beauty from the niche in the wall.

24. The religious image to which Laurent compares the Sultan's bed is _____.

25. Nicolas and the Captain of the Guard use _____ to transport the slaves out of the palace.

ANSWERS TO TRIVIA

MATCH THE EVENTS:

1. A	6. D	11. B	16. B	21. D
2. A	7. A	12. B	17. B	22. B
3. B	8. A	13. C	18. C	23. C
4. C	9. C	14. B	19. C	24. C
5. D	10. A	15. D	20. D	25. B

SHORT ANSWERS #1:

(Who?)

1. Lord Gregory
2. Prince Gerald
3. Captain of the Guard
4. King Lysius
5. Lord Gerhardt
6. Prince Jerard
7. Princess Lynette
8. Princess Claire
9. The Prince
10. Prince Alexi
11. Prince Roger
12. Prince Tristan
13. Lady Julia
14. Lord Nicolas
15. Lady Elvera
16. Squire Felix
17. Queen Eleanor
18. Jennifer Lockley
19. Princess Lizetta
20. Lady Julia and Lord Nicolas

(Where?)

1. In the soldier's encampment outside the village
2. The kitchen
3. In an empty chamber in the castle
4. On the Public Turntable

5. The Public Turntable
6. In Nicolas' bed
7. At the Farm
8. In the Queen's chamber
9. At Beauty's father's castle
10. In the Sultan's garden
11. In his own bedchamber
12. In the Harem of Beautiful and Virtuous Royal Wives at the Sultan's Palace

13. In the Slaves' Hall
14. To the Punishment Shop
15. At the Square of the Inns
16. At the Place of Public Punishment
17. In the kitchen
18. In Nicolas' bedchamber
19. In the village where he is put on display
20. On the Lord Mayor's farm

(What?)

1. Golden balls

2. Golden chains on nipple clamps, bracelets, a necklace, a navel jewel, earrings and genital clamps

3. Cinnamon

4. Monotony and routine

5. They both love (and lose) their slaves

6. Impertinence

7. The corpses of princes who failed to get inside

8. "Only if it pleases you, my Prince."

9. Notices the male slave, Alexi

10. That the males are more vulnerable because of their exposed penises

11. Auburn

12. Gather the blooms in her teeth, one at a time, before Juliana can spank her too many times, and give them to the Queen

13. To whip him for his good looks

14. That Alexi has a rebellious core that he does not surrender
15. Wisdom, self-control, and greater understanding of the world
16. Black
17. Moroccan leather
18. Coffee
19. Examine him
20. The examination table in the Great Hall

MATCH THE LOCATIONS:

1. A	6. A	11. C	16. B
2. B	7. B	12. C	17. D
3. D	8. A	13. A	18. B
4. A	9. A	14. B	19. C
5. A	10. B	15. A	20. D

FILL IN THE BLANKS:

1. Horseshoes	12. Lord Gregory
2. Maze	13. Wine
3. Doubled	14. Cat
4. Yielder	15. Dagger handle
5. The Queen's Chamber	16. The Sultan
6. Boredom	17. Cages
7. Special Punishment	18. Beauty's parents
8. Tristan	19. Juliana
9. Lord Stefan	20. Sultana
10. Slave	21. Midsummer
11. Cousin	22. Prince Richard

23. Violet-blue   25. Festival
24. Two

MATCH THE NUMBERS:

1. H	6. J	11. K	16. E	21. E
2. F	7. H	12. L	17. H	22. G
3. D	8. E	13. A	18. M	23. P
4. C	9. D	14. O	19. D	24. I
5. G	10. B	15. G	20. N	25. H

MATCH THE SLAVE TO THE MASTER:

1. G	3. D	5. H	7. C	9. B
2. F	4. E	6. A	8. J	10. I

MATCH THE TRAIT WITH THE SLAVE:

1. E	4. J	7. A	10. M	13. H
2. B	5. O	8. C	11. D	14. K
3. L	6. G	9. I	12. F	15. N

MATCH THE TRAIT WITH THE MASTER:

1. N	4. O	7. K	10. M	13. J
2. C	5. A	8. G	11. L	14. E
3. I	6. B	9. H	12. D	15. F

SHORT ANSWERS #2:

Beauty's Story

1. By making love to her
2. Poisonous rose vines
3. In her room on an upper floor

4. She touched the spindle of a witch's spinning wheel

5. They had served as love slaves in the castle of his ancestor

6. On the floor

7. Ribbons

8. A partridge and a kitten

9. The nobility are her peers and she feels more exposed and more harshly judged

10. The Prince is in love with Beauty, and he may try to protect her from discipline that she needs

11. To her periods of monotony in her life at her father's castle

12. She resents Juliana's clothing and privileges

13. Never complain; never plead to be released

14. He adorns her nudity with jewelry that makes her feel more exposed

15. When the Prince described the village as "sublime punishment"

16. To resign herself like he had repulsed and frightened her

17. Being hung high and doubled so that her genitals are exposed to passersby

18. As decoration in a niche in the wall

19. The Captain of the Guard

20. She discerned that they all wanted to be submissive to her, and she desired a real Master

Alexi's Story

1. He commands Alexi to be impaled on a stone statue with a phallus extending out

2. Felix sucks on his erection

3. Princess Lynette, because she is fearless and dominating

4. He resists his position as a slave and shows a lot of spirit

5. Prince Gerald, her valet

6. How to give them pleasure

7. She thinks he needs to learn better self-control

8. That the Queen's discipline is preferable to that imposed by the kitchen staff

9. In the garbage pit

10. The stable boy who most abuses him, because he loves the attention

11. He obeys her perfectly, although she tries to command him to do things that would humiliate him too much to obey

12. To move his naked hips in a humiliating dance for the Queen

13. She allows him into her bed

14. Opening his buttocks for all to see

15. Three

16. To learn to yield and resign herself with serenity

17. He kisses her between the legs

18. A leather cock-ring

19. Eat for the staff's entertainment

20. A sign noting that he is willful and clumsy, and in need of correction

Tristan's Story

1. In the pen of slaves waiting to be sent to the village

2. Lord Stefan was too weak to master him properly, so he decided to try his luck in the village

3. That he is a model of surrender

4. He tells Beauty that they should strive to obey their Masters, whatever their fate

5. "Strong, attentive organ . . . excellent buttocks . . . quiet of temperament"

6. She can read and write, which is rare for a woman

7. Pulls out two large phalluses for "measuring" him

8. Jerard

9. Nicolas treats Tristan as an equal when it comes time to make love; Tristan sleeps with Nicolas in his bed

10. "No fetters"

11. That he secretly loved it because it pushed him to his limits and made the experience exciting.

12. To tell him news of Beauty

13. That he has to sexually satisfy the others but gets no satisfaction himself

14. Nicolas allows Beauty to go to bed with Tristan and he listens in on their conversation

15. Tristan thinks they must obey, while Beauty wants to disobey; Tristan also wants to love his Master, a concept that confuses Beauty; Tristan surrenders his soul

16. He loves Nicolas and does not wish to be parted from him

17. Beauty

18. He is pitted against Laurent and he triumphs; the Sultan allows him to remain in his bed

19. He has decided that he loves the feeling of order and sense of being part of a larger design that the Sultanate offers

20. Nicolas does not immediately master Tristan, which makes Tristan desire a better experience

Laurent's Story

1. He chased, caught, and ravished Princesses in front of her

2. He was bored with the castle routines and wanted adventure

3. He puts Laurent on a Punishment Cross and rolls him through the village for all to see

4. Two

5. As an adventure; he looks forward to what lies in store

6. Beauty

7. Mocks him to get Lexius to take him to a private place for special discipline

8. Drops his whip while Laurent is satisfying him

9. He sees the Sultan as personable and innocent, not at all formidable

10. How to be a Master even while being a slave

11. How to enjoy his desire to be subservient despite his formal role as Master

12. She sentences him to serve in the Public Pony Stables

13. The degradation of it, as well as the opportunities to master the other ponies

14. He dreads the villagers who want to pump his organ, because he gets punished for losing control

15. The groom favors him and makes love to him in his stable

16. He likes to master the other ponies, particularly Jerard, and get pleasure and relief from them

17. Nuzzles up to Tristan in the stall

18. His father's death, which means he must return and rule his people

19. Golden nipple and genital clamps

20. The intimacy of being with only one person

MULTIPLE CHOICE #1:

1. C	4. D	7. B	10. A	13. D
2. A	5. A	8. C	11. C	14. D
3. A	6. C	9. B	12. B	15. B

SHORT ANSWERS #3:

Forms of Discipline

1. To remain on her hands and knees

2. Breaking the slave

3. Decorated him with sticky concoctions and feathers

4. To show Beauty that she belongs completely to the Prince and must submit to his every whim

5. She is tied to a post for display

6. Gracelessness

7. Like an animal being put through a circus performance

8. He believes Alexi remains rebellious despite his perfect show of obedience

9. Princess Lynette

10. The Master makes money from the audience, who give more if the show is good

11. A princess hanging from her heels

12. She must keep her legs wide apart and stay on her hands and knees

13. Their Masters rent them for any purpose from common labor to sex

14. The crowd's attention magnifies his experience

15. The slaves there are privileged with being able to master slaves sent to them for special discipline

16. It provides spanking services for those who cannot discipline their slaves themselves each day

17. To scrub the floor with the brush in her mouth

18. Golden mesh shields over their genitals, to prevent them from pleasuring themselves

19. To speak

20. As decoration

21. To serve at the Public Pony Stables as common rental ponies

22. They are to deliver the discipline necessary to punish and reform rebellious slaves

23. She commands them to do humiliating things to determine whether they are slave or Master

24. P

25. Flour and honey

WHO SAID?

1. B	3. A	5. D	7. B	9. A
2. C	4. D	6. A	8. C	10. D

BONUS QUESTIONS

1. He cut the poisonous vines at the roots

2. Height and arm strength

3. She is able to freely experience pleasure

4. In front of the Queen's stand

5. That she offers gestures of love to the one who punishes her

6. The slaves can be used for common labor in the village and may not receive the attention of a personal master; the punishments are also more severe and more is expected, with less allowances made

7. "Soften"

8. They have a slave auction and can buy slaves from the castle

9. They want to train ponies for the Queen's use

10. Quarter moon

11. The Captain of the Guard, who personally trained him for the Queen

12. Offer himself as a slave
13. They are marched in on foot
14. Her rebellious spirit
15. Angels
16. Tributes
17. Five
18. Two
19. Eugenia
20. Maypole
21. Two-way mirror
22. Purple
23. Man
24. An altar
25. Rugs

Two Original Chapters from *Exit to Eden*

Elliott: The Garden and The Bar

I suppose I had thought those crowded terraces facing the sea comprised the whole club, that now we should be sheltered by the sprawling branches of the trees from adoring eyes.

But again, Martin's words came back. "It is large beyond your imagining," and I bowed my head, panting with the others, my body moist from the run, only half believing what I saw: the garden stretching out endlessly, linen-draped luncheon tables everywhere crowded with elegantly dressed men and women, naked slaves in attendance with trays of food and wine.

Scores moved back and forth from the buffet tables, under the lacy limbs of the pepper trees, laughing, talking in small clusters, and of course there was still the crowd on the terraces of the main building gazing down on the throng below.

But it wasn't just the size of the gardens, or their crowds. It was the odd way that the crowd resembled any other, the flash of sunglasses and jewelry on tanned arms and throats, the sun exploding in mirrored glasses, the chink of silver on china, men and women in dark tans and Beverly Hills chic, lunching as if it were perfectly normal for naked slaves to attend them, it happened everywhere, and of course there was the usual gathering of some fifty naked and trembling newcomers with their hearts in their mouths at the gates.

It was as devastating to see backs turned, faces in earnest conversation, as it was to see bold stares and smiles.

But again, everything happened very fast.

The mass of slaves were writhing with movement, men and women trying to huddle together, and the handlers surrounding us, apparently waiting only for us to catch our breath before we were ordered to follow the path.

A strong red-haired slave broke into the lead when ordered, and another followed, whipped by the handlers who seemed now an altogether different lot.

These men, young and as well built as the blond sailor, were dressed all in white leather, tight pants, vests, and even held white leather straps.

They seemed made to go with the pastel tablecloths, the huge flowered hats worn by the women, the white or khaki shorts and stiffly pressed bush jackets of the men.

I braced myself for the sight of a woman handler but there was none, though there were plenty of women scattered all through the garden, and everywhere I looked, I saw short skirts, exquisitely shaped legs, bright sandal high heels.

I knew there would be women trainers of course, the real masters and mistresses here, who worked for and with the club members. And my mind flashed back compulsively to the few women trainers I'd known under Martin's regime, those "feminine" bedrooms, the eeriest and most drenching experiences of the secret life. . . .

But we were being run too fast now to see much of anything, plunging under the green shade of the trees as we followed a path through the great mass of tables, the conversation seeming to roar in my ears.

The grass, soft as it was, scratched at the balls of my feet. But I was dazed by the lush growth on all sides, the jasmine and roses everywhere, and the birds I glimpsed in gold cages, giant Macaw parrots, snow-white cockatoos.

Paradise, I thought, and I was a pleasure slave in it. Well, I had asked for it, hadn't I? To be used and enjoyed like the food being eaten, the wine being poured. It was surrounding me just as surely as if I had slipped into some unexpurgated history of decadence, and found myself being driven into the garden of a powerful Persian lord. And though there were limits here that made the cruelty of other times unreal, the vision of this place was so overpowering that all limits seemed unimportant. It was devouring, and I was staggered, lost.

My earlier avowals haunted me.

But the mere physical spectacle of the place was becoming something of a blur. One of the handlers, a young dark-haired boy with powerful arms for his small frame, was lashing me repeatedly, and the more he whipped me for nothing the angrier I became. My cock stayed hard, too hard, for all the energy the run took from me, but I made my face a mask.

I would give nothing, no response to him, I thought, but at the same time I was afraid I couldn't keep it up.

The blows were beginning to cause real discomfort, that creeping, swelling warmth that excites and weakens at the same time.

And never before had my legs been whipped so much before the rear was punished, and I wasn't used to the soreness all over, the blows coming on without rhythm so that dignity was hard.

The slaves around me pressed to the middle of the path to escape the straps, but I refused to do this, letting the blows fall.

The red-haired slave kept ahead of me, and I could see the same stubbornness in him. His body was in beautiful condition, and the sight of the strap scoring him suddenly incited me worse than anything else.

The path twisted and turned through the garden. I realized we weren't being driven to one spot. We were being shown off. A tiny psychic explosion went off in my brain. There wasn't any escape from this. It was happening.

Heads turned when we passed, members, guests—whatever they were—pointing, commenting. And as the young dark-haired handler sought me out again for a hail of whacks with the strap, I became furious, forcing myself ahead, away from the strap, which was a mistake. He was in hot pursuit, smacking at my ankles. He caught me twice on the soles of my feet.

On some level, my reason said, "It's his job to do this, and what's the difference? You're here to be reduced to nothing, to surrender your will." But I couldn't concentrate on this.

And I realized I was losing some vital perspective, and with that realization came a heightened sexual torment, one of those torrential feelings of nakedness and exposure that can wash over me at any moment, as if the experience with all its terrors had just begun.

I fell back into the herd, but he stuck with me. I wondered what I had done to deserve such love. I sensed if I cried out, winced, he might be satisfied, but I wouldn't, no matter how much the belt hurt.

But the scene around us was changing. We were driven past crowded swimming pools with vast flagstone terraces, past the high mesh fences of the croquet courts.

The walls closed in as we were driven through a grove of high ferns and weeping willows, and glancing up I saw men and women leaning over railings above to observe.

I was sore now, a mass of tingling aches, and each new sight stunned me gently, nudging me forward as surely as the handler's belt.

But as we moved back into the thick of the tables again, I saw one of the many guests motioning to the handler and pointing to me. I was being pulled out.

I thought I had seen this happen earlier to one of the other slaves but I wasn't sure.

In any event, I was yanked off the path and to a halt, and it was my relentless young handler with the dark hair who had hold of me, and though he pulled me roughly I didn't remove my hands from the back of my neck. I didn't break form.

My body felt swollen and hot. Another wash of self-consciousness. Cock jutting out, and my hair snagged in my face.

"On all fours with your legs straight," said the handler with a surprisingly calm voice. No anger in it after all those blows, just the job being done expertly, and not the abominable luck of this position.

I find it infinitely worse than being on hands and knees, because the head is thrown so far down and the rear end is elevated and all the more easy to violate or merely to see. And as soon as my hands hit the grass and the handler smacked me, I felt myself choking on discomfort and fear. Another point of renewal. It was as if the flogging with the belt had just begun.

Shoes surrounded me, yellow patent leather around naked toes, high cork clogs with pink straps, moccasins, and the inevitable boots, and the conversation was rising like impenetrable smoke. I was forced forward in this awkward position towards a collection of men and women about a table and heard a loud, almost raucous babble of foreign speech.

My feet were kicked wide apart. My neck was whipped with the belt, so I lowered my head.

And as I looked at a particularly beautiful pair of brown boots before me, one voice distinguished itself, crisp, and coming very rapidly in an Arabic tongue, and I heard a woman give a deep soft laugh.

I wanted to run. I don't mean I really thought to do it. I would never have gotten away, but I was terrified that I would lose control and bolt. My chest was heaving and I saw my own hard cock again, and suddenly the immensity and the closeness of everything was too much. I was moaning against my will.

The handler slipped his hand around my thigh, forcing my legs wider, and I was ordered by him in cool polite English to run in a small circle in place.

I found myself scrambling awkwardly, my calves and thighs taut and aching from this position, and the foreign voices rose and fell in obvious commentary, and then, again there was that soft laugh.

The belt cracked me and I must have stiffened indignantly because there was immediate responsive laughter again and I felt a hand stroking my head. I was facing the table. The man in the smart brown boots reached out and clasped my chin. He pulled my head towards him, and lifted my face.

I was almost dizzy. I was absolutely lost. I could see all the dark olive-skinned faces for an instant—the woman with her eyes shaded by two perfectly round black lenses, the man smiling as he held me, a young man taking a long draw on his black cheroot—before I obediently dropped my eyes. A stylish bunch, none of them older than me, my equals out there in the unreal world, the man who held my chin leaning forward and asking questions in French of the handler: When could I be examined, when could appointments to use me be made? And the handler answering in French that I was a postulant and that it could only be done later tonight.

I knew my upturned face was blood red. My body was trembling with the violent inner struggle to keep still, to forget that my legs were spread apart, my backside up, my scrotum, penis, exposed.

And even as this sense of exposure deepened, this sense of being immersed without name or other identity in what was happening here, I heard the moan grow louder and without choosing it, I struggled desperately, madly, to free my chin from the hand that pushed my face up.

Bad. Really bad. Breaking form. I gained control again but it was too late. There were loud scornful noises at the table, like those of elders scolding an impertinent child, and I heard the angry outburst of the handler as the strap came down. Another handler materialized immediately and caught up both my ankles, bringing them together high in the air.

I was thrown forward on my outstretched hands.

And as my legs were swung roughly to one side, the handler lifted my face again.

"So we have a proud young buck who thinks he's too good to show his face to his Masters and Mistresses," he said. The handler holding my ankles propelled me forward. "Kiss those shoes, all of them, and do it well and do it quick."

OK. Do it, no matter what this feels like. This is just the beginning. I pressed my lips repeatedly to the leather, scrambling on quickly to one pair of boots after another, the belt coming down on my backside all the harder, as laughter and conversation roared all around. I was stroked, scolded, ridiculed and pitied, not as a handsome and expensive slave but as a dog who'd displeased.

And yet my cock never faltered, registering every humiliating pinch.

But abruptly my ankles were released, and I was told to crawl on my hands and knees, with my chin lifted, the handler's voice angry now, impatient—"You need a good lesson!"—as hard cracks of the strap drove me on.

Impossible to analyze this. I tried to tell myself, "What difference does it make? They'll punish you, humiliate you, do what they want with you." But it made all the difference in the world. I'd blundered already, goddamn it, I'd already failed.

All around were the noisy little luncheon circles, the thick grass scratching my knees and open palms. Someone gave me a naked-handed spank as I went by; someone reached for my chin and stroked it upwards, pinching my cheek.

I tried to show perfect submission, perfect willingness. But tears were threatening, actual tears. What had it taken before this to bring tears? But forget all that. Forget it for two years.

The thought of the other slaves being commended on their control, being displayed with flawless poise and compliance, filled me with a staggering anxiety. Again I thought, "What does it matter?" But it did matter. I wanted to be perfect within this decorous and devouring system. That was the whole point, to obey.

Ahead I saw the little herd of fifty postulants, and prayed desperately that I'd be allowed to join them again.

But in a moment, my little blunder of "pride and insolence" was reported to the Trainer in charge. The Trainer took a shock of my hair and lifted my face.

"Proud Slave," he said, fixing me steadily with his cold black eyes. He held something before my eyes and I saw it was a broad grease pen. He bent over me and quite suddenly I felt the jab of the pen into the sore flesh of my backside as he said "Proud Slave" again, obviously writing the same words.

I was gasping, unable to wipe the picture of it out of my mind. I moved forward, chin high as ordered, driven round in a circle around the little herd of obedient ones, the belt flailing as before. And twice we made the little journey. I was frantic. There was no way to show contrition, no way to correct the error. To be a slave meant to be mute, powerless, to be caught in a momentum beyond one's own control.

I thought of Martin in San Francisco and how disappointed he would have been at this little failure, this botched beginning at The Club of all clubs, how he would have seen it as a reflection upon himself.

But I was allowed to rest for a second. The Trainer conferred with the handler and told him to take me to The Bar.

"Give his obedience a good testing," he said.

And numbly I watched the others being driven away before I was made to crawl as before ahead of the whipping strap.

The Bar was just that, a dimly lighted sanctum of chrome and glass and tufted black leather, opening off the garden, where a great many men crowded together at the proverbial brass rail.

The memory of all the bars I'd ever known, and the flirtations in them, and the pickups, and the tension of sensual expectation, charged the atmosphere as I was forced inside on my hands and knees. I wasn't fantasizing over a drink at a table, I was *in* the fantasy, locked into some purely degrading role.

For a moment I couldn't see as I was led across the sawdust floor. The light of the garden had been too bright. And then it materialized before me, faces in the dim silvery glow, video screens flashing pale blue and red, the ebony billiard table with its severe Art Nouveau carvings, surrounded by its shifting figures, the crack of the ivories, the unmistakable smell of hard liquor mingling with the cooled air, the smell of the beer.

I saw the flash of muscled arms, white shirts and tight pants in the shadows, caught the faint fragrance of expensive male cologne. A trace of music pulsed from some hidden source; and as I was whipped along the floor, I heard a ripple of laughter as someone read aloud the words written on my rump, and I carried myself with a remembered notion of dignity that was growing more fragile and illusory all the time.

I was being shown to the men, driven to turn and move back towards the door again, and trembling all over, I did exactly as I was told. One of the tall figures above me snapped his fingers and leaned back on his elbows as I paused.

A soft, almost gentle voice told me in English to kneel up. I complied, trying not to see those nearest me, my hands sliding behind my neck. I was pushed forward until I was staring right at the man's broad leather belt.

"Unzip my pants," he said in that same gentle manner, "and not with your hands either, Proud Slave."

I had expected much worse than this. I was shaking badly as I obeyed. I glanced only very quickly and furtively at the new Master. I saw the gold watch on his wrist, the dark hair of his chest above his open white shirt, something like a smile on his face. Maybe forty, I thought, no more, and something mingled in the face like affection and contempt.

A swimming sense of the whole bar came over me, the men watching, the low throb of the music and the conversation, an undiluted male atmosphere that made a catch in my throat.

I got the small metal zipper in my teeth and at once the bulging cock freed itself from the nest of moist, black glossy pubic hair. Strong clean smell of a man.

The sight and the smell maddened me. My own organ moved almost convulsively, so I had to tense my hips as I'd done so many times on the yacht the night before.

I struggled for command, but I was shaken by the Master reaching forward with his lowered hand. My balls were still thrust forward and bound to my cock by the little leather strap put around them on the ship. And he stroked the tight skin now with his nails, pulled at it, and then yanked me forward by my cock. I couldn't keep quiet.

He laughed softly, rubbing my head hard with the flat of his hand, and running his thumb down my cheek. The lump in my throat was rising again, thickening, almost suffocating me. And I could feel my eyes glazing over and the bar melting into a blur.

But he was offering me his own cock now, and brushing my hair back from my forehead with his open hand, he murmured a sort of wordless command under his breath.

At once I had the cock in my mouth.

It pulled me out of the chaos into which I was slipping. Its heat, its thickness against my lips and the roof of my mouth made the hunger between my legs into a knife.

It doubled as I sucked on it, stroking it with my teeth, tightening my teeth around the very tip of it and then going down on it until I could feel and smell that soft, wet pubic hair.

I drew back the full length of it and then plunged into a steady rhythm, my own hips pumping helplessly, and quite suddenly I felt the handler's strap.

Only I don't think it was the handler because the blows were worse. And as they cut across my backside, they came with the rhythm of my sucking and my thrusts.

It was almost unendurable, the pleasure of that thick, swollen organ and the humiliating, stinging pain of the strap. It brought me back to the bar and my place in it, while the cock connected me to the pure pleasure, and wrenched between the two I was able to forget the garden, the earlier failure, to think only of giving pleasure, the thing I came here to do, and when I thought of the other men watching me, the pleasure shot to a high pitch, going on and on as I locked my arms around the Master's hips. The pain throbbed all through me even in my temples at the very moment that the cock shot its sour salty fluids in my mouth.

For a moment it seemed I would come, my cock spurting into the air. I clung to the man, licking the cock even as he withdrew it, and the noise of the place pulsed through me like a light.

The Master laid his hand on my forehead again and I was told to look up as he drew back. My desire was so heated and desperate that I couldn't focus well. Yet I saw his flushed face again in the dim light, black eyes dazed and almost dreamy, thick graying hair at the temples, and a thin smile on his lips.

He held up a small object in his hands.

"Well, don't you know what this is?" he asked as if he expected something. He had the tone of one talking to a child. And I heard the handler explain I was only a Bad Postulant, and the man very patiently held the object closer so that I saw it was a small cylinder made of shining metal, and he withdrew from it now several large bills which he returned to it once I had seen, and snapping his fingers told me to turn around.

"You're very good for a postulant," he said.

I think I guessed what was to happen, the little ritual, and I swallowed hard. I turned on my hands and knees, and the handler told me, "Up," so that I was standing on all fours again, my rear exposed, and I shuddered, expecting his touch.

The sounds of the bar melted away. I felt that metal cylinder going into my backside, and then driven in deep with a sharp shove. I didn't dare wince or move, that intimate touch infinitely more annihilating than the thrust of a cock. And to be made to stand still for it gave me the most pervasive feeling of subservience. I almost moaned. I felt the man's hand conferring one last demeaning pat, and then a hard pinch and I was pushed gently on.

The handler had already found another man for me and I was being cracked hard to make me hurry to the end of the bar, the cylinder inside me shifting as if it was alive.

This man was taller, leaner than the other, and when I saw the length of the cock, I almost drew back. It hit the roof of my mouth, driving hard as I tried to close my lips on it, a low laughter erupting around me, and the man took hold of my head and started to drive the cock at his own rhythm, his full weight pushing against me with each stroke.

I don't know how many men I gave pleasure to before it was

finished. Probably six. Four of them "tipped" me, as the handler explained it, and each time I felt that odd terror when I was made to turn around and offer my backside for the little cylinder.

I say odd because it was nothing like the fear of humiliation when I was finally driven back out onto the lawn.

It was fear connected to passivity. On the lawn I felt a war of feelings, and my tears almost came.

I'd felt sheltered in the bar, by the darkness, and lost in the pleasure giving.

But now we were back in the throng, my backside humiliatingly red, scarred with the lettering Proud Slave, and the handler seemed more determined than ever to have my chin held high and to make me move as fast as I could.

The desire had become a dull pain in my organ and in my head. I saw the cocks in flashes before my eyes. I could still taste them and their fluids. In my rectum I could feel those little cylinders and had to tighten my muscles not to expel them, ever in fear that I might not be able to hold them in.

But with relief I realized we had left the crowded garden. I was being whipped alone down a narrow ribbon of grass that ran along the side of a vine-covered wall, told to move fast, and in the silence the strap sounded very loud. I felt a new vulnerability to be so alone with this handler, and the sound of his calm authoritative voice.

Finally no one was in sight.

"Stop," he said, "and squat."

I did it, feeling the cylinders poking at my sphincter. I couldn't hold them.

"Now drop that load, all of it," he said. And with a sudden groan, I started pushing the "tips" out. My face was blazing as I felt them slip one by one on the grass. And I hated the son of a bitch in a confusing, intimate way, not for his obvious little theft (he pocketed them immediately), but for the shiver of feeling that came with expulsion of each cylinder, and the way that he smacked me again immediately with the belt.

ELLIOTT: BELOW STAIRS

What was happening to the obedient ones? What was it like being chosen, led away to some private room for examination? Could Lisa choose more than one?

Maybe my mind kept going back to it to avoid what was really happening. Dangling by my ankles, the strap playing on me whenever the handler chose, I was jogged and pulled through a dizzying labyrinth of rooms and pathways and corridors, elevators and ramps, watching as the various slaves were packed off to their punishments, whipped on hands and knees into the vast tiled kitchen with its stainless-steel sinks and counters, thrashed through the haystrewn stables, and into the laundry with its sweet smells of freshly pressed linen and scented soaps.

A flock of fancy uniformed maids received the frantic Gregory, chasing him before them with their brooms.

But finally we were below stairs, in a vast basement room full of buckets and mops and the pungent smell of cleansing chemicals.

And to a handful of young and rather cheerful male servants I was unceremoniously delivered, an amusing enough surprise it seemed, as they looked up from their card games. I was set down on all fours on the white tile before them and told to bow my head so they might see the writing on my back. They looked trim as hospital orderlies in their smart belted white cotton coats as they went back to their card playing.

There were others in the basement, men coming and going, and even some naked male slaves, and though these men seemed slightly rougher than the handlers above they had about them the same air of refinement I'd seen everywhere at The Club. They weren't really coarse men, just sort of ordinary. Excellent builds, routine faces.

"Come here, Elliott," said the one who appeared the oldest, snapping his fingers and then tugging my hair as I neared the table where he shoved me hard to show me that I was meant to turn around. He gave a low whistle as he inspected my sore legs and rump.

"Have they ever been to work already on you," he said almost casually, then to one of the others he made some small comment on the card game. There was something plainly humiliating about all this that no one at Martin's house could have ever rigged it. I heard the splat of the cards on the table, and felt the tip of his boot in my anus. He pushed me forward. "And is it ever going to be sorer than that by twelve o'clock tonight."

There was a round of laughter.

"Look at those muscles," said one of the others. "We're going to make good use of them, Elliott. Ever done any hard work in your life?"

"No, Master," I said before I realized it. Not a very clever answer. There was more laughter.

"Well, you're going to work here, young man, and I'll tell you something else too, a postulant who gets himself this duty on his first day comes back to see us often as time goes on."

"That's 'cause we're so charming!" said one of the others.

"You'll get to be a regular," said a third one, with a rather low, almost velvety voice. "Come over here and let me have a look at you."

The mercy of it was I could keep my head down. Same exquisite boots that the others wore; it was the uniform of the place undoubtedly, classy boots. Even the maids must have had them. And the black-wash pants were tapered, and the coats made of heavy cotton, almost as heavy as khaki. The hand that pinched my butt now was rough. I must have given some little movement because I received an immediate hard spank. Rough as a paddle.

"See those bucket handles, Elliott?" said the deep-voiced one. "Know why the handles are coated with soft material? That's to protect your pretty teeth. And you'll find some brushes over there with soft leather handles. You'll learn to scrub with your teeth, and wipe with your teeth, and maybe a few other things with your teeth." More laughter. The card game continued with a new shuffle and deal.

"Kneel up, let me see that cock."

I didn't take time to think. And I heard the immediate mockery, pretended shock. "Oooooh, that's beautiful, Elliott, I'll bet that feels good, doesn't it!" And the dreaded slap to the cock, and then another.

I flinched, unable to help it, keeping my eyes focused on the tile floor.

"And look at the rest of that equipment, it must weigh ten pounds."

The hand slipped under my bound testicles. It was almost too much. I knew my cock was dancing, carrying my hips forward with it. And for two days, I had to put up with this. I couldn't make it, not that long. I'd go down on the floor, rubbing it against the floor. I couldn't think about that.

But I was shoved back down on my knees.

"All right, all right, let's outfit you for the job," said the older man, sliding his chair back with a scraping noise on the tile.

Again the snap of the fingers and the command, "Heel." No one had ever given me that command! But I knew what it meant and I followed fast.

He stopped. "Is that how you obey when I say 'heel'?" he demanded. And that big hand slammed my rear almost pushing me forward. "When I give you any command, to come, go, heel, you move! Now let me see you trot."

I tried to comply.

"I said 'trot'!" The hand again smacking my rump and then grabbing hold of it hard. I let out a little whistle of pain between my teeth. Two days.

"Trot means lift those knees and hands off the floor. It means sprightly. Didn't anyone ever teach you that? You're at The Club, young man, you're one of four thousand slaves at The Club, and whether you clean the lavatories, or give My Lady her silver handmirror in your teeth, you move!"

At once I trotted forward, struggling to give the desired effect. My face must have been purple, but the psychic miracle was working again: I *had* to please. To please, it was all I focused on. Anger coming from them would have been too much.

"Halt, now heel." I scrambled, trotted to obey, twisting about to kneel at his right, and immediately there came a mocking applause from the others.

"Good Boy, Elliott." And, "That cock knows it's Master's voice when it hears it."

"All right," said the elder moving forward to a row of metal lockers. "Now kneel up, and let me see your hands go where they should. All right, good."

He had removed a leather leash with a thick collar on the

end of it, but much too small for my neck. And in a moment I knew what it was for as he snapped open the old strap on my cock, and put on the little collar pushing my balls even further forward than before. The scratching of the new leather, his hand on the balls almost drove me crazy. A bit of liquid seeped from the tip of my penis. I felt it bubble up over the crown.

"Oh, you behave yourself, young man," he said in mock outrage as he buckled the strap. Straightening up, he gave the leash a jerk and I struggled to follow him on my knees, the pressure of the strap stroking and tormenting my cock much worse than the other, so that a loud gasp came out of me before I could stop.

He didn't notice or care.

"Now, you take the handle of this leash in your teeth," he said, giving it to me, "and that's where I'm to find it whenever I want it, you understand?" he said.

He was about to say more as he shoved the leather into my mouth, but something had caught his eye. I could see a light flashing up on the wall.

"You see that, young man? You're to watch for that. And whenever you see one of those lights flash, you're to trot out from wherever you are and come to one of us with that leash handle in your mouth. That's the signal that the lavatory in question needs attention, and we're going to it right now. And we don't clean the private bathrooms, young man, not the nice little ones with the Carrara marble and the coordinated colors opening off the quiet little bedroom suites. We clean the public lavatories of The Club on every floor. As you're about to see for yourself."

The leash handle was yanked from me again and I was pulled forward, but mercifully I was allowed on all fours, running in the trot after the man as he strode down the carpeted hall. Other uniformed servants passed us, with mops and buckets or stacks of towels, and other scurrying punished slaves.

I had a close look at one of the others in the service elevator as we went up, a stocky young man heeling anxiously beside a young orderly, not daring apparently to glance at me, his backside striped in pink with a map of white welts.

"Remember what I told you, Elliott?" said the man who was leading me. "About bad little boys who start out with us coming back again and again? Take a good look at Andre. He's been with The Club for years, but every month or two, he's back with us for a nice long visit."

This seemed to increase the slave's tension, and when the door opened he scrambled out behind the orderly without having to be told.

A strip of very rich champagne-colored carpet stretched before us when we left the elevator.

We must have been four floors up, and immediately I heard the soft free-flowing chatter of a crowd. How big was the place? I couldn't imagine. But the size was its own source of subjugation. I felt lost. We were passing enameled doors with brass numbers. Then I saw out of the corner of my eye a huge salon full of sunlight and cigarette smoke, potted palms and other tropical plants rising here and there over the heads of the crowd.

I glimpsed on the edge of the room two model-perfect women, wraith-like giants with skillfully lacquered hair in haute couture gowns speaking to one another in nasal French rapidly. No eyes moved towards us as we hurried past, as invisible it seemed as servants always are, and were very quickly inside a blue tiled lavatory, with some twenty marble stalls. It looked clean enough for surgery. But my new master unlocked a cabinet and threw down a small broom expertly made for me to use with my mouth as he had told me before.

"Be sure to keep that leash handle in your mouth, too; sweep hard and fast," he said. "Start at the far end, and I want the floor spotless right now."

I started sweeping at once, the movement of my head causing it to ache, but nothing in the world was going to cause me to displease these men, to get this punishment increased, and as my master saw to towels and soap, I swept the entire room, finally gathering the bits of paper and dirt into his dust pan and getting a kind pat on the head.

The doors opened and two men in mid conversation moved past us, one of them pausing at a basin to carefully wash his hands. They gave us not so much as a glance as my master locked the cabinet and snapped his fingers, whispering the word "Trot" as he gestured to the door.

The halls were streaming with guests now. Gleaming patent

leather shoes brushed close to me, the flash of red toenails under nude stockings, white sandals, the inevitable boots. But I kept my head down, following as fast as I could the tug of the leash, my heart racing from the relentless pace. A woman's chiffon dress brushed my hip, but there wasn't the slightest evidence anyone took notice. I didn't know whether it was worse than being scowled at, mocked.

The next lavatory had to be scrubbed.

The mixture of chemicals was mild enough so that it didn't burn my eyes as I moved the scrubber back and forth with my teeth. But my neck ached, and the Master, apparently seeing me slow down, gave me that rough hand again.

"You want a good old-fashioned spanking, Elliott?" he laughed almost genially as I tried to work faster. "They tell me my hand's the best paddle in The Club." He swatted me again with so much force that I dropped the brush, struggling to get hold of it.

"Did I hear a little whimper, young man?" He had thrown down a handful of white towels.

Not from me, you didn't, I felt like saying, but it might have been a lie.

"Now put that brush back in the bucket and wipe that floor dry. You can use your hands and use them well. And in the future when I point to a floor and the bucket, you'll know what to do, and if you don't, you go over my knee."

My head was swimming when I finished. Some crucial change was taking place in my mind, the exertion breaking down the barriers, and a primitive titillating fear taking the place of thought. I scrambled to put away the bucket and drop the towels down the linen chute.

"That's not what I call fast, beautiful, now move through that door!" And that hand came down again almost sweeping me out into the corridor.

I was only saved from it by the crowds in the corridor, and the press in the elevator, and I knew it.

As soon as we reached the cellar room, I was told I was going to "get it."

"Might as well get down to business right now."

The others were still playing cards and didn't look up from

their game, and those at other tables went on as before, slaves obediently at their feet.

I was pulled along roughly to the wall, the leash was stripped off me, and I winced as I saw a long-handled wooden paddle being taken down from a hook.

"You ready for your spanking?" he demanded.

I started to answer, but my voice evaporated. My pulse was pounding. I'd been lashed all day, but I hadn't been really spanked. Careless blows with the belt, angry blows, blows full of annoyance, driving blows. That was one thing, but at the thought of the utter humiliation of a real spanking, my cock felt ready to explode.

And it was these men, these priceless specimens of ordinary masculinity, servants of The Club, not some elegantly turned out guest above ordering me thrown over a padded chair in his suite for the "honor," it was to be a hard brutal job below stairs.

I knew I was going to lose all control. A picture of that beautiful Trainer flashed into my mind. What would it be like, being punished by her, really humiliated by her? I couldn't think. But I was reaching out to her in my mind as if she were a lifesaver. Did I want that instead of this?

But the man had seated himself near the card table this time. And he was beckoning to me and slapping his heavy thigh. It was like some nightmare memory from early childhood, maybe of something that had never actually happened to me, but had always been threatened, glimpsed happening to others. It was being inside one of those crude cartoons I'd secretly pored over as a boy, in which some naked-bottomed little delinquent was paddled over a knee as the tears flew out from his squinted eyes. I wouldn't stand it—it was too sublime—I'd lose all control.

"I should spank you right through the cellar," he said under his breath, grabbing a shock of my hair and pulling me towards him. "I should spank you right through the furnace room, and the storage rooms, and make you repeat their names to me, and find your way back to them under command. But we have a long night ahead of us and I'm already tired."

"No, give it to him right there," said one of the men at the table, the one with the velvety voice. "I haven't really *heard* that young boy yet."

At a distant table somebody called for action, saying it had been too long since one of these spoiled brats really got it, and the master moved, pulled me up.

"Over my lap, young man, and you're to keep that cock back out of the way."

I bent over his lap as I was told, my bowed head towards the other card players, who egged the Master on as before. The paddle needed a workout. And "I'd whip these other beauties," said one of the others at another table, "but they've been whipped full sore."

I lay still, unable to understand what I was feeling, how the dread alchemized into paralysis, trying to keep my cock away from his leg. I felt his left hand on the small of my back. I kept my head low down, and it felt good to be able to cover at least my neck.

I was shaking as violently as I had all day when with a loud smack he began. A groan came out of me immediately. And the second time it came again. I couldn't keep it back.

The third and fourth wallop was so hard I couldn't keep quiet. I was going to lose this battle and it was nothing but a little sport for the broom-and-mop crowd. I tried to clamp my mouth shut.

But he cut loose as though he would make me cry out or wear himself out and it seemed his paddle was bouncing off my rump and I was rocking across his lap. One of the men let out a whistle. I heard someone clap his hands. "Give it to him, Tony. Whip that boy."

I tried to think of Martin in San Francisco, we were in The House in San Francisco, this wasn't happening. Only trouble, it was.

My butt was on fire. The spanking pounded on. One of the men had come over to watch. "Look at that boy dance," he said. "You're too quiet, Elliott, too reserved, let that ass move!"

I gave a low open-mouth cry just as I vowed I wouldn't, each crack of the wooden paddle an explosion of pain that shook my whole frame. I could hear my cries now, I couldn't stop them, I was choking on them, but still I held back the tears.

The paddle smacked at my thighs. It cracked hard on my rear again. It rested flat and still for a moment, pressing on the burning flesh before it shattered me into a loud guttural moan that almost sounded like a plea. Again the men laughed, one of them clapping his hands. And as the blows came faster and faster I could hear nothing but my own open-mouth moans, coming so rapidly they were one long cry.

"Atta boy, atta boy," my Master was saying. "Just what the Master ordered, and now we're going to hear that polite, gentlemanly voice again, saying 'Thank you, Master.' "

"Thank you, Master," I cried out to a general round of laughter.

"Again? Again?"

"Thank you, Master, thank you, Master, thank you, Master." I was trying to say it, not cry it, but I couldn't control it, and I realized my body was rocking, undulating completely beyond my control. I felt my penis like a great throbbing shaft jutting from between my legs, and I was gasping "Thank you, Master!" over and over as if it were a plea.

Suddenly I realized my eyes were filled with tears. I couldn't see the floor below me, and my voice had grown thick and quivering, "Thank you, Master," coming in choking noises. I could not believe my failure, I couldn't believe it, and yet I had lost everything, letting go of the words "Thank you, Master," the paddle slamming me over and over again.

Roughly I was thrust off the Master's lap onto my knees. "Trot!" I heard the loud command, but it was coming from a younger man, the one who'd risen from the table, and I felt the paddle crack me with new vigor. "And I'll take a little 'Thank you, Master' with it loud and clear."

I rushed forward, my tears almost blinding me, the paddle right behind me, smacking me forward, as I cried out "Thank you, Master," and the boots beside me kept easy pace.

Applause came from a table as we passed it.

"Pick up those knees, young man, trot!" someone called out. And another, "Move it, young man," as desperately I tried to obey. I had come to the end of the room, and I was turned and spanked hard back along its length, my backside steaming with pain, and suddenly the words I was crying died again into wide open-mouth cries that were almost gasps.

"Bring him here," said one of the men at the first table, "and give me that paddle, I want to have a go at those thighs."

I was thrust over his right knee, head dangling, and I felt the paddle wallop my legs as he promised in a riff of blows until I was passed to another who shouted:

"Kneel up!" that dreaded command as he pushed my face high with the palm of his hand. Tears were washing down my face. It was excruciating to show it. My hips were knocked forward by the paddle, my cock quivering. I couldn't brace my hips hard enough and there was laughter all around.

One of the men was standing before me unzipping his pants. "Keep it up," he said to the other, and as the paddle kept smacking, he drew my head towards his erect cock. My mouth opened for it, my hands still locked obediently to the back of my neck. And as I held my shoulders firmly, he drove it back and forth through my lips.

It was delicious, it was the reward, the prize, the brass ring, having it, but even my noises weren't stilled by it but went on, muffled by the cock.

When the hot sperm shot into me, I swallowed greedily but even then I was crying, and now my head was forced down into the warmth of another man's crotch. I was ready for the cock, but there was another man behind me for whom I was being prepared, and the paddle had stopped.

My rear throbbed with its own humiliating rhythm, and I felt the flesh being pulled roughly and the nudge at my anus which meant the man was about to go in. I pressed my lips to the crotch in front of me, and the thrust came hard and dry.

My own cock tugged me mercilessly forward. And suddenly I felt a hand on it, hot, silky fingers batting at it that made me give a long groaning sound.

They opened, slapped at the length of it, smacking the tip over and over and then clamped on the tip hard, stroking roughly, and I came in a riotous explosion, my hips convulsing, the cock in my mouth and the one in my backside jetting with equal force.

It went on and on in sharp throbs, my moan rising and falling and then one at a time they pulled themselves free and I lay down, butt back on my heels, head to the floor.

"Oh, that felt good," the man behind me whispered, "that tight little asshole. Good."

I was as exhausted as I'd ever been, as utterly spent.

For a long moment, I was let to breathe, and then I felt a little humiliating spank of the paddle and a hand before me pointed to a long wooden table against the wall.

I moved to it, the paddle coaxing me just a little, and I was shoved up to lay my chest on the table, my legs spread out behind me. And when I heard the zipper, and felt his hands spreading my butt, I moved my hips to receive the new cock.

BIBLIOGRAPHY

"Playboy Interview: Anne Rice," *Playboy*, March 1993.

Apter, Michael J. *The Dangerous Edge: The Psychology of Excitement*. New York: Free Press, 1992.

Beevers, John. *St. Teresa of Avila*. New York: Doubleday, 1961.

Bluestein, Ron, "Interview with the Pornographer," *Vogue*, April 1986.

Carotenuto, Aldo. *Eros and Pathos: Shades of Love and Suffering*. Charles Nopar, tr. Toronto: Inner City, 1989.

Chapple, Steve, and Talbot, David. *Burning Desires: Sex in America*. New York: Doubleday, 1989.

Chester, Laura. *Deep Down: The New Sensual Writing by Women*. Boston: Faber and Faber, 1988.

Cowan, Lyn. *Masochism: A Jungian View*. Dallas: Spring, 1982.

Dworkin, Andrea. *Woman Hating*. New York: Dutton, 1974.

Edelstein, Andrew J., and McDonough, Kevin. *The Seventies: From Hot Pants to Hot Tubs*. New York: Dutton, 1990.

Garber, Marjorie. *Vice Versa: Bisexuality and the Eroticism of Everyday Life*. New York: Simon & Schuster, 1995.

Gitlin, Todd. *The Sixties: Years of Hope, Days of Rage*. New York: Bantam, 1987.

Goodman, Paul. "Pornography, Art, and Censorship." In *Perspectives on Pornography*, Douglas A. Hughes, ed. New York: St. Martin's, 1970.

Halberstam, David. *The Fifties.* New York: Villard, 1993.

Hopke, Robert H., Carrington, Karen Loftus, and Wirth, Scott, eds. *Same Sex Love and the Path to Wholeness.* Boston: Shambhala, 1993.

Hyman, Stanley Edgar. "In Defense of Pornography." In *Perspectives on Pornography,* Douglas A. Hughes, ed. New York: St. Martin's, 1970.

Jackson, Graham. *The Secret Lore of Gardening: Patterns of Male Intimacy.* Toronto: Inner City Books, 1991.

Knode, Helen. "The Naked and the Dead," *L.A. Weekly,* October 19, 1990.

Michelson, Peter. "An Apology for Pornography." In *Perspectives on Pornography,* Douglas A. Hughes, ed. New York: St. Martin's, 1970.

Moore, Thomas. *Dark Eros: The Imagination of Sadism.* Dallas, Spring, 1990.

Moravia, Alberto. "Eroticism in Literature." In *Perspectives on Pornography,* Douglas A. Hughes, ed. New York: St. Martin's, 1970.

Mordell, Albert. *The Erotic Motive in Literature.* New York: Octagon, 1976.

Nabokov, Vladimir, *Lolita.* New York: Berkeley, 1955.

Phillips, William. "Writing About Sex." In *Perspectives on Pornography,* Douglas A. Hughes, ed. New York: St. Martin's, 1970.

Preston, John. *Entertainment for a Master.* Boston: Alyson, 1986.

————, ed. *Flesh and the Word.* New York: Plume, 1992.

————, ed. *Flesh and the Word II.* New York: Plume, 1993.

Ramsland, Katherine. *Prism of the Night: A Biography of Anne Rice.* New York: Dutton, 1991.

————. *The Vampire Companion: The Official Guide to Anne Rice's "The Vampire Chronicles."* New York: Ballantine, 1993.

———. *The Witches' Companion: The Official Guide to Anne Rice's "Lives of the Mayfair Witches."* New York: Ballantine, 1994.

Réage, Pauline. *The Story of O.* New York: Blue Moon, 1993.

Rice, Anne. "Nicholas and Jean," *Transfer*, #21, June 1966.

———. "Katherine and Jean." Unpublished Master's thesis, San Francisco State University, 1972.

———. *Interview with the Vampire.* New York: Knopf, 1976.

———. *The Feast of All Saints.* New York: Simon & Schuster, 1979.

———. "The Art of the Vampire at its Peak in the Year 1876," *Playboy*, January 1979.

———. *Cry to Heaven.* New York: Knopf, 1982.

——— (as A. N. Roquelaure). *The Claiming of Sleeping Beauty.* New York: Dutton, 1983.

——— (as A. N. Roquelaure). *Beauty's Punishment.* New York: Dutton, 1984.

——— (as Anne Rampling). *Exit to Eden.* New York: Arbor House, 1985.

——— (as A. N. Roquelaure). *Beauty's Release.* New York: Dutton, 1985.

———. *The Vampire Lestat.* New York: Knopf, 1985.

——— (as Anne Rampling). *Belinda.* New York: Arbor House, 1986.

———. *The Queen of the Damned.* New York: Knopf, 1988.

———. *The Witching Hour.* New York: Knopf, 1990.

———. *The Tale of the Body Thief.* New York: Knopf, 1992.

———. *Lasher.* New York: Knopf, 1993.

———. *Taltos.* New York: Knopf, 1994.

———. *Memnoch the Devil.* New York: Knopf, 1995.

———. "Playing with Gender," *Vogue*, November 1983, p. 498.

Schmidgall, Gary. *The Stranger Wilde*. New York: Dutton, 1994.

Scott, Gini Graham. *Erotic Power: An Exploration of Dominance and Submission*. Secaucus, N.J.: Citadel, 1983.

Sontag, Susan. "The Pornographic Imagination." In *Perspectives on Pornography*, Douglas A. Hughes, ed. New York: St. Martin's, 1970.

Steinberg, David. *The Erotic Impulse*. New York: Tarcher, 1992.

Steiner, George. "Night Words: High Pornography and Human Privacy." In *Perspectives on Pornography*, Douglas A. Hughes, ed. New York: St. Martin's, 1970.

Stoller, Robert J. *Observing the Erotic Imagination*. New Haven, Conn.: Yale University Press, 1985.

Strossen, Nadine. *Defending Pornography*. New York: Scribner, 1995.

Wheelis, Allen. *The Path Not Taken: Reflections on Power and Fear*. New York: W. W. Norton, 1990.

White, Kristen E. *A Guide to the Saints*. New York: Ivy, 1991.